THE MODES
AND MORALS OF
PSYCHOTHERAPY

THE MODES
AND MORALS OF
PSYCHOTHERAPY

PERRY LONDON

University of Southern California

HOLT, RINEHART AND WINSTON, INC.

New York · Chicago · San Francisco · Toronto · London

3495

PREFACE

At the cost of militancy and persistence over many years, the craft of psychotherapy has gained a position of eminence in our society. Its professors and practitioners, once contemptuously regarded as eccentrics mumbling arcane obscenities at the fringe of medicine, have advanced from relative obscurity to chairs of eminence and couches of opulence in the finest universities and neighborhoods in the Western World. America, with its mixed traditions of hospitality toward all kinds of ideological novelty and of personal self-seeking, has been the kindliest of hosts to this endeavor.

But there are reasons to think that psychotherapy has gained more of social respectability than of intellectual integrity. A detailed examination of the surfeit of schools and theories, of practices and practitioners that compete with each other conceptually and economically, shows vagaries which, taken all at once, make unclear what it is that psychotherapists do, or to whom, or why.

If these remarks are critical, they are not meant to be hostile or destructive, but are mainly intended to imply that psychotherapy requires more careful analysis and articulation than it sometimes gets, for it can be best used only when it is most understood.

This book essays to systematize and make explicit some issues and ideas that are critically important to every aspect of psychotherapy but are often only implicit in its practice. The burden of its argument involves two main dimensions of discourse.

First is its contention that psychotherapy is a *moralistic* as well as a *scientific* undertaking to such an extent that it cannot be properly understood as the latter unless it is also thoroughly evaluated as the former. Therapists use their technical skills and scientific opinions as the basis for studying and treating their patients, but it is in terms of moral concerns that they decide the ultimate goals and objectives of their treatment. In fact, our society only sanctions the practice of psychotherapy and the existence of therapeutic guilds because of a tacit assumption that the moral order to which therapists address their skills is one that ultimately benefits the social order through its treatment of the needs of individuals. The ambiguities of value inherent in a democratic society make it easy to overlook this fact, just as the ambiguities of the theraputic process make it easy to overlook the implications of therapy's outcome, but therapists may compromise their integrity by doing so and patients may sacrifice full value of the experience by letting them.

The second major argument of this book is that while the morals of psychotherapy have not been attended to enough, the modes of therapy have multiplied at such a pace that it becomes impossible to attend to them enough if they must be examined one by one. The winds of change in psychotherapy have reached gale force, for better or for worse, and new positions, schemes, and remedies come up so fast, especially among the Action modes, that some of the material in this book is already dated as it goes to press. The very speed and quantity of developments make it vital to design some systematic conceptual scheme in which all kinds of psychotherapies, including many yet to be discovered, can be comprehended, interpreted, and evaluated. The best basis for such a system, it is argued, is the dimension of therapeutic technique, where schools may be positioned according to the normal activities of their expositors. Some thoroughness of understanding of each school is lost thereby, but much is gained, I hope, by way of clarity and perspective.

A word on form: This work is addressed both to a general and to a scholarly audience, and its organization has been designed with the intent of satisfying the specialized needs of the latter without excessively trying the patience and indulgence of the former. For this reason, the body of the work contains no technical references, and footnotes are kept to a minimum, permitting the main arguments to be studied without too many distractions. The Commentary, which contains parenthetical information and arguments, opinions of different authorities, and occasional gossip, also contains complete citations of the many works that were used in the preparation of this one. An index of names is also provided.

ACKNOWLEDGMENTS

Many dozens of students and colleagues were kind enough to criticize part or all of this book while in preparation. Their comments often resulted in alterations of the text that salvaged many parts from falsehoods, errors, and incivilities. For this, I am especially grateful to Professors Joseph Becker, Charles Leonhard, and Donald R. Peterson, all of the University of Illinois; Professors Albert Bandura, Kenneth Mark Colby, and Albert Hastorf, and to Mr. Byron Klorfine, Mr. Paul Verden, and Mrs. Suzanne H. Troffer, all of Stanford University; Professors James H. Bryan and Lowell Storms of the University of California at Los Angeles; Dr. Norman Matlin and Mr. Erik Wensberg, both of Columbia University; Dr. David Rosenhan, of Educational Testing Service.

This work was undertaken at the suggestion of Professor O. H. Mowrer of the University of Illinois and the insistence of Mr. Erik Wensberg, founding Editor of the Columbia University *Forum*. The work of writing it was encouraged and supported by Professors Lloyd G. Humphreys and Donald R. Peterson, respectively Head of the Department of Psychology and Director of Clinical Psychology Training at the University of Illinois.

I am also grateful to Miss Carol Kupers of U.C.L.A. for many hours of congenial help in clerical crises.

Finally, I am indebted to Vivian London, my wife, for a multitude of editorial and personal aids, of both kinds too many, varied, great, and private to be decently detailed.

Los Angeles, California   P. L.
February 1964

Dedicated to the beloved memory of
my father

MAX LONDON (1895–1963)

who urged and inspired me to write books

and

to the memory of
my student

BYRON KLORFINE (1940–1964)

for whose critical approval this book was meant

CONTENTS

DIMENSIONS OF PSYCHOTHERAPY

CHAPTER ONE

THE MORALS OF PSYCHOTHERAPY

Insofar as he is concerned with the diagnosis and treatment of illness, the modern psychotherapist has grown up in the tradition of medicine. But the nature of the ailments he deals with and the way he treats them set him apart from the physician and in some ways make him function much like a clergyman. He deals with sickness of the soul, as it were, which cannot be cultured in a laboratory, seen through a microscope, or cured by injection. And his methods have little of the concreteness or obvious empiricism of the physician's—he carries no needle, administers no pill, wraps no bandages. He cures by talking and listening. The infections he seeks to expose and destroy are neither bacterial nor viral—they are ideas, memories of experiences, painful and untoward emotions that debilitate the individual and prevent him from functioning effectively and happily.

Our traditional understanding of the physician is that he relieves men of their suffering regardless of their moral condition. Historically, the dedicated physician has treated the good and bad alike, ministering to their physical needs as best he could.

He has done so for reasons that are both technically and theoretically sound. In his technical work, the physician rarely needs to be concerned with the moral attributes of his patient, for they generally have no bearing on the diagnosis he will make or how he will combat an illness. In theory, the physician is committed to the task of saving and enhancing the life and physical well-being of his patients. So he treats them all, and treats them as they come—and this is perhaps the noblest tradition within medicine.

Psychotherapists have been nobly moved to adapt this tradition to their own practice. In so doing, they argue that the mental therapist is no moralist, that he has no business becoming involved in the moral, religious, economic, or political beliefs of his client, and that he has no right, in the course of his practice, to make value judgments of his client, to moralize or preach at him, or to try to dictate to him some "good" way of life. His purpose is to alleviate the suffering, the mental anguish, the anxiety, the guilt, the neurosis or psychosis of the client, not to change his way of life along moralistic or ideological lines.

This argument has a great deal in its favor. It has served the historical purpose of permitting students of mental health and illness to investigate objectively the conditions that predispose people to mental troubles and the kinds of people who suffer from such difficulties. It has allowed therapists, free of metaphysical concerns, to develop a technical armamentarium that, though limited, can often be used much as the physician uses his store of pills and skills. It has been largely responsible for the creation of a new "helping" art, one that has not only demonstrated its usefulness, but has also been able to entertain legitimate pretensions to being a scientific discipline.

It is impossible to overstate the importance of freedom from metaphysics and morals to the conduct of scientific research, especially to the objective analysis and interpretation of data. But the psychotherapist, in his actual practice, does not usually function as a researcher. He is a clinician. And much of the material with which he deals is neither understandable nor usable outside the context of a system of human values. This fact is unfortunate and embarrassing to one who would like to see himself as an impartial scientist and unprejudiced helper. It is a fact none the less, and one which, for both technical and theoretical reasons, may be painfully important to students of human behavior in general and to psychotherapists in particular. Moral considerations may dictate, in large part, how the therapist defines his client's needs, how he operates in the therapeutic situation, how he defines "treatment," and "cure," and even "reality."

Many psychotherapists are poignantly aware of this. Students of mental health find that it is difficult even to define such terms as "health," "illness," and "normality," without some reference to morals; and worse still, they cannot discuss the proper treatment of what they have defined without recognizing and involving their own moral commitments.

The issue is the same whether the problem is a social one like prostitution or an apparently individual one like obsessional neuroses. Neither can be called an illness on the grounds of invasion by a foreign body or of the malfunctioning of specific organs. Nor do people die directly from them. They may be abnormal in a statistical sense, but this is hardly a basis for worry. Living one hundred years or making a million dollars is also deviant in that sense. The objectionable feature of these problems concerns the violation of the public moral code, in the one case, and the experience of apparently unnecessary personal anguish—which either presupposes the virtue of comfort or abjures the discomfort of preoccupation—in the other. In both, the assumption of a moral desideratum underlies the definition.

Yet psychotherapeutic training programs in psychiatry, psychology, social work—even in the ministry—often do not deal seriously with the problem of morals. Psychotherapeutic literature is full of formal principles of procedure and somewhat vague statements of goals, but it generally says little or nothing about the possible moral implications of those procedures and goals—indeed, it often fails even to mention that there are any moral, as opposed to scientific, implications to psychotherapy, though the objectives of the latter are rationalized by the former. It is as if therapists were themselves unconscious of some of the most profound difficulties in their own work. Or perhaps the opposite is true—that they are well aware but find that, as Marie Jahoda puts it, "[it] seems so difficult that one is almost tempted to claim the privilege of ignorance." Perhaps so, but ignorance can serve no useful purpose in this matter, and may even impair the uses of the craft.

At some level of abstraction, it is probably correct to declare that every aspect of psychotherapy presupposes some implicit moral doctrine, but it is not necessary to seek this level in order to say why it is important for therapists to recognize the moral concomitants of patients' problems and the implied moral position of some of their solutions. Some problems are inevitably moral ones from the perspective of either client or therapist, and some can be viewed as strategic or technical ones and treated without reference to particular value systems. In the one case, the therapist must fulfill a moral agency in order to function at all, whereas in the other he may restrict himself to the impartial helping or contractual function with which he is usually identified. But if he does not know the difference, then his own moral commitments may influence his technical functioning so that he willy-nilly strives to mold men to his own image, or his technical acts may imply moral positions which he might himself abhor.

MORALS AS TECHNICALITIES

To be sure, there are many people and problems that clearly do not require much moralistic concern by therapist or patient. These are in fact purely technical problems and can be assessed, for the most part, on purely empirical grounds. An example might be the case of a phobia in a child. Such a condition will often succumb to fairly specific techniques without much thought to the value systems that may underlie their use. Similarly, many psychogenic physical symptoms in children and adults may be treated without seriously invading the patient's value system and without challenging his moral code or, for that matter, knowing anything about it. Some familial conflicts are resolved by fairly simple means —helping people to improve interpersonal communication, to discover that their feelings can be voiced without disastrous consequences, and so forth.

Such problems require few moral commitments from the therapist beyond the belief that children ought not have phobias, people should be free of allergies, members of families should not be in continuous conflict, and so on. It would be precious for most of us to labor these as moral issues, not because they are free of moral underpinnings, but because the consensus which exists about them almost everywhere is so great that it makes them virtual universals.

The technical problem that becomes a moral problem in psychotherapy, often in a critical way, might be stated like this: How does a psychotherapist properly deal with a client who reports that he has perpetrated a theft or been sexually delinquent? Or suppose a religiously devout patient reports that he is conflicted, guilty, and anxious about the use of birth control devices. What defines a therapeutic reply to a person who feels that his behavior, or thoughts, violate the word of God, or the Church, and that at the same time he cannot control them?

Suppose, for that matter, the converse—a patient reports particularly opprobrious behavior about which he does not experience guilt, anxiety, or conflict; suppose, in effect, he thereby violates the moral code of the therapist.

What should the therapist do? Avoid comment? Refer his comments to the ostensible code of the client without reference to his own? Should he circumvent the moral issue itself and attempt to penetrate the dynamic, or unconscious, or historical situations that may have "determined" the behavior?

A common technical objective of therapists of all schools is to help the client to be free of his unrealistic conflicts—but when conflicts revolve around moral issues, how is it possible to help without becoming directly involved in the moral issue? How is it even possible, for that matter, to decide whether a conflict is realistic without moral involvement? It is specious to argue, as some therapists do, that moral concerns are simply manifestations of "resistance" and that the underlying dynamics of the client's situation never relate to moral problems. It seems viciously irresponsible for the therapist to argue that, at such times, he must formally remove himself from the discussion by telling the client that the therapy session can be helpful for discussing "personal, emotional problems, not moral ones." The naive injunction that, regardless of what approach he *does* take, the therapist must *not* moralize at the client, has little value here—it is hard to imagine that the failure to moralize alone arranges things so that the client can then solve his own moral dilemmas.

Within the framework of technical therapeutic objectives, independent of his own scheme of values or his awareness of the relevance of the client's morality to the conflict situation, it is unclear what the therapist should do here. Most therapists, regardless of the particular psychological orthodoxy to which they adhere, would probably agree that there are a number of perfectly valid, even necessary, technical actions which may be considered in such a situation. The therapist might reflect, interpret, probe the origins of the symptom, or its intensity, or its continuities and discontinuities; he might ask the client to free-associate in general or in response to particular words or phrases. He might challenge him to explain clearly why he deprecates his own impulses, or to explore deeper underlying motives for his anxiety or his preoccupation, to describe this or think about that or understand a third thing. What unites all these technical operations in most actual cases, I believe, is first, the fact that the therapist *says something*, and second, the fact that he almost inevitably avoids expressing an opinion about the *moral issue as such*. Morality, religion, the oughts and shoulds of human behavior, are not his ostensible concern.

But these issues are surely the concern of the client; to the extent that he is in touch with reality, let alone has any care to serve his own best interests, he must necessarily be concerned with what he should and should not do. This kind of concern may be one of the things that brought him to a psychotherapist in the first place, and however independent a soul he may be, one of the main things that keeps him there is the hope that he can be helped to guide himself along lines of behavior that will make his life more meaningful and satisfying. It is largely this hope that may compel him to invest the therapist with greater importance than most other people and to view the therapist, more or less realistically, as the agent of the resolution of his conflicts. It is my contention that the force of this agency, in those conflict areas in which morality figures, propels the therapist into the practical position of moralist whether or not he wishes to assume it.

That he should not wish to assume such a role is understandable, but the studied attempt to avoid doing so sometimes leads therapists into logically untenable positions. A therapist of my acquaintance, for example, once offered her students as a cardinal rule of psychotherapy the dictum that one "does not get involved in the politics or religion of the patient." At the same time, she could not advise how to avoid doing so—once the client has made them explicit issues—except by declining to offer one's personal politics or religion as solutions to the client's problems. While this may be sound negative advice, it is of questionable use to either therapist or patient. The strategy itself requires some rationale—it seems unreasonable to propose a list of ideas, beliefs, and attitudes that are outside the scope of the therapist's function, without similarly defining relevant alternatives that are appropriate to his function. Such a task is, at best, very difficult to do, and still harder to justify. And considering only tactics, how does one explain to the patient that it is legitimate for him to talk about anything, but it would not be proper for the therapist to talk back about A, B, or C?

Another analyst of my acquaintance said to a patient, in response to queries about certain guilt-provoking behavior, "Why should I give a damn how you act?" but on another occasion, in relation to the same behavior, told him that therapy would have to terminate if the patient did not discontinue his "acting-out." In the first instance, the analyst was referring, albeit for technical reasons, to his own moral view of the patient's behavior, while in the second situation he was considering the behavior as a technical problem in the therapy. But the behavior was the same in both cases! It seems unrealistic to discuss the same behavior as a therapeutically irrelevant issue in the first instance and a therapeutically critical one in the second. Could one seriously expect the patient to honor the distinction?

The "neutralist" position is most clearly stated by a third analyst who says, "When I am working in the privacy of the analytic session, I don't care if the world is coming down around my patient's ears on the outside." He does not stipulate, incidentally, whether his attitude would be the same if the financial world of the patient were collapsing, indicating that he would no longer be paid, or if the patient were, on the outside, "acting-out" in a fashion which "interfered with the progress of the analysis."

It is obvious that, in most therapeutic situations, there are choice points at which the therapist must manifest some very real concern with the life the patient leads outside the therapy situation proper, and that some of that concern will be directed towards how the patient ought or ought not to act.

MORALS AS GENERALITIES

Consideration of the foregoing as a purely technical problem also forces a more general issue into bold relief: This concerns what the therapist wishes ultimately to accomplish: the long-range goals of his therapy. The technical problem deals with immediate goals, but this asks what he wishes to see happen to this person, not merely in therapy, but in life. In what ways does he, as therapist, want his ministrations to alter the client's life?

Ultimately, I believe, this is a moral question that is always answered by the therapist in practice, whether or not it is ever posed in words; and the answer in fact is formed in terms of some superordinate, if unvoiced, moral code of his own. Sometimes the nature of the answer is masked by the impersonal scientistic language of mental health—but it is less subtly hidden in the words of the minister who counsels against premarital intercourse because of its "unfortunate psychological consequences"; of the Catholic caseworker who opposes his client's divorce because of its "mentally disrupting effect"; of the libertarian who helps his client accept the "psychological legitimacy" of extramarital affairs. Such therapeutic goals reflect personal morals and not scientifically validated conclusions.

Perhaps the most general, and accurate, answer that sensitive and self-conscious therapists could offer to the question of their goals could be put so: "I want to reshape this person's existence so that he will emulate values which I cherish for myself, aspire to what I wish humanity to be, fulfill my need for the best of all possible worlds and human conditions."

It is a truism that the therapist is himself a human being, that he lives in society, and that wisely or unknowingly, responsibly or casually, he has made moral commitments to himself and that society. But the present argument carries this platitude to its own logical, if unheeded, conclusion—that the very nature of his interaction with the people he serves involves a moral confrontation which, at the very least, renders communication of some part of his own moral commitments an inescapable part of his therapeutic work.

No one seriously doubts the validity of this argument in the case of the pastoral counselor, for he is almost always publicly committed to a religious-moral system whose content is usually well known to his clients before they ever approach him. No one believes, for example, that a priest will "accept" crime or sexual misconduct when confessed, as something less than sinful, regardless of the immediate response he makes to the confession. And while he may be understanding of the cause of this behavior and eager and able to temper judgment of its severity, and may deeply empathize with the guilt and anguish of its perpetrator—there is still little doubt that he looks upon the action as sinful and the behaver as a sinner, independent of the determinants which contributed to the act. For the priest, despite all else, is publicly committed to the notion that every individual is ultimately responsible for paying the price of his choice—and the person who confesses knows this all along.

The notion that the psychotherapist's situation differs much from the priest's is, I believe, a convenient fiction. To any given incident revealed by his client, the psychotherapist makes some kind of response, or so he is seen. He may carefully avoid making a very emphatic positive or negative response—he may manifest a studied, neutral attitude, and he may sincerely and devoutly feel neither censure nor approval of the situation at hand. But to regard this neutrality as an amoral position, to salve his own democratic, egalitarian, or relativistic conscience, to convince himself that he "is not imposing his own value system upon his client"—merely because he does not want to impose it—is ultimately to deceive both the client and himself. For this belief implicitly denies the essence of the psychotherapeutic relationship: that its most critical points are those involving the *interactions* between participants, not the private experiences of either of them. In other words, psychotherapy is a social, interpersonal action, char-acterized by an exchange of individual, personal ideas and feelings. The verbal content of the exchange differs with the respective roles of client and therapist, but the relationship is, in vital respects, a reciprocal one.

The very fact of the exchange relationship dictates, I be-lieve, the inevitability of the therapist's functioning practically as a moral agent for three reasons:

1. He influences the moral decisions of the client because the client necessarily interprets the therapist's response to his moral concerns. If the therapist approves his behavior, he may reinforce it. If the therapist disapproves, he may change it. If the therapist appears neutral, he may interpret this as either tacit approval or tacit disapproval—and in many instances, it may be either one, complicated by the therapist's fears of upsetting the client or his reluctance to "dictate" ground rules of propriety. In any case, the very fact that the therapist permits discussion of these issues largely legitimizes any attempts on the client's part to interpret the ther-apist's reaction to his remarks.

2. Therapists are affiliated with professional societies. These societies have generally published codes of ethical conduct that dictate ground rules of propriety to the therapist, codes that at-tempt to establish minimal bounds to his conduct. Breach of these codes generally results in expulsion from the professional society. Whether or not he makes the binding limits of his code explicit to his client, the ethical therapist must act on these limits at criti-cal points in therapy—and whenever he does so, he serves an ex-plicit moral agency.

3. Therapists have personal value systems, and it is difficult to see how they could possibly form relationships with clients even for the sole purpose of understanding them, never mind helping them, without being cognizant of their own values and making implicit comparisons between themselves and their values and those of their clients. The failure to respond in any way to those

comparisons, by some process of suspension of his own beliefs, may be possible, but it may also eventually commit the therapist to suspending his interaction—for it is hard to see how he can respond to his patient without cognizance of himself, and once aware of his own values, how he can completely withhold communicating them and continue to interact. This communication is precisely what occurs whenever, for example, a psychotherapist makes the continuation of treatment contingent on the patient's performing or refraining from some behavior. That the value involved for the therapist is a technical rather than a moral one is beside the point. It is *his* value, not the client's, and unless he can communicate it, he cannot function therapeutically.

IMPLICATIONS

If one accepts the notion that psychotherapists are moral agents, and that this agency may be intrinsic to their functions and goals, some important issues take shape.

It becomes apparent, for one thing, that not all the matters dealt with in therapy are mental health matters, even within the broadest meaning of that term. Some of these matters refer to religion, politics, and social and economic behavior of great importance both to individuals and to society. Psychotherapists cannot claim special knowledge or competence in the discussion of such issues, but neither are they apparently free on that basis to disengage themselves from their patients' concerns.

I do not believe that this is an entirely soluble dilemma, but certainly a first step towards its solution would require that therapists become vividly aware of their own personal commitments. Students of therapy have too often been encouraged to regard their clients and themselves exclusively in terms of "dynamics," "relationships," and "perceptions." Insufficient attention has been paid to those aspects of both clients' and therapists' ideologies, philosophies, and moral codes, many of which cannot be interpreted as merely incidental aspects of people's lives.

Secondly, it is apparent that so-called moral neutrality in the psychotherapist is as much a moral position as any more blatant one. It is, from the therapist's side, a libertarian position, regardless of how the client sees it (indeed, in some respects, he may justly see it as insidious). Expressed in a variety of ways, this position is currently in vogue among psychotherapists of quite dissimilar orientations. Some of the concepts that serve to legitimize and popularize moral neutrality are "democracy," "self-realization" or "-actualization," and "existence." All these concepts are oriented towards people's freedom to do as they please. But even the most democratic general theories, in specifying assumptions and goals, limit their generosity with other terms such as "social responsibility" or "productivity." The latter kind of language seems to suggest that psychotherapists regard themselves as a genuine social force. If so, then to what extent are therapists obligated to represent themselves to the public at large, and to their clients, as a committed social agency? And according to what set of codes? For societies reflect within themselves systems of morality, and a relatively open society, such as that in America, reflects competing and contradictory codes. Is the therapist as moralist obligated, further, to participate publicly in moral arguments as they are reflected in political and economic life—or is he entitled to reserve his participation to his special area of competence?

The question becomes more immediate when it is asked in relation to the individual patient rather than to society at large. At what point, and by what means, is the therapist obligated or entitled to involve himself actively as moralist with his client? Is he entitled, perhaps obligated, to challenge the moral intent of his client when he thinks it inadequate—or immoral? Can he, in good conscience, permit in his patient any kind of behavior that serves to free him permanently of guilt, anxiety, neurosis? If so, will he not thoughtlessly be elevating the goal of personal adjustment to a supreme value—and is this not an inadequate goal for a community of men? And if so, is the therapist free of moral responsibility to that community?

Starting with an altogether technical matter, the sequence of issues that evolve seems inescapable. Either therapists can successfully influence behavior or they cannot, and they have little choice of what to claim. If they wish to say they cannot do so, or may not do so in just those areas where human concern is greatest, and are therefore not at all responsible for the behavior of their clients, one must ask what right they have to be in business. The very validity of the disclaimer destroys their most important function, so the help they can give must then be very narrowly defined.

But if, on the other hand, they affirm some technical expertise and wish to claim a genuine ability to influence people, then they must also assume some responsibility for the nature of that influence. In that event, they must ultimately see themselves as moral agents as they are confronted with moral problems. And the extent to which they are confronted with moral problems depends on the significance of the problems with which they deal, for morals are the ultimate values we assign to our acts.

It is not clear that psychotherapists are suited to assume this role, but it seems certain they cannot escape it. In such a strait, they may best serve themselves and those they hope to aid, by examining this agency to see what it entails.

THE SOURCES OF THERAPEUTIC MORALITY

Until recently, both physicians and patients were generally content to define health by its absence (in illness) and illness by the presence of symptoms. People went to doctors to be cured of ailments, however vague, that were accompanied by symptoms, however vague. For some centuries now, doctors have been increasingly successful at accomplishing their cures by discovering more and more specific sources of ailments and specific agents for their relief. Despite current adjurations to treat "whole patients," there are few medical practitioners who are loathe to use the scalpel quite specifically on a bloated appendix or an antibiotic drug with equal specificity on a pneumonic lung. Thoughtless of any philosophic need for a theoretical definition of health, doctors work with implicit regard for an empirical definition of illness. Essentially, illness is defined by the presence of symptoms.

In this view, health is simply the state in which symptoms are absent, treatment is the process of removing them, and cure is the state in which they are continuously absent after the termination of treatment.

The term *mental illness* has been used somewhat ambiguously to refer both to peculiarities of thought or feeling that result from some physical disturbance of the body and to peculiarities of bodily function that apparently result from some irregularities of thought or feeling. It is the latter use which has given most impetus to the development of psychotherapy, a craft which capitalized on the discovery that some symptoms which have no obvious organic basis are vulnerable to psychological assault.

While both these concepts of mental illness still have some currency, neither of them is adequate to describe the great bulk of conditions for which people seek psychotherapy in modern times. Especially in the case of educated and sophisticated people, it is probably fair to say that they seek help mostly for irregularities of thought and feeling which result from irregularities of thought and feeling. Simply stated, they have "psychological problems" or "emotional difficulties" or "disordered personalities" or are merely "maladjusted" or unhappy.

It seems strange, at first blush, that this once crude, inefficient, and little known branch of medicine should, in barely three generations, have given rise to an enormously popular, lucrative, and influential profession which has little apparent connection with the scientific practice of medicine. It seems even stranger, perhaps, that an originally narrow scientific endeavor should have generated a secular moralism which has impressed itself so quickly on the Western world, and so profoundly, and without much benefit of scientific validation. Yet these developments have occurred, and they cannot be attributed, I believe, either to historical accident or even primarily to the personal genius of psychotherapeutic pioneers such as Freud. They are perhaps more the result of two inevitable problems that arose when people first started trying to cure ailments by talking:

1. Psychological approaches to symptoms tended to elicit information of much broader scope than the details of individual aches and pains. This process starts quite naturally when a physi-

cian begins to treat by talking instead of only prescribing, injecting, or cutting. It is extended when he invites or permits the patient to join in discourse. And it becomes prolific when, as in Breuer and Freud's early work, he enjoins the patient to talk about anything that comes into his head. The invitation to talk confers the blessing of relevance, and the presence of a willing audience tempers the stigma of shame and dishonor that may cloud one's private concerns. What started as a visit to an alienist for the relief of migraine headaches or paralyzed limbs may then expand to an outpouring of problems in living, of interpersonal conflicts and frightening sexual and aggressive themes, of sin, horror, agony, and fear. If, in the course of this process, symptoms are relieved, it is small wonder that the doctor connects the contents of the discourse with the origin of the symptoms, and some tribute to his genius that he invents sequential explanations of a mental process creating bodily symptoms when he cannot identify an organic process which does so. The niceties of *post hoc, ergo propter hoc* are trivial matters to the practicing physician.

2. The definition of symptoms was expanded to include issues that had no conventional scientific relationship to health or illness, such as happiness or satisfaction in life. Once a connection had been made between disorders of body function and psychological conflict and discontent, permitting the argument that the basic problem which gave rise to ailments was a psychological one, it became reasonable to think that psychological problems were legitimate objects of treatment even if they had not yet produced physical ailments in a person. Finally, and equally plausibly, it was argued that psychological problems should be treated even if they would never give rise to physical illness, for physical ailments are peripheral events and psychological problems central ones in the lives of modern men.

The horizons of psychotherapy thus widened naturally as medicine found increasingly formal and elegant theories for defining an ever-broader range of human distresses as being within its scope. Armed with rationales apparently consonant with the spirit of scientific inquiry and independent of overtly religious Messianism or denominational buffoonery that might supernaturalize its goals, psychotherapy gained increasing appeal among educated people as a potential means of relieving their problems of living even if they are not plainly sick.

SCIENCE AND MORALITY

But if the scope of practice was broadened by these inevitable problems, the scope of inquiry was extended even further. For the first problem, the sources of symptoms, forces the question "What is most real?" especially when reality is hidden from the naked eye. If the observable symptom is not the real problem, but something overlaid upon it, is it not equally likely that the underlying problem is itself an overlay? The problem is not merely one of what to look for but of when to stop the search. The idea that there are levels of problems implies the existence of some core or basement of concern. Thus working backward step by step, always potentially in infinite regress, inquiry is focused more and more narrowly on the nature of things. For psychotherapists, the self-imposed limit on the question is addressed to the nature of man.

The second problem, the elaboration of symptoms, raises a less academic and thus more practically difficult question. If psychological distress in the broadest sense is a legitimate object of psychotherapeutic endeavor, then the breadth of the effort to relieve distress must be measured against some potential cost and valued in terms of some potential gain. Willy-nilly, the abstraction "ought" must be invoked to mediate objectives. "How ought people to behave? How ought they to feel? What ought they to want?"

Now the central difference between these problems is that the first poses a question of *fact*, the second a question of *morals*. The distinction between them deserves much thought, especially in discourse about scientific enterprises, for facts define science and morals are excluded from it.

For scientific purposes, a fact is anything potentially susceptible of measurement, and that is all that scientific work is about. A hypothesis in science is a guess about a fact that has not yet been measured, and a theory is a body of logically related guesses, based on a collection of known facts, about still unmeasured things. Scientific work identifies facts—that is, measurable realities—and attempts to predict the consequences in fact of measured or inferred reality, but by definition it avoids any evaluations other than factual ones. The desirability of any consequence, as opposed to its predictability, is a contingency outside the scope of science; it is a problem in morals.

Morals are not logically contingent on facts, but in practice moral systems are always ostensibly based on conjectures about the factual nature of things. Moral theses may start with the argument that "such and such is the way to be" and rationalize some reality from which to explain the moral, or "such and such is the nature of things" and propose some ideal behavior which is consonant with nature. Social and religious movements develop in both directions. Science starts and ends with consideration only of the nature of things, but scientists do not. They are as concerned as anyone else with the desirability of things and, their lives devoted to the rigors of discovering what is true, may feel themselves possessed of a better platform than others have for judging also what is good. It is understandable, then, that what may start them off on a narrow technical or scientific work may end them up with a sweeping Weltanschauung and a moral philosophy that engages more than they ever dreamed. Far from being conscious and deliberate, however, this progression is likely to take place almost thoughtlessly, with technicians operating more or less unaware of the points at which their technical enterprises overlap with and imply moral systems.

THE MEANING OF NORMAL

A good example of this transition in the psychotherapeutic arts comes in the generally ambiguous use of the word "normality." Technically, "normal" is a term that describes a particular kind of mathematical graph and statistical phenomenon. If certain measurements are made of a very large number of individuals, for example, and half of them fall above and half below a certain point on the measuring rod, with most falling very close to it and diminishing numbers falling further and further from that point in precisely equal proportions on both sides of it, then the entire array of measurements is called a normal distribution.

Viewed this way, normality can never be considered a property of *persons*, but only of *characteristics* that are shared in some specified degree by everyone. Used in this statistical sense, things like height or intelligence may be said to be normally distributed among all people, but it would not be correct to say that someone has normal height or intelligence. The latter phrase is more appropriately used in connection with the term "norm," which essentially means *average*; thus, to say that someone is normally tall or bright means that he has about average height or intelligence. In this sense, abnormal means unusual, that is, much different from the average.

Now, neither of the meanings above has any reference to what is good or bad, holy or profane, desirable or abhorrent. They are purely descriptive. Any scientific use of these terms will remain purely descriptive, and anything that looks evaluative and is still scientific will be evaluative *only* with respect to some specific function or fact. Thus, it is good to be abnormally tall (above average in height) *if* one wishes to play basketball, and it is good to be abnormally short *if* one wishes to drive a Volkswagen. Such statements imply nothing about the desirability of either playing basketball or driving Volkswagens, and no such scientific statement is possible except in terms of some further function that may be *measurably* served by either behavior.

In common parlance about people, however, "normal" is generally used to mean either *optimal* or at least not bad and "abnormal" is used synonymously with *bad, sick,* and so forth. Were this only a popular misuse, it might be no more significant than the current fad of describing things "electrical" as "electronic." But this misuse is rather widespread within professional psychological circles, and one cannot help wondering what the mislabeling contributes to misunderstanding. Textbooks in abnormal psychology, for example, are concerned almost exclusively with pathology; they have no chapters on the intellectually gifted, the artistically creative, nor the unusually happy, well-integrated, or productive people, who by virtue of the epithet deserve some space. Not that they should have; it is the title, not the practice, which is questioned here.

The concept of normality is a most attractive one to many

scientists, particularly to those whose work, like that of psychologists and psychiatrists, is related to the biological sciences. How has it happened, then, that this scientifically valuable notion has been damaged in its handling even among those who should know better? How has it come about that abnormality has passed from a descriptive statistic to a moral pejorative? I think it has happened in much the same way that science and morality have generally been confounded in psychotherapy—unwittingly, by the imposition of value and fact upon each other, by the casual assumption that there exist norms which suit values when the former have not been measured and the latter not defined, by the failure to weigh means (techniques) against ends (goals) and both against fact. And much of this, I believe, is a natural consequence of the derivation of therapeutic theory from therapeutic practice, which forces upon the conscientious healer such an urgent need to allay the distress of the individual who confronts him, that he will be likely to employ some patchwork of that which seems to work, mindless at the time of both science and morality in their broader sense. And if what seems to work works well enough for some poor souls to gain relief, then he will recollect what he has done long enough to repeat it and well enough to teach it. He will rationalize it too, but maybe not very broadly nor very well nor with intent of seeing it beyond itself. For he is fascinated by his "case," and even were he not, the entire public seems to pound on his door and plead for help that he must give as best he can. He is a busy man, not stupid and not malicious and not given much to the possible tedium of aloof reflection on his work—and often not very effective. If he knew a little more of astrology or charlatanism or faith healing or the development of priestly castes, he might see some ironic and perhaps worrisome parallels between his own and some less-honored crafts. But purity of motive may itself restrict vision and besides, he is too busy. Thus surfeit of busyness elicits straitness which, lacking perspective, makes wasted effort which, delaying success, promotes busyness . . . and on and on.

PROFESSIONAL CONFUSIONS

The results for the public of the therapist's activities have not been as much as their promise, as we shall see. For the circle of his colleagues, they have been prodigious, and prodigiously confusing. One such result is economic, another academic.

For the former, psychotherapists have responded to the need for service chiefly by expanding training and promoting the expansion of professional training and service facilities. Training in psychotherapy is mostly a matter of apprenticeship, in which one learns to perform in ever greater accordance with the demands of his teacher. This is most unlike training in engineering, in which the person of the teacher has no great bearing on the performance of what is learned. Bridges stand or fall in their own right. Neither is it entirely like learning to play the piano, paint pictures, or carve furniture, for performance in these arts can be repeatedly submitted for judgment to very large audiences. Nor is it even quite like learning medicine, in which a goodly number of erstwhile patients may, through incompetent performance, become patent victims. In psychotherapy there is no clear body of truth that stands apart from its discoverer and no great audience to listen all at once to its performance; evidently too, nobody dies from it. Finally, if one is not entirely sure the patient is sick before treatment, how can he be judged to be well after it? Under the circumstances, training in psychotherapy necessarily involves the perpetuation of error in some degree, and worse, in some unknown degree. Perhaps ignorance comes to seem less ignorant as it bcomes more venerable, expanding error in the same direction. Or maybe it grows stale with age and pallid, inviting novel truths—or errors. No one knows.

But it is plain that when the main measure of performance is the experience, perspective, and instruction of the teacher, some changes will occur from one professional generation to the next. For bright students will think their own thoughts, and they will almost inevitably come upon experiences beyond the conceit of their tutors. And the more personal a man's teaching, the more divergent the pupil's learning by dint of his own personality. Then if the teacher has low tolerance for dissent, and if the student has small need to remain with him or great need to stand free of his shadow, they will separate. And when, as often happens, the student has become enamoured of his new experience or thought and too busy exploiting it to refrain from generalizing about it, a school is born. Thus Freud begat Jung, Adler, and Rank, and Rank begat

Rogers, and so on. It is unfair to say that the main reason there are more therapists than therapeutic schools is because it takes two or more people to make a school, but one investigator, without joking, has identified thirty-six schools or techniques—and missed some.

It is true that the profusion of schools signifies intellectual ferment, but it is probably also true that new schools have about the same value as old ones, for they are built on about the same structure—reverence for the person of the founder, fascination with individual cases and easy generalization from them, a strange confusion of theory with technique, the former usually struck from the latter mint, the casual assumption of opinion as fact, and the weird interposition of science and morals. The very profusion can be considered symptomatic of the poverty of psychotherapy as an applied science, for it does not represent different assaults on different kinds of problems but competing tactics in the same battle.

Another clue to the doubtful scientific status of psychotherapy lies in the close identification of therapeutic positions with the personalities and circumstances of their creators. I know few medical students who can identify Sherrington or Fleming, much less separate Galen from Vesalius, but still fewer psychotherapy students who are not interested in Jones' life of Freud. A favorite bait of "neo-Freudians," such as Thompson and Fromm, is that Freud's theories cannot be properly evaluated outside the context of the intellectual currents of the late nineteenth century and the social environment of Central Europe, or the emancipation of the Jews from the ghetto or their traditions of religious mysticism. If the intended evaluation were a historical or sociological one, they would be quite right. But if proper evaluation means judging the scientific veracity of Freud's theories—that is, their power to predict still unknown facts—the demand for context is absurd. Can Newton's physics be properly understood only in the context of the seventeenth century or his calculus in the light of his religious mysticism? I have heard therapy students disparage the scientific status of the theories of C. G. Jung on the (unwarranted) grounds that he was a Nazi sympathizer, but no parallel proposal from mathematicians to abolish Cartesian coordinates because their creator was a devout Catholic. There is a striking correlation between the

extent of validation of a science and the lack of necessary reference
to personalities in the teaching of it.

THE COMPONENTS OF THERAPY SYSTEMS

It is not necessary to probe the historical origins of any system of thought to analyze either its scientific or its moralistic implications, but it is necessary to identify the components of the
system. I believe there are three signal elements explicit or implied
in all systems of psychotherapy. These are: (1) a theory of personality, which addresses itself to the nature of man and behavior,
(2) a superordinate moral code, usually a social philosophy, which
addresses the organization of society and the relationship of individuals to it, and (3) a body of therapeutic techniques, which are
deliberate means of manipulating or influencing behavior.

Personality theories are inherently scientific enterprises in
that they refer entirely to questions of fact. They have bearing on
morality, however, in two respects: (1) The limiting principles of
behavior may determine the theoretical limits of moral expectations.
If, for example, men of necessity behave in certain ways under
certain conditions, then they cannot sensibly be adjured to behave
differently in those circumstances. (2) So little is actually known
about the principles of behavior that all personality theories of
much relevance to psychotherapy are thoroughly speculative. Insofar as they are neither tested nor currently testable, the implications for morality that derive from them have no more scientific
validity than do the moral adjurations of revealed religion. They
are predictions based on faith, not fact.

Put differently, this says that if what scholastics called
Natural Law existed, it would be embodied, for our purposes, in
the facts which verified personality theory. But so few of those
facts are themselves known, that no moral code which refers to a
personality theory for authorization can correctly claim any scientific status.

Social philosophies, like other moral orders, are more often
implied than explicated in psychotherapeutic systems, and inevitably have more pretension than title to be called scientific. Insofar
as they derive from theories of personality, they pile speculation

upon speculation. As apparent derivatives of historical or sociological fact, however, they do much the same. It is not clear that there has ever been a single original social organization or that there exists any natural social organization or natural relationship between individuals and society. Anyway, psychotherapists are really concerned only with the possibility of an optimal social organization, not a natural one. As such, social philosophies of psychotherapeutic systems are almost exclusively moral doctrines, either suggesting how individuals ought to live to optimize society or waiving the obligations of individuals to social orders unworthy of their efforts.

Systems of therapeutic technique are scientific insofar as they predict specific outcomes of particular activities. Most therapy systems, however, have been less than incisive in specifying either outcomes or activities. Most of those that specify have not troubled to test their predictions. Most of those that test have produced rather unimpressive results. Most results that look impressive also appear untrustworthy.

The most important moral implications of techniques arise from the assumption that they work, which is obviously tenuous. Nevertheless, the moral issues that develop in this connection are more immediately significant than those related to behavior theory or social philosophy, for it is technique, not theory, that is actually imposed on people. They refer to the possibilities that the very application of technique, even if it is unsuccessful, violates existing moral systems of patient, therapist, or society, and that if successful, the resulting change in the patient will foster the violation of some extant moral standard or the creation of a dubious new one.

If this analysis of the components of psychotherapeutic systems is valid, then it is even more evident than before why this discipline is in a somewhat muddled intellectual state, for neither analysis into their components nor evaluation along separate scientific and moral dimensions, to my knowledge, characterizes many works on psychotherapy. The bulk even of the most thoughtful and considered psychotherapeutic writing fails completely to recognize as well as separate moral from scientific issues. Most of it derives from case studies that are used to illustrate theory with little mention of technique or social philosophy, as for example

Greenwald's compendium, *Great Cases in Psychoanalysis*. Or it specifies theory proper, tending to identify technique with theory, even though they may be largely independent, as in Fenichel's *Psychoanalytic Theory of the Neuroses* or Salter's *Conditioned Reflex Therapy*. Or it specifies technique alone with what sometimes looks like cavalier indifference to both behavior theory and optimal sociality, as in Wolberg's *Techniques of Psychotherapy*. Or it is largely social philosophy, rationalized by behavior theory or speculative doctrines of social science and totally indifferent to technique, as in Fromm's *Man for Himself*.

The development of this intellectual muddle, as suggested above, was a sort of natural one, a function of both historical and professional exigencies that were not entirely avoidable, but there is no good reason to maintain it. On the contrary, it undoubtedly must inhibit the legitimate development of the psychotherapeutic enterprise, if nothing else, by preventing therapists from defining their own functions. If psychotherapists wish to be considered applied scientists, they will have to start acting like scientists, which could mean sharply curtailing their activities and divesting themselves of deeply ingrained myths. If they wish to function as arbiters of morality, they would do well to say so. If they entertain hopes for discovering some scientifically viable moral system, they will have to become more sharply aware of the problems involved before they can even launch the search, let alone find anything. In any case, it seems unlikely that a society as hell-bent as ours on using science for the development of some kind of good life will permit them to muddle through the next three generations in plying their trade as they did the last. And it is as well for the profession as for the society that this is so, for it demands of psychotherapists that they improve themselves to maintain the decent regard of those they wish to serve.

THE MODES OF PSYCHOTHERAPY

Before psychoanalysis achieved much prestige in professional circles, a common defense by its supporters against unfriendly criticism was the claim that one had first to have the experience of being psychoanalyzed before he could really understand its significance. Transporting this argument to psychotherapy in general, it might read for patients: It is easier to partake of psychotherapy than to understand it. For psychotherapists themselves, read: It is easier to practice psychotherapy than to explain it.

I think the latter may be true, not because the subject is so abstruse or esoteric, but because the usual explanations of concrete practice so commonly invoke a theoretical discourse quite removed from what is really practiced. The practice of psychotherapy revolves around a body of techniques, but most of the discourse that tries to explain it is about one or another personality theory.

The relationship between them is often tenuous, and the failure to distinguish them can create serious confusion, the upshot of which in this discipline is that nobody can say quite precisely what psychotherapy is, or to whom it should be addressed, or how, or why.

It is difficult to know just how some clear understanding can be best achieved, but this essay contends that a good place to begin an exploration of psychotherapy is with an examination of techniques, for these have been the stepchildren of therapeutic discourse. And if in so doing, we examine not the minutiae of techniques, but their thematic qualities, then I believe we may discover a narrow range of therapeutic schemes from each of which derive some critical ideas. This says, in short, that understanding psychotherapy begins by looking at what psychotherapists do or say they do; from there, we may deduce more nuances and implications of this work.

PUBLIC CONFUSIONS

But how necessary is such an analysis? Is the allegation of confusion real, with its unhappy implications for the therapeutic professions, or is the confusion actually a network of quibbles in the mind of the accuser? Let us see.

One would think that people who need psychotherapy have enough troubles already so that they ought not to have imposed upon them the added task of sorting out one kind of therapist from another. But sort they must if they are wise, as even popular magazine articles on how to choose a psychiatrist now make clear. And if they make much use of the plethora of soft-cover case histories, psychic autobiographies, and sophisticated advice available on the subject, they must face at least some of the following problems.

First and least important, there are several different professions with strong vested interests in the public practice of psychotherapy: psychiatry, psychology, and social work all officially use it. Most people do not know the differences between these professions—and indeed, with respect to the practice of psychotherapy, most differences that are not financial are probably fictitious; psychiatrists earn more than psychologists who earn more than social workers.

More confusing perhaps is the fact that psychotherapy is practiced by many more different kinds of professionals who, unlike those above, differ in most functions as well as in their titles. Some of these find it impolitic to identify their therapeutic work with this label. Ministers who do psychotherapy call it "pastoral counseling," educators do therapy called "guidance," and a host of persons with credentials in any or all or none of these professions label their particular therapeutic practices "marital counseling" or "psychoanalysis" or some such term which refers to no formal profession and overlaps in meaning with several other terms all properly equivalent to "psychotherapy."

But neither having different kinds of tradesmen plying the same craft nor calling it by different names offers the wealth of confusion or requires the delicacy of distinction that is demanded by the very number of psychotherapeutic schools and styles proclaimed by its practitioners, by now so acclimated to multiplicity that they see no ironies in it. Robert A. Harper, for example, has written a book entitled *Psychoanalysis and Psychotherapy—36 Systems*, for the ostensible purpose of enlightening both "the professional person . . . and the intelligent layman who has heretofore looked in vain for an understandable map of the psychotherapeutic maze." Now if this plentitude of treatments involved much variety of techniques to apply to different persons under different circumstances by different specialists, there would be no embarrassment of therapeutic riches here, just as there is not within the many specialties of medicine or law or engineering. But this is not the case, and psychotherapeutic "systems" (or "orientations," as they are often glibly called) speak more to epithets than entities, and more to the perspectives and labels of their founders than to the facts of human behavior. One hardly goes to a psychoanalyst to be cured of anxiety and a nondirective therapist to be treated for homosexuality, as he might to a cardiologist for one condition and a radiologist for another. Nor does the same doctor use Freudian therapy for psychogenic ulcers and Rogerian treatment for functional headaches, as a physician might use medicine for one ailment and surgery for another. On the contrary, being a certain kind of psychotherapist has little bearing on treating a certain kind of problem, but refers rather to the likelihood of treating all problems from the vantage of a certain system. And its champion may see his system either as implying something more grand than mere technique, so that he feels no need for technical precision, or alternately as positing a technique comprehensive enough to apply in general rather than particular, so he feels no diagnostic limit on the ailments it can treat.

And though his system should tell much of how he is likely to treat whatever it is to which he lays his hand, it may in fact reflect less of true or significant difference from another's healing work than is suspected by him, his patients, or his competitors. It is not unfair to generalize that most advocates of most systems will treat most people for most problems for which most therapists of most other systems would treat them. Such differences in clientele as exist among therapists are generally matters of preference, source of referral, and the like, and not the studied consequence of orientation or system.

But far from being altogether bad, the very indifference in fact to differences in theory on the part of therapists makes it possible for clients to find help without first having either to learn much about psychotherapy or to be shunted around from one specialist to another. And the willingness of most therapists to take on most patients for most conditions reflects neither a cynical attempt to mulct the public nor a fanatical one to missionize any school; it is simply a direct response to what is probably the chief article of faith of the profession: that the skillful application of psychotherapy by a trained practitioner will be of definite positive value to most patients.

This common creed of therapists itself belies some claims of differences among the schools, implying that there must be terms in which some elements of difference make no difference. If we then seek among the therapeutic schemes not nuances of difference, the fine details of Dr. Harper's map, but the bold relief of thema, a topographic view that, losing subtleties, still gains perspective breadth, the schools of therapy might seem fewer and less varied than some of their advocates believe.

I earlier proposed that there are three major components

specified or implicit in all psychotherapy systems; these are a theory of personality, a social (moral) philosophy, and a more or less consistent body of techniques. Of these, theory of personality has received the most attention by far both in the literature and in training programs, and it is disputation over schemata of personality that has been chiefly responsible historically for the growth of different schools. Differences in social philosophy have not been the topic of much discussion among professional psychotherapists, and have thus understandably failed to produce much professional difference. Divergences in technique have always been important, of course, particularly to practitioners, but they have also been a source of potential disdain. They are important, on the one hand, because they are the most conspicuous aspects of different psychotherapies, and thus eminently suitable as foci for argument. On the other hand, sophisticated people tend to cherish the myth that technique is a nearly inevitable corollary of valid theorizing, an almost obvious application of true understanding. This is not so, of course, since the same theory may suggest several techniques and a single technique be deduced from many theories. But the belief makes it embarrassing to create or affiliate with a school on the basis of "mere technicality."

Embarrassment is both unfortunate and unnecessary, however, in this case, for the analysis of techniques serves understanding more than any other possible approach to this discipline, mainly because techniques are relatively concrete things, and to that extent are not only simpler to describe accurately than theories or philosophies but also more relevant indices of what actually goes on in therapy. The concreteness or specificity of techniques gives them some special advantages over other elements as grounds for understanding psychotherapy; three of these are (1) a scientific value, (2) an educative value, and (3) a dialectic value.

1. The scientific value of studying therapy techniques is that they are subject to exposure, thence to measurement, in a way that therapy theory is not. Techniques can be observed in a fairly straightforward way, and they can be described and labeled in the operational terms that are absolutely required for measurement and experimentation. It is effectively impossible to assess the practical value of psychotherapy in any terms other than technical

ones. However interesting, plausible, and appealing a theory may be, it is techniques, not theories, that are actually used on people. Study of the effects of psychotherapy, therefore, is always the study of the effectiveness of techniques.

2. The educative value of techniques is that they are easily described and thus are more intelligible and meaningful both to psychotherapy patients and to the general public than are theories, the more so as they have very direct bearing on the primary concern of patients, their symptoms. It is the presence of symptoms that makes people seek therapy to begin with, and it is the presumed availability to the psychotherapist of techniques that makes them go to him. It is not entirely facetious and not at all imprecise to say that the patient contributes his symptoms and the therapist his techniques to the mutual relationship called psychotherapy, and the successful exploitation by each of the other's contribution defines successful treatment in both their minds. Just as symptoms are overt and easily seen compared to their causes, which may be hidden and have to be inferred, so techniques are overt and plainly seen compared to theories, which, though supposedly underlying them, are always inferential and abstract.

3. The dialectic value of examining techniques, like the other values, is a function of their explicitness. To understand the principles of an unfamiliar system, whether of machines or of human relations, one must first examine its operations—what it does. Possession of that information, which is most apparent, then makes it possible to trace the less obvious connections backward between its operations and their source and forward between the operating limits of the system and its applications. Learning what the machine does, so to speak, precedes learning how it does what it does, then why it does what it does in the way it does it, and finally what its doing implies. In the same way, the most efficient means for understanding psychotherapy is to observe first what it is that therapists do, then how they go about doing it, and finally why they do things just so and what their doing implies. Using the components suggested above, this means first examining therapeutic techniques, then the personality theories that underlie them, and finally the personal and social moral schemes they imply.

In order to distinguish the scientific and moralistic components of the major psychotherapy systems and to evaluate their status both as scientific enterprises and moral systems, it is necessary to categorize them into a manageably small number. This categorizing could, of course, be done from the vantage of their personality theories or social philosophies, but only with more difficulty in the one case and less precision in the other. Personality theories are not all stated in ways equally applicable to psychotherapy, so some amount of translation is necessary to make them parallel each other enough to compare for this purpose. Techniques, moreover, are simply less complicated than personality theories, and therefore less confusing. As for moral ideologies or social philosophies, psychotherapists have, with few exceptions, been silent or naive about such implications of their trade, with the effect that ideology or social philosophy usually has to be read into a psychotherapeutic scheme because not enough has been said about it to permit its being read out of one.

At all events, one must choose some starting point, and I believe that from the vantage of technical operations, it is possible to assess the various brands of psychotherapy thematically but without oversimplification, and to conclude from this survey that there are essentially only two categories of psychotherapy, such that all the many systems and schools can be reduced to expositions of one or another of these or of attempts to compromise between them.

THE TECHNICAL MODALITIES

In general, the activities of psychotherapists are efforts to implement either of only two gross kinds of therapeutic operations, one of which characterizes what may be called *Insight Therapies*, and the other what may be called *Action Therapies*. These labels properly describe some of the signal features of all the treatments that fall under either heading, but are not themselves the official names of any psychotherapeutic schools. The name *Insight Therapy* is not original with me (cf. Wolberg, *Techniques of Psychotherapy*), but is used here to include several schools that ordinarily do not see themselves as particularly concerned with insight. The name *Action Therapy* is used here to refer largely to schools that call themselves "behavioristic," a term whose meaning is essentially historical and polemic and which is now functionally obsolete.

Almost all of the practice of psychotherapy in the United States and Western Europe is the practice of one or another brand of Insight treatment, and the Action therapies as formal systems are almost completely unknown to the general public. Indeed, psychoanalysis, the most venerable of the Insight therapies, is often popularly taken to be identical with all psychotherapy. Insight therapies, as represented by psychoanalysis, have had a somewhat longer history than the Action therapies, but since their beginning have been more fractionated and have had considerably fewer pretensions to any scientific basis for their development. To this day, they have had much more influence on all the psychiatrically connected helping professions. Psychotherapy training institutes in the United States tend to teach only single Insight systems, but even most university facilities and the psychotherapy institutes of Europe, which give training in several Insight systems, generally offer no training at all in the Action therapies. This situation is changing rapidly, however, for the voices of the Action therapists are stridently raised, not in an appeal for equal attention, but in a crusade for the erasure of the Insight treatments from the books of therapeutic practice. Armed with the canons of scientific evidence, the Action therapists claim that their counterparts at best have failed to demonstrate the usefulness of Insight Therapy and at worst have perpetrated a vile, if unintended, fraud upon the public. The public as yet remains unconvinced, but the attention of uncommitted professionals is given increasingly to the Action therapists.

THE HANDLING OF SYMPTOMS

There is a technical focus of conflict between these systems that tends, on the one hand, to define the difference between them, and that permits, on the other, the many different Insight systems, subject to conflict and disputation among themselves, to be lumped together. I think the difference can be most clearly understood as an orientation towards the problem of *symptoms*.

Regardless of the kind of therapist to whom they go, people only seek psychotherapy because they have some kind of symptoms, which means, for our purpose, that something is bothering them. Insight and Action therapists could readily agree on this casual definition of a symptom, but they would differ over the relevance of the symptom to what they do about it. If the therapist is oriented towards Insight methods, he will probably try to assail the ailment that lies beneath the symptom, bypassing the immediate problem. If he is an Action therapist, he will probably behave as if the symptom were itself ailment enough, and try to remove it. From another angle, the Insight therapist will try to help his patient with the reflected problem rather than the symptom, thus undermining the symptom or at least permitting the patient to understand the character of his symptom and its relationship to his life so that he can exercise better control over the latter if not the former. The Action therapist will try more directly to eliminate the symptom so that the patient will feel better, and it makes no difference to him what the patient does or does not understand about anything.

The technical source of disputation is thus a function of the importance the therapist attaches to symptoms in the first place, for the more finally important they are in the life of the patient, the more cautious and critical must be his attack upon them. There is a lot at stake. But if the significance of psychological symptoms is no greater than the rash of measles or even the sputum of pneumonia, which is after all, even at its lethal worst, still less than the essence of its victim, then it were best attacked perhaps with gusto and élan and little fear of burning down the house together with the rubbish.

The difference between the Insight and Action schools comes clear in what may seem like a paradox between them, but which sets the tone for describing the details of each. For the object of the Insight therapist is grand and dangerous, demanding of him at his moral best the utmost in discretion and circumspection —he aims towards the core of meaning of his patient's life, prepared to reshape and mold it to new designs whose implications, though unknown, must be great indeed. Symptoms do not occur in vacuo, and however troublesome themselves, they only condense the vast significance of what they symbolize. In such a vital game, the therapist risks more by winning than by not, and he may be less afraid of failing to cure the symptom than of curing it to make a golem or a convert for whom he has no faith. And thus he orients his practice towards a gentle stance in which he mostly checks himself, exerting no control, but watches, guides, and counsels, Socratizing with the anxious hope that clearing off the cobwebs from his patient's soul will by itself reveal some splendid creature fit to live with men.

Not so the Actionist, a ruder man, contemptuous of subtleties at first, whose fear of symptoms is limited only to the thought that there may be other symptoms underlying them or that they may themselves, once vanquished, somehow still recur. If he can solve these problems he has done enough, with no examination of the meaning of this or any man's life. What symptoms reflect in his concern is pain and nothing else. He is a modest man thus far, like the mechanic who, proud of his ingenious repairs, has neither wish nor fear that they are inventions. And this very modesty cuts his risks, he thinks, permitting him a boldness in his work that Insight doctors hardly dare. He shapes behavior (in the lower case), not tampering with "selves" or "souls" or even "personalities." And if he can, by argument, seduction, threat, or even skillful violence (as a surgeon does), excise the symptom's painful barb, then he has done enough, but not too much. For the moment, his control is as intense as he can manage, but it is a momentary autocracy only, and meaningless enough to the totality of life to be permissible.

Time honors the development of schools, permitting each its institutes and seminars and spokesmen and prophets, whose identity is partly clarified by contrast with their counterparts. Thus accusations grow between these schools: The Insight advocate alleges that the Actionist is sterile, superficial, and mechanical, failing to apprehend the great variety of human ways, and ultimately sacrificing the meaning of any man's existence to a quest of comfort and adjustment that, freeing him of the need to discover his self and the meaning of his existence, deprive him of his best potential traits. The Actionist in turn contends that true compassion recognizes even symptomatic pain as painful and, not stopping there, as scientist decries the house of inferential sand his Insight colleagues burrow out beneath the patient's pain, permitting them

to disdain the palpable as superficial and felt anguish as irrele-
vance. If he is mechanical, says the Actionist, mechanics work
some tangible effects that literary pseudo-scientists do not; and if
he seems sterile, he at least refrains from grandiose and philosophic
quests. And finally, if nothing else, he says, regard for truth alone
dictates that he free himself of the mythology which, lending whatever meaning or security to Insight therapists, may give nothing to
their patients but expense and long travail and maybe finally
neither meaning nor comfort.

THE LIMITS OF THE SYSTEMS

Each system, earnestly pursued, must somewhere lead to
choice points where consistency creates absurdity, which in turn
unveils delusions of the total scheme. For there are purely symptomatic wounds which so engross the lives of victims that to disregard them as mere externals in honor of an unseen primal cause
is surely idle cruelty. Such is anorexia, a sometimes lethal loss of
appetite, or altophobia, a fear of heights which, when writ large
in urban man, and operating if he merely tries to walk upstairs,
may almost invalid him. No decent therapist, in deference to insight, will sit quietly and watch the (symptomatic?) self-destruc-
tion of a manic state, or gently authorize compulsive washers in
symbolic flight from guilt to rub away their flesh. For all of these,
symptomatic treatments always have priority, if not respect—if
nothing else, some vessel must be kept in which to pour awareness.

And perhaps as many times, there must be men who, freed
of all their symptomatic woes, discover then a truer misery, until
now buried underneath a host of petty ills. Preoccupied no more
with pedantries, with headaches, phobias, or vile thoughts, a nau-
seating emptiness appears to them ahead, a nameless terror of a
nameless end. Can this be still a symptom, and if so, still violable
by some concrete Act, by formulation of a habit or association with
some pleasantness-arousing stimulus pulled from a bag of therapeutic tricks? May not men leap from cliffs for other reasons than
those for which dogs salivate to bells? Are there not meanings,
goals, and fears, and aspirations which, subject to words, to understanding and appraisal, dictate some pains and balms alike, rooting

themselves more firmly as they settle into consciousness and intertwine with all man's myriad thoughts of self? Even the most devout Actionist probably will not deny *his* consciousness or will or complexity, and should he do so, we may suspect his actions will belie his words. Whether life has meaning or not, there are men who think it does, or can, or should; for these, perhaps the search alone or lack of it brings repair or suffering. Such miseries, by their nature, take the Actionist off guard; his system is geared to lesser aches and pains.

Happily, the contest between these systems, the mutual allegations, the sources of delusion, and the moral implications are not constant matters in the thoughts of their adherents, who quite sensibly devote their practices more to their patients than to their colleagues. And since patients do not always fit the theoretical molds to which their doctors incline, and do not always respond graciously to the "technique of choice," but must nonetheless be treated, a certain flexibility of manner is likely soon to mark the doctor's work regardless of his continued devotion to one or another school. The clear-cut differences then argued here appear to become oversimplifications as even the most extreme practitioners are gradually transformed from militant fanatics to casual eclectics, borrowing one or another technique or operation that seems appropriate to the person and the occasion. There is a quiet blending of techniques by artful therapists of either school; a blending that takes account of the fact that people are considerably simpler than the Insight schools give them credit for, but that they are also more complicated than the Action therapists would like to believe. The paradox is only apparent, not real. It is the other extreme of absurdity in both systems, in which Insight theorists attribute too much significance to nail biting and thumbsucking and their like, while Actionists cannot believe that any man, ever, really bears in his heart personal anguish for "the suffering of all living creatures."

All this suggests a caveat on catalogues like this one, but it is a two-sided warning.

There is a straw man clothed by my model, and some care must be exercised to avoid seduction either into too literal an acceptance of it or too hasty a rejection of the similarities and distinctions it proposes. It takes only a personal experience doing psychotherapy to recognize diversity and variation among people that will not permit any neat plan of treatment to be effective for everyone; no sensible therapist operates with as much loyalty to doctrine as has been implied. But were there, on the other hand, no real distinctions possible, then the *Sturm und Drang* that marks this craft is nothing but the prattling of fools, and I do not think that is the case. When Action therapists allege that insight schemes reflect compassionate incompetence, or Insight advocates portray the Actionists as petty men slinking into scientific rigor to hide their inability to countenance significance, each touches on the other's nerve and somewhat rightly so.

However much the blending of techniques occurs to mask the differences, one must not disregard them and argue more consensus between the schools than exists in fact. Practitioners blend mostly for practical reasons, but at all events are always more inclined to see their work as part of a self-contained body of ideas than as a set of reactions to a foreign scheme. It may be even more useful for the observer who wishes to compare the Insight and Action positions with each other, to see them first in some detail as independent entities. But in reality they are hypothetical points on a continuum of technicalities, and nothing more.

Approaching therapy by a description of such technical systems serves clarity, but it is not quite sufficient for comprehension; techniques must finally be seen in the context of their application and related both to the assumptions from which they are deduced and to the goals to which they are addressed. A technique is nothing but a means for doing something, and the study of means in psychotherapy falls midway between the study of personality theory and the study of the goals of therapy's outcome, for means derive partly from the content of some underlying theory and are directed partly, or should be, at some specific goals. To some extent then, the procedure to be followed here is one of starting in the middle and working both ways. This is not absurd, however, for we must finally come full circle anyhow, to find that the separation of theory, technique, and objectives is largely fictional. It is a useful fiction, and one from which we may be best enabled to understand and criticize the entire elusive process of psychotherapy.

———————————————————————— PART TWO

THE HEALING MODES

THE SECRETS OF THE HEART
INSIGHT THERAPY

Magazines, movies, plays, television programs, novels, short stories, and learned texts have all told much about Insight psychotherapy, often very accurately. Artists, poets, composers, and movie scenarists have all borrowed from it for their work, and if their renderings are less than clear expositions of it, still they are illustrations of its pervasiveness in this culture. It is unnecessary, to say the least, to introduce sophisticated readers to this discipline, for they have been introduced almost endlessly to one or another aspect of it in education, in entertainments, in cultural pursuits, in social relationships, and perhaps in their personal lives. This is even more true in metropolitan than in rural areas, for large cities have the resources to sustain formal societies of psychotherapists, and in such settings the educated public is likely to learn a good deal about the different trademarks of different psychotherapeutic denominations. The less initiated, on the other hand, are more likely simply to equate psychotherapy with psychoanalysis, a confusion which is given unwitting support by the many Insight therapists who simultaneously affirm and deny that they are psychoanalysts, usually by calling themselves "psychoanalytically oriented."

Far from belittling this equivalence, however, I shall argue that the apparently ignorant gathering of many psychotherapeutic sheep into a single fold is more justified than not, and that the many different Insight schools of therapy, instead of differing vitally from each other, as they allege, in practice are united by more significant commonalities than they are separated by discords. The areas of disagreement are worth some attention because, among other reasons, they have been sources of intense personal argument among psychotherapists and have given rise historically to a large number of schools, some of which feel so strongly about their differences that they avoid contact or interaction with members of rival camps.[1] These differences have also consumed considerable space in the psychotherapeutic literature. But they are here regarded chiefly as curiosa, and one purpose in citing them will be to discount them.

The progenitor of all modern types of Insight therapy, if not of all psychotherapy, is Sigmund Freud's psychoanalysis, and as prototype, it has continued to this day to serve both as bible and whipping boy to all the subsequent developments in this field. It will do as much for this characterization of Insight psychotherapies, for the most vital attributes of psychoanalysis apply equally well to its progeny, justifying the allegation that they are all "psychoanalytically oriented" whether they say so or not.

Insight therapists vary considerably both in the degree of and the reasons for their divorcement from Freudian psychoanalysis. Disciples of the American psychiatrist Harry Stack Sullivan, for example, himself only a vicarious disciple of Freud, are likely to say that they differ radically from Freudians because of their different theory of personality, which asserts a cultural rather than biological origin of neurosis. But they also claim to differ on the

[1] They sometimes try to protect patients from them too, as when a Freudian therapist told a patient to make his wife stop seeing a Jungian because "we can't have two kinds of therapy going on in the same family."

technical grounds that the patients of Freudians have to lie down where they cannot see the therapist during their appointments while their own patients are permitted both to sit upright and to face their doctor.

Perhaps the Insight school which claims the greatest difference from psychoanalysis and for the most reasons is that founded by the psychologist Carl Rogers. It is variously known as Rogerian, nondirective, or client-centered therapy, and not only does it fail to specify any origins in psychoanalysis, but it also identifies the most critical aspects of its operations as critically different from psychoanalysis. Like the Sullivan school, it is an American product.

Existential analysis, on the other hand, originates in Europe and has become widely known in the United States only within the past few years. This movement, as its name implies, tries to blend the insights of psychoanalysis with the insights of existential philosophy to elicit insights from troubled people. Without totally disavowing psychoanalysis, it claims to be and do more than analysis.

THE TECHNICAL EQUIVALENCE OF INSIGHT THERAPIES

To begin with their operations, there are two gross commonalities among all the Insight therapies, one positive and one negative, which dwarf both their many differences and all their other likenesses:

1. The single allowable instrument of the therapy is talk, and the therapeutic sessions are deliberately conducted in such a way that, from start to finish, the patient, client, analysand, or counselee does most of the talking and most of the deciding of what will be talked about.

2. The therapist operates with a conservative bias against communicating to the patient important or detailed information about his own life, that is to say, the therapist tends to hide his personal life from the patient.

There are considerable differences in the rationale of these procedures among different schools, just as there are differences between them in the actual conduct of many details of therapy.

But the foregoing characteristics are still sufficiently vital to determine the general appearance of all Insight therapy sessions, and even a superficial description of them does not require very many qualifications to incorporate the differences from one school to another.

The actual conduct of an Insight therapy session might proceed as follows:

The patient and doctor greet each other and take positions in the doctor's office. If the patient lies down on a couch (classical psychoanalysis), the doctor generally sits behind his head towards the side, in order to see him without being seen. If the patient sits (client-centered, Sullivanian, and so on), the doctor usually sits facing him. In either case, the positions tend to be fixed and constant for all sessions; neither party will ordinarily get up or move around the room during the session, nor will there ordinarily be any physical contact between them. Talk is the legal tender of expression and communication here, talk and not motion; there are therapists who say one must never take notes, but listen in rapt attention, motionless. For some even, talk means only speech and no other kind of words, as with therapists who discourage or forbid patients to make agendas or other notes about themselves or read them during the session; notes are words, but not talk.

As physical positions are established, and patient and doctor get "set," there may be some brief exchange of a conventional social kind, though many therapists frown on this. In any case, it is always desultory and impersonal, about the weather, the traffic, and so forth, a part of the preparatory activity. It is usually introduced by the patient, not the therapist, who probably makes no more response to it than necessary, partly because of its baldly social character, with its implications for his role in the relationship, but more because it is plainly not the res gestae of the therapy session. Some talk is worth more than other talk. Thus, if the patient begins the therapy session with irrelevant pleasantries rather than diving headlong into serious things, the casual conversation is as likely to die off into silence as to blossom into more momentous talk.

And the silence is likely to be maintained until and unless the patient begins talking, for it is the rule that, in the ordinary course of Insight therapy, all possible options on decisions belong to the patient. Once the decision to undergo therapy is made, along with arrangements for the business of its conduct, such as hours and fees, there is nothing left to opt except the decision to talk and the content of the talk. The explicit responsibility for both of these is never assumed by the therapist,[2] though he may appear to prod the patient into talking by comments or reflections upon his silence.

Even after the patient has begun to talk, the therapist is unlikely to make very explicit evaluations of his remarks, such as indicating that one thing is important and another not. Nor is he likely to assume even such passive responsibility for the interchange as directly answering most direct questions. Should the client hesitate, for example, to choose between two things to talk about, the therapist would not choose either one—and if the client named the things and asked him outright which to speak of first, the therapist would almost certainly not say. On the contrary, Insight therapists devote a good deal of their energy, particularly in the early part of treatment, to subtly turning the patient's attention in upon himself and to accustoming him to become completely self-responsible for the entire flow of his consciousness. And this is done by practice rather than precept, for the therapist accomplishes this end by taking on himself essentially the reverse of that role he wishes the patient to adopt, leaving the patient with only the alternatives of carrying the ball himself or having no interaction. The therapist does not discourse or lecture; he merely responds suggestively.

If the foregoing description applies more literally to classical psychoanalysis than to other forms of Insight therapy, it is only because analysis is practiced more consistently and lasts longer than other Insight therapies. The procedural bias of them all lies in this direction, and it has long since been shown that the operations of trained therapists of different Insight schools are relatively hard to tell apart.

[2] Freudian psychoanalysts are kind enough to try to remove this responsibility from the patient as well by their "cardinal rule of analysis," which is to say whatever comes to mind. Analytic hypnotherapists may go even further by suggesting not only that the patient assume no responsibiliy for what he says, but also that he does not have to listen to it or remember it afterwards.

Fiedler's study is now more than fifteen years old, and its result apparently still stands, but the practical similarity in therapeutic work of different schools still comes as a surprise to many Insight therapists, the more so as they have been schooled in the comparison of differences. It might be useful therefore, at this point, assuming some general knowledge on the reader's part of individual Insight schools, to explore the semantics of technique they employ and see how critical their differences really are.

PSYCHOANALYSIS AND CLIENT-CENTERED THERAPY

The extremes of technical difference among the Insight schools are represented by the systems of Freud and Rogers respectively. Their differences in technique are mainly concerned with the therapist's instrument of response, his remarks, and the kind of material to which they should be addressed. Rogerians place primary reliance on the technique called "reflection," while Freudians give similar weight to one called "interpretation." Reflection is a therapist's remark which tries to communicate that the patient has been thoroughly understood, while interpretation is one which, in addition to understanding, implies some elaboration, explanation, or assessment of meaning by the therapist. When a therapist reflects a remark, he might repeat the patient's very words or synonyms for them, whereas in interpreting a remark he would be freer to say things whose meaning was less obvious from the patient's words.

The distinction between reflection and interpretation is more apparent than real, however, when they are both considered in the context to which Rogerians and Freudians respectively recommend that psychotherapists apply themselves. Rogerians limit the therapeutic attack to the exposure of feelings in whatever connection they are presented to the therapist, while Freudians, though similarly interested in dealing with feelings, are concerned with identifying their sources as well. This difference may seem great, but its significance depends entirely on the extent to which reflections and interpretations can be distinguished from each other and can be seen to have different consequences. Neither is easy to do.

Since feelings are the pivotal contents of client-centered therapy, reflection is meaningfully directed towards feelings alone. The impact of the therapist's reflection of feelings is likely always to be greatest when the relevant feelings are implied rather than spoken, for it is in such situations that the reflective response can be most clearly seen to contain more empathy than mimicry. But to the extent that it addresses the implicit rather than the explicit, the reflection is itself interpretive, for it both assesses and elaborates upon the actual content which has been presented.

Even when the feeling is explicit though, reflection may still be seen as nothing more than a relatively restricted response on precisely the same continuum where interpretation lies—both are counter-remarks or responses of the therapist to something the patient has elected to say. The difference between them would then be quantitative only, and since reflection is quantitatively more restricted than interpretation, its consequences might differ simply by being less effective in communicating the very messages of "acceptance," "empathy," and so on, for the facilitation of which it is specifically prescribed. In effect then, the risk of failing to communicate empathy may be no greater for an interpretation that says too much than for a reflection that says too little. In either case, moreover, the therapeutic effectiveness of the remark will depend upon the interpretation lent it by the patient, not the intention of the therapist. The peculiar emphasis that the Rogerians lay on reflection may thus have no operational significance.

But what of the importance of interpretation, the equivalent cornerstone of psychoanalytic responses? It involves a somewhat greater latitude of content on the part of therapists, but does it have any greater significance than reflection? Perhaps not, especially if interpretation eventuates as a communication from the Freudian therapist of meanings equivalent to those the Rogerian conveys by reflection. The difference between them would then be a function only of the difference between the theories on which they were based. My contention is that these distinctions of devices serve to satisfy some theoretical preferences of the therapists who use them, but without much difference in effects on patients.

The Freudian scheme of things is more complicated than

the Rogerian, which suggests that it requires a more complicated approach for its implementation. Since the source of feelings may involve the examination of an individual's history, and since some people find history a less than obvious subject for discussion, the Freudian therapist permits himself greater latitude for comment than does the Rogerian. It takes more to direct the patient's attention where he wants it to go. The Rogerian, on the other hand, theoretically does not want to make the patient's attention go anywhere, which is one reason his therapy is called nondirective. Consequently, he neither requires nor permits himself the same latitude of deliberate interpretation. Of course, he does want the client's attention to be focused on his own feelings, but he regards his part in getting it there as a mirroring function only.

The difference in usage is then a matter of exposing feelings in the proper context. The Freudian requires more interpretive latitude in order to get them to appear in the context of history, while the Rogerian can afford merely to reflect because he will in any case interpret the exposed feelings with no reference to time. These different techniques are, then, both equally closely related to the different theories of the Freudians and Rogerians respectively. And therefore, to the extent that the theories have similar objectives in therapy, the techniques will mean the same thing. Both Freudians and Rogerians would argue that the differences in therapy theories are of cardinal importance, but there are some grounds for questioning this.

In the first place, the Freudian emphasis on history in the development of neurosis is not challenged by the Rogerian scheme; on the contrary, the latter simply does not consider it important to deal with history in the course of therapy, attending instead to phenomenology. Any contradictions between them must then be sought in the present tense, where the sum of the differences seems to be that the Freudians claim to know a great deal about the structure and content of neurosis and the Rogerians claim that they do not. On the basis of what they believe to be their knowledge of neurotic development, the Freudians deduce a rather plausible scheme of treatment to unravel the neurosis. The Rogerians challenge the psychoanalytic genetics of personality as involving both unknowns and unknowables, but rather than contradicting it as wrong, they seem to believe simply that analytic therapy involves procedures which are unnecessary. The Rogerians then describe a treatment strategy of their own, which limits the therapist to doing only that minimum which is indispensably necessary for treatment to succeed. Their scheme thus ends up as a distillation of the Freudian, which does no real violence either to the theory of psychoanalysis or to the essence of its technique.

The single difference on which the whole technical controversy hinges may be seen as a dispute over the extent to which it is cricket for the therapist to cue the patient, and the difference here is not all that great. Freudians, for example, regard dreams as rich sources of therapeutically useful information and are therefore eager to hear their patients' dreams. But they do not prod the patient to produce them; they are much less likely to *ask* for dreams in the first place than they are simply to respond in a reinforcing way if a patient spontaneously brings up the subject. Similarly, they believe that the therapy sessions, to be completely effective, must involve a microcosmic repetition by the patient of important emotional experiences of earlier life, with the therapist placed in the same light as were the loved and hated figures of childhood. But the therapist hardly lectures to the patient about this expected transference of feeling, nor does he ask the patient to watch for it and let him know when some such mental spots appear. Essentially, the therapist simply waits for signs of its occurrence, and when they appear, he responds to them in such a manner as to support their exposure without demanding it. The Rogerian may accuse him of wasting time on irrelevancies by fiddling with dreams or history, but of little else, for he himself uses precisely the same general technique: he responds selectively to those unsolicited remarks of the patient that are most critically important for his treatment. The Rogerian tries to limit himself to selecting feeling tones and responding only to them, while the Freudian permits himself to respond to other things as well and to look for connections between things; but both regard the feelings as centrally important, however complicated they may be to untangle.

THE PERSONAL RETICENCE OF THERAPISTS

From the preceding discussion, it is clear that Insight psychotherapists of all kinds will go to some lengths to avoid giving information about their own personal lives to their patients. From the purely tactical side, this practice seems to be corollary to the rule that patient-opted talk be the focus of therapy. In other words, if the patient must do all the talking, then the therapist had better not, and if the patient is to be encouraged to talk about his most private feelings, then it might be ill advised for the therapist to talk about himself in any terms.

But it is not simply relevance that dictates this procedure, and it is anything but corollary—for by and large, the therapist masks himself from the patient outside the therapy session as well as within it, avoiding even casual social relationships. If that is plainly impossible to begin with, he will probably not accept the patient for treatment, and if social contacts later occur unavoidably, he will limit them and probably discuss them at length as part of the therapy. At all events, it is considered extremely improper by all Insight schools for therapists deliberately to undertake or even permit social relationships with their patients or clients.[3] However personal this relationship may be in some sense, it is not in any social sense—for to make it so would be to make it an extension of that ordinary existence in which people are mostly preoccupied by their engagements with other people and with objects, and the recipient of Insight therapy must be permitted to engage with nothing but himself. His interest in the therapist as a person must be transmuted into transference projections for the Freudian and deflected away from himself and onto others who, by virtue of their physical absence, are no more than extensions of the patient's thoughts. And for the Rogerian, this interest must be reflected back onto the patient from a therapist who, operating at his best,

---

[3] This analysis pays no attention to those mundane reasons which have nothing to do with either technique or theory of therapy, but may still be important, such as the fact that therapist and patient may both be embarrassed by a tea party relationship after the intense interactions of their sessions, or that therapists in particular would just as soon not be bothered with the same people after hours, or that neurotics may be unpleasant company.

is suffused with empathy, that is, who feels the patient's feelings proper, not mere sympathetic kinship with them, and who, to the extent that he succeeds, is himself the patient's self in kindly form, so that the patient may learn to see himself in the image of this beautifying mirror.

To summarize the techniques of Insight Therapy: The patient initiates all critical talking and assumes responsibility for it, while the therapist reinforces that talk which is of the most personal and feeling kind, always maintaining himself as an object but never subject of what has its meaning ultimately as an elaborate monologue. He guides the patient, as it were, by following his lead, always without letting his own identity be fully known, and without forewarning the patient where the path will lead, however many times the therapist has earlier guided others over similar paths through similar forests.

But where does the path lead? Curiously enough, for the Insight therapist this is a very secondary question to that which asks from where it originates, for the former is inexorably tied to the latter, and it is towards the clarification of that tie in the patient's mind that the therapist directs his functioning. This takes us to the examination of the theory that underlies the Insight techniques.

THE MOTIVES OF BEHAVIOR

If "insight" is the critical term that incorporates the technical objectives of the psychotherapy system we are discussing, then "motive" is the parallel term to caption the theory of personality it employs. For the cardinal assumption which unites all dissidents among the Insight schools is that the significant problems or behaviors which are the target of psychotherapy are the products of some equally significant motives, and that the solution to those problems and changes of behavior must result primarily from changes in the motives producing them. This same proposition can be put in several different ways, and it may be well to state them, for there is no overstating its importance to the understanding of Insight therapy:

In common parlance, it says that there are compelling

reasons for everything one does, that these reasons are the sources or causes of one's acts, and that the only effective way of changing the acts in question is by changing the reasons which compel them.

Yet again, this theory says that people behave in whatever ways they do because they are driven to behave so, and they cannot be persuaded or induced to behave otherwise unless they are otherwise driven or their energies reduced.

What motivates a man, what drives him, what his needs are, or his tensions, what gratifies him, what his reasons are, or goals, or objectives—all these terms mean essentially the same thing, and all may be employed equally aptly in the basic formula of motivation theory, that motives determine and dictate acts. In the order of behavioral events, motives seem to occur prior to the acts they motivate. Their priority in sequence is taken as a basis by the Insight therapist, from which, adding on some secondary postulates, he builds an intellectual structure in which motives are prior in significance as well. At the extreme of this position, acts are left dangling as helplessly from their motives as puppets from their strings.

There is a biological basis to this argument which is so familiar to the experience of everyone that it seems like the most elementary common sense: We eat because we are hungry, sleep because we are tired, evacuate because our bowels are full, and so forth. In each case, these acts, which we may plainly observe in another person, are driven or compelled or motivated by things within him which we cannot see, but none can doubt that such acts are a consequence of their motives. And if this is the case in biology, it hardly strains credibility to extend it to psychology, proposing that more refined and less vital drives develop from fundamental ones, so that general hunger may eventually result in a specific craving for meat or bread or ice cream or even for money with which they can be procured. By such reasoning, one may finally reach the point of arguing that all behaviors may be explained by some motives which underlie them, and that all acts seek ultimately to satisfy unseen drives.

If this idea is applied to the symptoms that cause people to undergo psychotherapy, then all such symptoms can be properly understood as attempts to satisfy some need, as expressions of some drive, revelations of some longing or some fear. Far from being pointless, accidental, automated things irrelevant to the essence of one's life, as measles, broken legs, and staph infections are irrelevant, these symptoms are replete with meaning, derivatives of unseen needs, immeasurably significant of causes whose content may be vague, but that lurk beneath the symptom as surely as the symptom can itself be seen.

This view of symptoms bespeaks some hope or confidence that the world is a rational place in which results do not take place without causes, nor consequences without antecedents, and this suggests a strategy for treatment. Not only should the symptom be relieved, but tracing back its course to find its origin may make it possible to quell the flood of misery at its source—while failing to do so, and attacking the symptom alone, runs the risk of damming up one outlet only to leave the torrent free to break through at another point, in another symptom.

The implication for treatment is more ambiguous and has been less important, however, to Insight therapy than the model of disorder implied by this doctrine, for the suggestion that there is no such thing as a meaningless symptom, and that all symptoms have reference to ideas or feelings or impulses which go to the core of a man's being, intimates as well that all of his experiences are somehow important and worthy of his attention. And if he does not engage in any truly incidental behavior, then he must operate entirely on some pay-off principle that directs every motion, however minute, to the satisfaction of some need. But if that is the case, then the definition of a symptom is now clearly reduced to "that behavior which tries to gratify some need and fails to do so." Then the problem of understanding the nature of the disorder is one of tracing, in detective story fashion, the need whose satisfaction is the symptom's futile aim, and insofar as treatment involves the removal of symptoms, it becomes a matter of trying to do away with the need, which is generally unlikely, or more realistically, of finding and using means other than the symptom by which it can be satisfied. At all events, the belief that acts are essentially the consequences of their underlying motives forces one's attention to a consideration of the "meaning" of any act, for meaning means the pattern of events and circumstances which

antecede, surround, and "cause" events. The motive of an act
thus is its meaning, and this consideration ultimately demands, as
we shall see, that as therapeutic discourse involves motives of increasing significance, the therapeutic situation itself evolves into
an exploration of the meaning of one's life. This is least deliberately true, historically, of Freudian psychoanalysis, which is even
today "classically" articulated as a system aimed at facilitating personal adjustment, in other words, at reducing psychological distress
so that people may conduct their affairs without undue susceptibility to feelings of anxiety and guilt. The search for meaning is
fostered more strongly, albeit passively, in the Rogerian system,
which is built entirely on a concern with a capitalized, concretized
entity called the Self, whose very definition must incorporate the
meaning systems people use to judge themselves. But the search
culminates actively, explicitly, and deliberately in the writing of
the existential analysts, who identify psychological distress as a loss
of meaning and treatment as the effort to discover or construct a
meaning in life, regardless of the fate of the symptoms themselves.
This is the situation which describes the patient who, when therapy
is done, says that his tics and headaches are still there, but that his
attitude has changed for the better, so that they no longer bother
him. However ironical, this is a logical development in a system
which posits, as its first principle, that the most apparent behavior
is peripheral and less important than some unseen thing that lies
behind it. It says in effect that the "real problem" is never what
it seems to be.

The assumption of the prepotent effects of motivation lends
an aura of indirection to the operations of Insight therapists. Symptoms must be flanked rather than attacked outright, not because
they cannot be assaulted directly, nor even because symptomatic
changes, when induced, might be unstable in and of themselves,
but for another reason: The vital task is, to begin with, the discovery of the complex of motives from which the symptoms spring.
And this is no simple matter, for not only are motives less than
evident to others, but they are also often hidden from the sufferer
himself. The significance of consciousness, or rather unconsciousness, is second in importance in the theories of Insight systems
only to that of motivation. The main reason why people continue

to manifest their symptoms over long periods of time despite their efforts to change is that their motives are hidden from themselves. The task of therapy is to expose those motives, not so much to the therapist as to the patient himself. The techniques of therapy are then systems for facilitating this exposure, for producing consciousness. And the occurrence in one's awareness of things of which he was previously unaware defines insight.

Insight is thus synonymous with consciousness, and the expansion of consciousness is indeed the productive goal of all Insight therapies. What then is the significance of the widely touted phenomena called unconscious processes? With the exception of classical psychoanalysis, this is a moot point. The Freudian system has assumed that motives were effective in producing neurotic symptoms somewhat in proportion to how thoroughly out of awareness they were, and a large scholarly industry has developed within psychotherapeutic writing and research on personality, as well as in practice itself, for analyzing, exploring, elaborating, elucidating, and otherwise inquiring into Unconsciousness and the mental mechanisms which sustain it. But the secondary position of such processes in Insight systems is clear enough if we keep in mind that unconscious contents are never dealt with directly; they are always inferred, never measured, and thus far, are not clearly measurable.[4] Most important, they are inferred primarily from that material which occurs in consciousness, whether free associations, dreams, or straightforward reports of experience. The very assumption of the existence of unconscious processes can be seen as a means of facilitating the expansion of consciousness, for it suggests that there is an endless supply of content within the mind of the patient which can be coaxed into awareness.

The minimum assumptions of Insight therapists about personality are that symptoms, like all behaviors, are significantly motivated and that their operations are sustained and their re-

---

[4] There may be important exceptions to this with respect to some physiological and psychological changes that unconsciously accompany some psychological states and may be controlled by them (see Blum and Razran), and certainly a great deal of routine performance in everyday life is unconscious (Eriksen). The argument does apply to unconscious "content" that is inferred from verbal reports, however, and is therefore applicable to virtually everything that happens in Insight therapy.

moval impeded by a relative dearth of consciousness. The activities of all Insight therapists must therefore involve some kind of insight-producing sequence of (1) exposure, whether by requiring free association or passively letting people say what they wish; (2) therapist operation on the exposed material, whether by analytic interpretation or empathic reflection; and (3) consciousness or insight within the patient, whether intellectual, a greater understanding of himself, or emotional, a feeling of awareness of himself.

But what is insight supposed to do in turn? How is it supposed to change anything? We find in Insight therapy a body of techniques of practice and assumptions about personality that are reasonably consistent with each other, and we are returned once more to the question of where the system is supposed to go.

THE USES OF CONSCIOUSNESS

To be fair and accurate, I believe that this question must be properly answered at two different levels, a *scientific* one, whose value now appears chiefly historical, and a *moralistic* one, which may finally propose more questions than it answers. The scientific answer is that insight is supposed to produce relief from the symptoms which have been troubling the person and to provide him with a greater degree of control over himself than he has previously felt. The moralistic answer is that insight is not supposed to do anything, that it is a quantum desirable in maximum amounts and sufficient unto itself, and that its achievement in proper measure represents the point in therapy at which the doctor has fulfilled his responsibility and may discharge his patient as cured. Cured of what? Of ignorance of self.

SCIENCE AND INSIGHT THERAPY

Insight therapy began as a thoroughly scientific enterprise in the work of Breuer and Freud, both at that time practicing physicians deeply concerned with finding means for treating neurotic symptoms. The discovery of the techniques from which psychoanalysis evolved, and the later elaboration of those techniques into a formal system of treatment, was directed primarily at an attack on a limited set of symptoms. Even the intricate personality theory that Freud's genius constructed out of a medley of clinical observations, personal experiences, and literary acumen was intended primarily as a means for deducing how neurotic symptoms arose and for predicting the course that psychoanalytic therapy might take towards their relief. In other words, the system started with the technical problem of the existence of neurotic symptoms and worked itself both backwards to a theory explaining their origins and forwards towards a means of hastening their end; but theory of any kind was, for a long time, entirely adjunct and subsidiary to a concern with curing symptoms, and success or failure of the therapy could be judged entirely in those simple but eminently scientific terms.

Insight came to be regarded as a curative agent because early Freudians viewed the development of symptoms as an immediate consequence of an unconsciousness-producing mental mechanism—repression. Repression prevented its victim from recognizing his motivations, which, continuing to operate sub rosa, eventually expressed themselves in the unhappy form of neuroses. Lifting the repression, permitting consciousness, or eliciting insight, might therefore be expected to relieve the pressure of the motive, so that it would not force its expression any longer in the form of symptoms. Once insight occurred, the symptom might go away by itself, as it were, without further attempts at decision. If not that, the occurrence of insight still meant that the patient would recognize his motives clearly, and this done, he would be able to find ways of fulfilling or handling them which would make the symptoms superfluous, thus atrophying them.[5]

As stated, the foregoing scientific rationale for Insight therapy remains a basic tenet to this day of all those schools of therapy that orient themselves towards psychoanalysis, whether "neo-Freudian" or "classical," for it is just this rationale that justifies the therapy of searching for underlying motives. But there are

[5] The language of classical psychoanalysis is enormously more complicated than my statement suggests, but I do not think its ideas really are. Very many terms are used to describe the prevention of consciousness, such as "defenses," "denial," and "projection," but these are all variants of repression. Similarly, many terms describe the facilitation of consciousness—"abreaction," "working through," "screening," and so on but these all concern variations in the situations, processes, and experiences that culminate in insight.

probably few adherents of this system who nowadays would state its doctrine in such an elementary form, for in that form it is, by and large, invalid. For most of the problems of most people, it seems generally to be the case that the achievement of insight, however detailed and precise, into their motivations, however unconscious, does not by itself solve their problems, reduce their symptoms, or change their lives in any but a gross intellectual or economic sense—they have an enormous body of information for talking about themselves at cocktail parties, and they are out so much and so much in analytic fees.

It is possible, of course, that whenever insight does not produce relief, it is false insight, with the true motives still remaining hidden, or that the insights achieved are valid but incomplete, with their motivations actually more complicated than was thought. Puristic adherents of insight make precisely such claims, and analysts who keep patients in treatment for ten or fifteen or twenty years are implicitly making them.[6] The concept of "interminable analysis," a problem of some currency among psychoanalysts even during Freud's life, can be sustained by this argument. But if this idea is not false just because it is logically circular, it is still terribly wasteful; in scientific matters, merely reasonable arguments, which this one is, rarely succeed as explanations in competition with parsimonious ones, and a parsimonious argument here would be that insight is just not very effective by itself in solving most therapeutic problems.

Most modern Insight therapists have had too much experience with this situation to insist any longer that the achievement of insight spontaneously melts away all other problems, but they are still prone to approach therapeutic problems by asking about the underlying complexes of motives which produce them and by assuming, in the first instance, that these problems can be treated by insight methods. They are likely to rationalize the use of in-

---

[6] The figures used here are not literary but literal ones: a colleague recently brought to my attention that the analytic consultant to a distinguished mental hospital urged the psychotherapists there not to give up "too easily" on their cases. To illustrate, he told how he was now in the sixteenth year of treating a homosexual, though intensive treatment had been going on only for ten. He was pleased to report that the man was finally making such progress that "in another four years he should be able to make a heterosexual adjustment."

sight more in terms of somewhat indirect effects mentioned earlier. "True, achieving insight will not necessarily solve all problems or remove all symptoms," they say, "but what it will do is put the patient in a position where he can now control his behavior if he is sufficiently motivated to do so." To some extent, this position suffers from the same circularity as the previous one, for the only obvious index of whether the patient is sufficiently motivated is whether or not the relief of symptoms occurs. If it does not, then it becomes possible to say that the patient's claim was untrue that he wanted an end put to his symptoms, and the plea was itself the result of hidden motives which require exploration. We are then back where we started, but this kind of risk is inherent in any argument that puts much emphasis or credence on the efficacy of unseen and essentially invisible and unmeasurable factors—there is no clear-cut point at which they can be logically excluded as explanations of events.

The importance of the second argument is not in any logical superiority it may have over the first one, but rather in its implication that psychotherapy is a more limited or less specific endeavor than one might otherwise guess it to be. The idea that insight facilitates control rather than removes symptoms reduces the responsibility of the therapist—he is no longer required to seek to cure the patient, but rather to put the patient in a position where, if he so wishes, he will now be able to cure himself!

In one sense, this position is more consistent with the actual techniques of Insight therapists than is the argument that success is defined by relief. Throughout the actual course of treatment, initiative is left to the patient and the responsibility for what is done in the sessions must be assumed by him. Then why not responsibility for the cure as well?

The scientific difficulty with this position is brought on, not by making the patient responsible for the removal of his own symptoms, but by exempting symptom-removal itself from the requirements of cure, for this removes the most clearly measurable means of assessing what psychotherapy has accomplished. When the connection between insight and symptoms is loosened, as it is here, it may be proper to "successfully" terminate treatment with symptoms still present, or conversely, to say that treatment is a

failure even with all the symptoms gone unless insight has somehow been achieved. The first case is akin to saying that the treatment cured everything except what bothered the patient in the
first place, while the second says that it does not matter if the
patient is well unless he is also educated. Finally, since insight is
itself applied to hidden motives whose precise quantity is made
unsure by the very fact that they are hidden, how does one know
how much insight is enough? The scientific status of the therapy
depends upon its success or failure in terms of some measurable
relationships between the insight it produces and the object towards which that insight is directed, and no object is more obvious than symptoms.

MORALS AND INSIGHT THERAPY

Despite these difficulties, the divorce of insight from such
practical effects as symptom removal is not altogether senseless. It
does not necessarily follow that, since the existence of symptoms
is what starts the search for motives going in the first place, the
discoveries which result will ipso facto satisfy the impetus for the
search. The fact that Columbus failed to find a new route to India
did not make the discovery of America less real or less important.
The Insight therapist, by the same token, may propose to start on
the motivational path suggested by the symptoms which confront
him without prejudice as to where it will lead, with only the faith
that it will lead somewhere worth going. But in so doing, he effectively abandons the elementary notions of treatment and cure
that are common to patients and doctors alike for most ailments;
for all practical purposes, he makes of insight an end unto itself,
which, insofar as it does not relate to symptoms, forces a redefini-
tion of his work; this new definition is one that casts him in the
mold of a secular moralist. As long as the prescription of insight is
rationalized in terms of its effect on some demonstrable set of
symptoms, the therapist can claim that his is a technical operation, more or less scientifically conceived and directed at some
measurable end. But the more the concrete ends are attenuated,
the less is this possible, till even the idea that treatment is a pre-
ventive against some future chain of events which can act on a

person to produce some specific symptoms is a weakened claim to practice. And when the justification of insight no longer bears on its effect upon some known distress, but on different ends, then the fitness of its dispensation is more a moral than a scientific matter.

The plainest moral problem in its dispensation is seen if we think of insight as having some moving effect upon one's life in every way except in its ability to cure symptoms, for the fact that the doctor is then trying to sell something other than what the patient intended to buy is morally questionable. The same question might apply almost as well, however, if insight cured symptoms too, for so long as it did more than that, it would do other than that; but in such events, it is usually easy to overlook the other effects. In any case, the point here is not so much one of establishing professional ethics, which are often no more than fair trade laws, as of assessing the very nature of the profession. It does not propose that Insight therapists, by doing something other than curing symptoms, are immoral rather than moral, but that they are thereby moralists rather than scientists. It is the generality of their efforts, not their efficacy, which forces this conclusion.

What is the morality they promote? By precept, it is the virtue of insight, or consciousness, or self-knowledge. By example, it is the necessity for each man to assume his own initiatives in the quest for insight and to be alone responsible for its achievement. By implication, it is the right of individuals above all else to live as they choose.

For the Freudian, the unknown self that needs knowing is ultimately one of violent and lustful impulses, denied as one's own, attributed only to the foulest parts of others, filled with the antitheses of the domestic or heroic virtues decreed by the culture and ordered to be exalted by the individual. For the Rogerian, it is a self of discrepancy, where exalted ideals and aspirations are masks for fear, and where deprecation of self is a false and unworthy treatment of an immeasurably acceptable, lovable person. For the existentialist, it is a self alone in a hostile universe who, to become capable of knowledge, must recognize its inevitable aloneness as the first step towards the imposition of meaning upon chaos. Regardless of the content to be exhumed, the supposition of all the Insight theorists is the same: that the self is valuable, that it is worthy of being known, and that its title to explication and intelligibility is its very existence rather than any behavior it undertakes or performance it sets in motion.

That one must in therapy assume initiative himself for the discovery of self is a technicality based partly on the assumption that he will refuse to hear or understand the meanings of self if they are delivered from outside. But it is also a means of reinforcing the moral doctrine of selfhood, by making the patient be alone even within the therapy sessions, by enforcing independence. And the moral goal this tactic finally serves—autonomy, freedom to experience the self, to enhance it, to gratify it, to unbind it, to give it rein to palpate itself and, so doing, to be fulfilled. What concrete acts subserve this end and constitute some therapeutic deeds? Exactly none, or any, or all—what serves the self, or fairly represents it to itself, can qualify.

The virtues of this moral are so popular among educated people in democratic countries that it would be redundant to recount them in any detail. It exonerates the individualism of the Protestant ethic in a more plausible context than could any believing Christian; it grounds the search for the justification of political autonomy in lawful biology; it poses man's right to independence in more elementary and final terms than could the best of eighteenth-century rationalists, offering in drive reduction theory a more "natural" order of things than Encyclopedists or natural theologians ever dreamed; it frees the artist from suspicion of perversity, both by assigning the same perversity to all mankind and by casting on conformism the shadow both of perversity and hypocrisy. It offers the ultimate justification of the individual, and so it has since its earliest, most conservative exposition at Freud's hand; his theory, for example, of the original bisexuality of man can be seen as an attempt to deny the biological sociality of humankind, and to assert the unique right of the individual to survive alone.

In its most modern and extreme form, culminating in existential analysis, Insight therapy strives to establish or restore meaning, not function, to life. This is as much as to say that the object of treatment here is not so much surcease of pain as the establishment of a context of meaning in life of which the pain is an intelligible part. This of course, is what religions have long since tried to do; and it is what, when they failed to maintain enough credibility for the intelligentsia of any age, philosophies tried to replace. Thus Stoicism and Epicureanism in the ancient world when the mystery religions gave up their strength. Now Zen Buddhism and such in the West, nonprofessional counterparts of existential analysis, all alike striving to replace the meanings that were lost with the loss of the extrinsic morality of Judaism and Christianity.

THE PROBLEMS OF INSIGHT MORALITY

The extent to which Insight therapy fails to restore function is the extent to which we must discount its scientific pretensions as an applied healing art, and any such scientific failure raises moral questions in its own right. But the evaluation of function is the bête noire of the Action therapists anyhow, so it is not necessary to look closely at it here. It is precisely to the meanings which are implicit in Insight therapy that the most significant moral questions must be addressed, and these questions, centering around the implications of hidden motives and the status of individualism, must be examined for more than their positive contributions to social philosophy. Insight therapies, particularly psychoanalysis, have become the psychological orthodoxies of our time, and like all orthodoxies, their moral orders have such a familiar ring that, at their worst, they may appear more comfortably familiar than repulsive.

The system proposes, for example, to operate by lending all initiatives to the patient. But does it really do so, or is the proposal itself part of a massive seduction that culminates when the patient voluntarily exercises the therapist's preferences? If the latter, then the seduction may become even more effective when the therapist shares the myth of his own psychological midwifery. By this idea, Insight therapists insulate themselves from all assaults—if they fail to relieve symptoms, they fail only passively, and are not much responsible for a condition whose cure resides within the patient alone to begin with; but if they succeed in changing him otherwise, and in ways that are opprobrious to the patient, or the therapist, or the society, they are not culpable there either—for all they have done is put him in contact with himself by catalyzing his own behavior, and the choices he makes are his, not theirs.

But are the choices really his either according to this system? The seeming endless chain of underlying motives, especially those *unseen* (and thus demanding *insight*), suggests that he is finally free of choice, or will, or all executive capacities. As Anna Balakian suggests, does not "the preoccupation with the subconscious . . . anesthetize the sensitivities of that faculty which used to be called 'conscience'?" That is, perhaps any moral sense must be attenuated beyond repair by introspection of a causal sequence that puts events so far in time and space from their inception that it makes the notion of responsibility absurd, literally *ab-surd*, rootless, unanchored in any recognizable self.

And if so, then the doctrine which espouses a search for some self hidden beneath the surface of behavior sustains this very rootlessness by claiming that there is a "real self" somehow different from what is seen. The assumption of massive complexity, the mental iceberg that Freud describes, by its denial of the relevance of parsimony and the possibility of measurement, will always witness in defense of nonresponsibility, leaving the individual free to see his self as unsullied and inviolable.

Perhaps the heart of the problem lies here, not in the question of whether the Insight therapist really can confer freedom of choice or even of whether he should want to, but rather that the outcome of his most successful efforts might be a person who, schooled in all the erstwhile hidden references to self, could be best described as a well-adjusted psychopath. This is not to say that such a person necessarily would be, except in the most conventional terms, amoral, but rather that his would be a moral order whose referents lay all within himself. If so, then the core question is whether the broad facilitation of this doctrine would create individuals who could support a social order. If the methods of Insight therapy are effective in making a person cognizant of his self as an entity, then may he not see it ultimately in isolation? In this sense, the existentialists are quite correct in speaking of "the ultimate aloneness of man." Such a self is, at best, asocial, and its possessor could presumably be as antisocial as might serve his purposes at any time.

If sociality meant crude conformity to mindless automata or to the brutal dicta of aloof tyrannies, then nurturing the lonely self would preserve humanity. But this is not the usual case, and it is least so in societies where psychotherapies all flourish best and individuals are most secure from harm. For those individuals, C. P. Snow puts the problem clearly: "Most of our fellow human beings . . . are underfed and die before their time. In the crudest terms, *that* is the social condition. There is a moral trap which comes through the insight into man's loneliness: it tempts one to sit back, complacent in one's unique tragedy, and let the others go without a meal" (*The Two Cultures*, p. 7).

The asocial implications of Insight therapy have disturbed its adherents as well as its critics, and they have made many attempts, both formally and casually, to incorporate sociality within one or another rationale of Insight therapy. Arguments in this direction sometimes take the form that real selves are discovered finally in interpersonal relationships such as love, or that, since in the therapy situation the self is discovered through the medium of a social relation, a generalized need develops for fulfillment through relationships. Sophisticated theories, like those of H. S. Sullivan, offer these principles as more than articles of faith, and offer plausible descriptions of how the self comes into being in the first place in a social context, implying that its existence must be maintained in one. But none of these answers satisfy the question, for they say simply that the self can make use of sociality— we are asking whether it can be used for society.

In some ways, this question is tangential to the purposes of Insight therapy. For societies exploit people in terms of *functions*, and this system is ultimately directed at *meanings*. A man's social functions are things outside his self, but his existence is finally meaningful only with reference to his self. This argument is, I believe, common to all Insight therapies, and since they tend only to discuss self, not social functions, it commits all of them equally to a moral order in which individuals, pitted against societies, have prior right. But it is a right without mandatory commitment or responsibility, and in this, it differs not only from classical social theory, which, as Phillip Rieff so eloquently describes it, sees society as the true therapeutic agent and good citizenship as the final mental prophylactic. It differs too from classical definitions of virtue, both religious and secular, which hinge human dignity, or worthiness, or finally even meaning, to moral codes that lie outside the self, whether revealed in thunder and inscribed in stone, or elected into law by common counsel among peers.

If the latter have no more claim to truth than Insight, and surely age alone can give them none, they at least have the qualities of being represented in functions that are identifiable, and measurable, and—relative to insight doctrines—simple. And this suggests a final question of the moral force of Insight therapy.

The essence of this system is that it rationalizes behaviors in terms of the motives which precede or underlie them. But when the behaviors under study are weak or stupid or vile, representative of some *malfunction*, the distinction between explanation and excuse becomes confused and arbitrary in fact, if not in theory. There is a danger then, since this system must in any case proceed this way, that the wholesale quest for insight into self which occupies so much of intellect in these times, is not so much a quest for truth at large, or even for control of self, as a grand apology for impotence in fact, which makes the search for meaning but a final desperate substitute for functions which were long since lost.

CONCLUSION

The earliest efforts of Insight therapists, as described here, were directed at the alleviation of symptoms. Later, more attention was paid to making it possible for the patient to increase control of his behavior, including control of some kinds of symptoms. Most recently, effort has been made to help people to discover meanings in their existence that would make life more worthwhile even if their symptoms were quite unchanged. In the first category, symptoms included things such as phobias and hysterical paralyses; the second class expanded the concept of symptoms, or at least of disorders amenable to psychotherapy, to things such as uncontrollable impulses, sexual perversions, and so-called disorders of character; and the third class expanded the scope of the Insight therapist to things such as a general concern with happiness, or death, or security. The last category clearly refers to matters of a traditionally moralistic rather than scientific nature, but it is the second category, with its obvious problems of perspective and of the social consequences of behavior, which requires that the finest distinctions be made between the roles of moralist and applied scientist. If Insight therapists have failed to concern themselves with this distinction, it is at least as much because they operate in a society basically sympathetic to individual liberty and rich and powerful enough to tolerate a great deal of deviation within it as because they have generally wished to reject the role of moralist. The latter is nonetheless true, as should be partly apparent from the very neutrality of their procedures. At all events, it seems plain that their theoretical positions are such that they would be thoroughly committed to a morality of individualism were they to specify their moral role. The single qualifier of importance currently popular among Insight therapists is that people, in doing what they please, should not hurt others. Adherents of Western religions and utopian social visions would, by and large, view this as an inadequate morality, however therapeutic for individuals. Opponents of Insight therapy among professional members of the therapeutic disciplines may see it as antitherapeutic for individuals, however moral.

The opponents of Insight therapy among psychotherapists are, if anything, even less concerned with morals than are Insight therapists. But they are, by their own lights, more concerned with science. Their indictment of Insight therapy has nothing to do with the category of problems of meaning, which they sometimes see as a meaningless concept, and not much more with the moral implications of the second category, problems of character. It is to the problem of symptom removal that they address themselves, proposing stridently that Insight therapy is, in the first place, generally incapable of relieving symptoms, that it is grossly uneconomical when it is successful, and that in those instances where successes are recorded, they have nothing to do with the achievement of insight, but are either accidental or the result of specific *actions* which can be identified and measured. Let us turn our attention now to these Action therapists to examine their origins, their indictments, their systems, and their prospects.

CHAPTER FIVE

AN EPITAPH FOR INSIGHT
ACTION THERAPY

When Breuer and Freud first came upon their odd discovery that physical ailments like hysteria could be cured by apparently simple means like talking and listening, they surely had no idea of the impact their work would have on the intellectual life of the twentieth century, nor even, for that matter, on the nature of the helping professions. Their early goals were as modest as their views were limited: to find a treatment for hysteria that would excise its symptoms close enough to the root to prevent their recurrence later on. Hypnotism had long been used with some success, but its effects were both unsure and unstable. Some symptoms did not yield to hypnotic suggestions, and some of those that did were later evidently replaced by still worse ones. Even at its unpredictable best, moreover, a hypnotic cure was as mysterious as a hysterical illness, compounding a medical puzzle even when it solved a personal problem.

The cathartic technique they used, and which Freud alone later expanded into psychoanalysis, differed from hypnotic treatment in two critical ways: (1) it did not require instruction on the doctor's part for the symptoms to go away, and (2) the doctor's role was reversed from one where he did most of the talking to one where he mostly listened. And listening of this kind was not preliminary to the treatment, as is that of the general practitioner who takes a case history, but was rather the essence of it. The doctor's role was shifted by this procedure from a very active one to a rather passive one, and with this shift of function came a shift of responsibility. The very fact that the doctor had to be a listener in order to function, and could not in any case force upon the patient the consciousness which was indispensable to his cure, altered the character of his responsibility for the effectiveness of the treatment. Under the circumstances, there was less likelihood of his bungling treatment by some error of commission than of his simply being ineffectual, for the commissions by which he could err were much reduced.

But if therapy was no longer a result of positive action on the doctor's part, neither was neurosis considered the responsibility of the patient. In the development of psychoanalysis, Freud adhered both to the scientific determinism and to the medical tradition in which he had been schooled, the upshot of which was the view that neurotic people were ill and could not meaningfully be held responsible for their troubles. As indicated earlier, this position is rationalized somewhat by the notion that behaviors are the consequences of their underlying motives, but even more by the idea, central especially to psychoanalytic thought, that motives are essentially unconscious, therefore out of the individual's control. A neurosis would thus be something like an infectious illness— once contracted, one could hardly blame the sufferer for having germs. In a sense, neurotics are even less liable, for one may actively disregard his health and thereby increase the likelihood of infection; but since Freudian theory in particular placed the origins of neurosis in childhood, under circumstances for which children could hardly be considered culpable, the development of difficulties could not involve even the breath of collusion between a responsibly self-destructive psyche and a cooperatively banal environment.

Even near its beginnings, when Insight therapy was directed almost exclusively towards relieving specific ailments rather than addressing larger questions of meaning and purpose in life, it was ripe for some conundrums and embarrassments. Deterministic theory said, in the first place, that patients were not responsible for their illness, so they could hardly be responsible for their cure. The studied indirection of analytic technique, in the second place, proscribed the use of blunt, direct, or surgical procedures to effect a cure. Then how did cures take place? When the accidental products of the patient were suitable for the delicate interpretations of the therapist? Or by some more deliberate activity of therapist or patient, for which neither one was formally responsible? Or not at all? The riddle here is, "what is the effective agency of treatment?"

But even if the treatment can be defined by some set of operations, however whimsical their proper order of occurrence, the problem of defining cure remains, with all the ambiguities described above: cure cannot simply be the disappearance of the preventing symptom, for the theory proposes both that preventing symptoms are not primary ones and that all symptoms are merely expressions of underlying maladies of motive. But if cure is defined by the exposure of the latter, it is unclear whether the symptom must also be relieved or not. And in either event, how much revelation of motive satisfies what criterion of cure? Do not motives themselves have motives, and must these then also be exposed and analyzed?

These questions may seem like casuistry, but they have, to the contrary, some practical and theoretical importance. Though they are articulated here in relation to early psychoanalytic therapy, the same questions apply as well to the expanded application of psychoanalysis to ever-broader kinds of human problems, to all the neo-Freudian schools, including the ego psychologists, and to workers as current as Rogers and the existentialists. For problems of this kind are intrinsic to any system that makes *insight* the primary therapeutic phenomenon and that views the symptoms of disorder as effects of *disease*. However much the creators of new psychotherapeutic systems deviated from Freud's ideas, all the systems classified as Insight therapies have remained loyal to these principles.

It is precisely at these points, of course, that the Action therapies take their departure and begin their polemic, for they deny both that psychological disorders have any more than casual relationship to disease and that insight has any more than a peripheral and incidental bearing on cure, if that much. But if their departure begins at these points, it hardly ends there, for they may be distinguished from Insight therapists on one count after another both of technique and of the theory that supposedly supports it. What is more, the Action therapies describe and evaluate themselves in the language of greatest modern currency, that of "hardheaded" experimental science, and to the extent that they are able to defend themselves in these terms, and Insight therapies are not, it is probable that the relative status and popularity of the two systems eventually will be reversed among practitioners and the public alike.

REACTION AND ACTION

Who are the Action therapists? Where are their historical origins? What are their intellectual pretensions? In general, these people are still relatively unknown to the educated public, either as "behavioristic psychotherapists" or "learning theory based psychotherapists," the two labels by which they most commonly refer to themselves. But this obscurity is not limited to laymen; undergraduate college courses in psychology still make no systematic references to the Action therapies either as psychotherapy or systems of "behavior modification," though both introductory psychology texts and books on abnormal psychology, psychology of adjustment, and psychology of personality almost invariably devote some attention to Insight therapy, generally describing some features of the systems of both Freud and Rogers, and often adding others as well. And though the titles and terminologies of Action therapy are becoming rapidly familiar to psychologists, and slowly perhaps to psychiatrists, social workers, and other professionals as well, there are still proportionately very few practitioners of this ilk at the present time (1963). This is not surprising, for there are probably very few professional therapists well enough acquainted with the technical details of Action therapy to be able to formally practice it without further study or to recognize that what they are doing is Action therapy when they informally practice it in the course of their regular activities.

For all these reasons, it will be necessary, in this section, to offer a more detailed description and exposition of Action therapy than was the case with Insight therapy.

THE GENESIS OF ACTION THERAPY

The progenitors of Action therapy were laboratory scientists, not clinicians, though its present practitioners generally got to the laboratory via clinics rather than the other way around. The Russian, Ivan Pavlov, who won the Nobel Prize in 1903 for his research in *physiology*, is usually credited as the forerunner of this system, but his contemporary, the American psychologist, E. L. Thorndike, made laboratory contributions of equal significance for the development of Action therapies. In both cases, it was principles deduced from experimental studies they made of the psychology of learning that provided the bases for the different Action therapies, and in both cases, the discoverers themselves never established therapeutic schools or practiced psychotherapy, though late in his career, Pavlov became vitally interested in the possibilities his discoveries held for it.

The therapists who applied the work of these men to clinical problems were, by and large, only vicarious students of the scientists to whose systems they appealed. Andrew Salter, Joseph Wolpe, Thomas Stampfl, and the larger number of workers, chiefly psychologists, who transported the psychology of learning from laboratory to clinic, neither studied under their mentors nor, in many cases, ever met them. More often, these people were raised professionally as clinicians and trained in one or another brand of Insight psychotherapy, generally some variant of Freudian analysis. By one means or another, they became increasingly disaffected with the results of the therapy they practiced, and either sought alternatives in scientific rather than clinical psychology or, in course of developing their own variants of the therapies they knew, discovered the systematization that scientific psychology in general and learning theory in particular seemed capable of offering their thinking.

A curious irony followed: Though the intellectual roots of Action therapy in almost all its forms are entirely independent of Insight therapy, indeed of psychotherapy altogether, its historical roots, expressed in the careers of its best-known practitioners, are not. On the contrary, some of them clearly specify the reactionary process that characterized the development of their systems—and where it is not specified, it still may often be inferred. This is particularly convenient for our purposes, for there are many differences, both apparent and real, between different Action therapies, and the common attack they all tend to make upon the Insight therapies makes it easier to see the basic principles that unite them.

THE ASSAULT ON INSIGHT

Their attack is mounted all at once on every level against Insight therapy: They accuse it technically of producing insight when it should properly elicit action, theoretically of inferring motives when it should be observing behaviors, and philosophically of wallowing in sentimental humanism when it should be courting tough-minded mechanism.

As for goals of therapy, the actionists allege that Insight therapists delude themselves and at their worst, defraud society, by claiming to sell self-knowledge, for this is what practically nobody comes to them to buy. Even knowing that their clients seek relief, not information, they stock their bazaars with certificates that license dispensation of a balm they do not have. Face to face with customers, they then produce a diagram of illness and a blueprint for repair, both always the same—they say he suffers from illusions that must dissipate when once he knows himself. Chief among them, and most illusory of all—he thinks that what he thinks is his trouble really is his trouble. Almost by sleight of mind,

the sufferer's surface troubles are made secondary, and the rationalization with which the therapist diverted his attention from them
to begin with, launches him on his introspective voyage, and perhaps keeps him there forever—for when does a man really know
himself? Perhaps this could all be justified, says the Actionist, if
in the course of this tortuous trip, the trouble went away, but
mostly this is not the case except for random errors of the therapist in which he slips and, accidentally using Action therapy, cures.
The Action therapies protest that they alone try to stop the endless spiral which extends the doctor's function by anchoring
their efforts on the proximate source of trouble: the symptom. In
this respect, they truly are reactionary, for they thus return to what
was also once the goal of Insight.

But far from trying to bring some secret motives into consciousness, the Action therapies' attack on symptoms cavalierly dis-
regards their source, and aimed at changes in fact, it likewise
disavows the crucial need for consciousness. This attacks the very
core of Insight therapy, for it implies that symptoms may not be
meaningful expressions of their motive states, but may be nonsense
learned by chance association with some unhappy event, and that
consciousness may be no help at all in gaining freedom from it.
If this were the case, and the entire labyrinthine network of motive
forces a myth, then not only would symptoms not be expected to
disappear when motives became conscious, but even if they did
disappear, this would not verify that the symptom was necessarily
a product of the motive! In that event, the entire structure of the
personality theory which informs Insight therapy might be shaken
and in doubt, for it was derived largely from hypotheses about connections between observed symptoms and the hypothetical events
preceding their occurrence.

There is another reason, though, for questioning the personality theory of most Insight therapies, particularly the recent
ones, and that concerns the humanistic orientation of these theories, with its implication that the difficulties in life which may be
resolved by therapy are connected to uniquely or fundamentally
human attributes of the patient or amenable to peculiarly human
behaviors of the therapist. Action therapists would say precisely the

opposite, that most of the difficulties which bring people to therapy reflect learnings of fundamental behaviors which are at least as easily observed in lower animals as in people. And the proper therapy for these problems, far from a suitable display of humanity, is the artful exploitation of a basically mechanical procedure in which the therapeutic problem is the discovery of which organismic buttons to push or switches to throw. There is a seemingly ironical difference between the systems that is explained by the difference between their respective humanistic and mechanistic leanings. The Actionists, properly disclaiming a disease model for their therapy, nevertheless operate animal-learning laboratories for experimenting with the production and treatment of neuroses and other ailments, using rats, cats, pigeons, monkeys, and guinea pigs as guinea pigs. One might think, on the face of it, that the advocates of disease models would be more prone to study animals and the students of learning to study only humans, but just the opposite is the case. The reason is that Insight therapists often disdain to study lower organisms because they feel that human problems are more or less uniquely human. They do not doubt that neuroses and such can be produced experimentally in animals, but they question the relevance of such states to the disabilities of human beings. Action therapists, on the other hand, believing that neuroses are the mechanical results of learning, see every reason to test this notion by manipulating the learning opportunities of mechanisms simpler than ourselves.

The final basis for the general criticism that Action therapies level against Insight therapies is an economic one. It proposes that Insight therapies are typically unsuccessful in outcome even in terms of their own requirements for success. With treatment so inordinately time-consuming and expensive, and so few persons much improved after the arduous process is completed, it is questionable whether the therapy is efficient enough to justify its existence even as a luxury of the rich. Indeed, some evidence exists that the rate at which people are cured by Insight therapy, even with cure defined by the Insight therapist, is no greater than the rate at which they spontaneously work their way out of their troubles without any professional help.

GENERAL TECHNIQUE OF ACTION THERAPY

In addition to their common negative reactions to Insight therapy, Action therapists share some common positive attributes with respect to their techniques, theories, and goals.

Perhaps the most important technical trait they share is a relative indifference to the origin of the symptoms they treat, and a concomitant concern with specifying the goals of their treatment. Contrary to the Insight therapist, who is often preoccupied with tracing the etiology and development of symptoms from specific motives, and who tends to be casual about the outcome of this process, the Action therapist is interested entirely in his ability to manipulate behaviors to eliminate symptoms, and is somewhat complacent about their origin. A better description of the technical stance involved may be to say that the Action therapist is interested only in producing some specific changes in behavior, and those in the shortest possible time and the most deliberate way— and in so doing, he cares not a whit what the patient does or does not say about himself or even know about himself except insofar as such *behaviors* have concrete and demonstrable value for producing change. Somewhat in the technological mainstream of Henry Ford, the Action therapist despises history.

There are two nearly inevitable tactical consequences of the planful, goal-directed character of Action therapy:

1. The therapist assumes a much greater influence over the detailed conduct of the treatment sessions, and possibly over the outside life of the patient, than Insight therapists would.

2. The therapist is much more responsible for the outcome of treatment, that is, for whatever changes take place in the patient, than are Insight therapists.

If the object of the Insight therapist is to free the patient, the object of the Action therapist, it may fairly be said, is to cure him. Again a seeming irony appears, that despite their rejection of the disease model of the development of neuroses, Action therapists would no more ask their patients to conduct their own treatment than doctors would ask patients to prescribe their own medicines. But neither would the teachers of a complex but specific skill ask students to compose their lesson plans, and it is with educators that a more suitable analogy is found. By and large, Action therapists plan specific treatment programs according to their interpretations of the specific ailments of each patient.

These plans are not necessarily imposed arbitrarily upon the patient, and some therapists find it useful, even indispensable, to enlist the active cooperation of the patient in planning the treatment. It makes sense that if patients help plan the concrete details of treatment and thereby have a better understanding of it, they may be better motivated than otherwise and more able to assume responsibility for its successful conduct. But the reader must beware of misconstruing this proposition to mean that insight is considered a critical agent of cure; at best, the Action therapist will grant that it has some facilitating effect for some purposes, much as do many other responses—but it is overt behavior change which defines cure for him, not verbal change, and the value of having patients help plan their treatments is that it reinforces a positive attitude towards treatment even in the complete absence of understanding of the treatment rationale. Besides, insight into a treatment program is quite different from insight into a system of motives, origins, or other unconscious mental things.

At all events, most Action therapists do not design their treatment plans around the patient's ability to understand them nor necessarily even in congress with their patients, and all of them do assume, for the most part, a very active role in the treatment session. Salter and Wolpe often argue and exhort, and both use hypnotic suggestion extensively; Stampfl does virtually all the talking in most of his therapy sessions; students of Skinner plan the details of treatment and control the sessions in such a way that it is generally irrelevant whether or not they ever discuss the treatment program with the patient.

Just as the Action therapist is deliberately responsible for the conduct of treatment, he tends to be responsible in large part for its outcome too; he tends, in other words, to select in advance the particular changes he wishes to effect in the behavior of his patient. This is more true of some Action therapies than of others, as will be plain later; the main point is that, in contrast to Insight therapists, who do not wish to control the patient's life, the extent to which Action therapists are unable not merely to predict, but to determine their outcomes, is an index of their failure. Once again, this description is not meant to portray the Action therapist as a scheming Machiavellian or a power-intoxicated mad scientist who uses human pieces in his chess games, though he may be both those things; it is rather a corollary of the planful character of his treatment. The more precise his goal, the more effective the treatment he requires to achieve it. Success is defined by the extent to which he has been able to do what he set out to do. And it is no more possible for him to shift responsibility for his plans to the patient by discussing the treatment in advance, than it is for a physician to shift responsibility by describing a variety of available medicines. Even if he gives his patient a choice of goals, as doctors sometimes do, he himself defines what goals are possible; Insight therapists, contrarily, leave the onus of defining treatment goals on the patient to begin with. And even if the Action therapist makes the patient responsible for the choice of goals, he himself retains responsibility for their fulfillment. He cannot shrug off his role as a mere agency, claiming that the patient selected it, however much he may be comforted by this fact in the event of failure or disaster.

So much for the common general techniques of Action therapies: The therapist tends to actively impose treatment procedures rather than passively await the introspections of the patient; he tends to plan the details and goals of treatment very specifically, with only secondary acknowledgment of or concern with the problem's history; he assumes serious responsibility for the kinds of changes resulting from his machinations.

Naturally, he cannot make any plans, exert deliberate controls, or assume meaningful responsibility for anything without making a number of assumptions about the character of the symptoms and the conditions to which they are susceptible. Some theoretical propositions about personality underly Action therapy just as they do Insight therapy, and in order to rationalize the procedures of Action therapists, we must examine the basic beliefs about behavior that inform their plans.

POLICIES FOR ACTION

The theories which Action therapists invoke as the basis for their techniques cannot, in any narrow sense, be called theories of personality, for that term is generally reserved for theories specifically concerned with human behavior. The most important commonality among the theories of the Action therapists is that all of them come under the general heading of theories of learning. Despite wide divergencies among them, moreover, they are all agreed that only a very few principles of learning are needed to understand even the most complex kinds of behavior to which psychotherapy is applicable, and these principles, by and large, can be as thoroughly and sufficiently demonstrated on lower organisms as on human beings.

The theories of learning that explain the Action therapies have all been identified at one or another time with the processes of *conditioning*, whether the so-called classical conditioning of Pavlov, the instrumental conditioning of Thorndike, or the operant conditioning of Skinner, a special case of instrumental conditioning. These processes have all been demonstrated repeatedly in rigorous laboratory experiments, but they are still subjects of considerable scholarly controversy, not the least part of which concerns the degree to which any of them can be considered truly applicable to human behavior, particularly to adult behavior. But the details of this controversy are not immediately important to Action therapists and have no immediately detrimental value for their therapeutic systems. For the purposes of all the major Action therapies, the term "conditioning" is simply a formal expression for the processes of teaching and learning—and it goes without saying that human beings are highly capable of that. What is more, and more crucial to the planful character of Action therapy, it is assumed that all processes of teaching and learning, regardless of the precise conditioning models which they fit, can be described in terms of stimulus–response patterns. In extreme form, this argues not only that particular fixed patterns of response will result from particular fixed patterns of stimulation in accordance with a few laws of learning, which merely means that learned behavior is lawful, but that this will happen in precisely and predictably the same way for a human being of any age, sex, or degree of sophistication, as it will for a rat, cat, or chimpanzee. This position does not imply that humans are no different from other animals, a patent absurdity, but rather that the same principles of learning apply to them, regardless of the content which they learn! On the face of it, this is no more sweeping a statement than that the circulation of the blood proceeds in precisely the same way in humans as in chimpanzees even though there are differences in the blood chemistry of the two species. The significance of the notion only becomes apparent in connection with another principle of learning theories: that of the interchangeability of stimuli and responses. The principle of interchangeability proposes that organisms will learn habitually to make a particular response to a once-unimportant stimulus if only that stimulus happened to occur when the response was already being made to some quite different and very affecting stimulus; conversely, it says that a new response will become attached habitually to a particular stimulus when it occurs at around the same time as the arousing properties of that stimulus are diminished. Now the details of the conditions under which these patterns develop are remarkably complex, as the principles themselves may seem to be, and are the subject of a vast area of study in experimental psychology. But the upshot of them is straightforward and clear: it says that, by and large, under the proper conditions, any stimulus can be attached to any response.

Talking has some value in Action therapy, but it does not achieve value from its *meaning* so much as from its ability to function as a stimulus. Treated as a stimulus–response phenomenon, not as a set of meanings, and with the principle that any stimulus may be trained to any response, the significance of talking would then come from its capacity for being easily associated with whatever responses are desired. This will become particularly apparent in the therapy of Thomas Stampfl, who deliberately uses speech in therapy as nothing more than a convenient substitute for physical objects and manipulations.

Viewing all behavior as a stimulus–response phenomenon,

the general description of psychological disorders that results is one that sees the individual as having undergone some unfortunate conditionings of one or another kind; the untoward things he has learned are his symptoms. In some instances, it might be said that he has predominantly learned the wrong responses to certain stimuli, as in compulsive rituals or sexual fetishes; in others, that he has learned inappropriately to associate a properly indifferent stimulus to a powerfully arousing one and thus learned the wrong stimulus to a suitable response, as in phobias or anxiety attacks. In either case, the task of therapy is the same: to identify unsuitable stimulus–response connections and to interfere with them to abrogate their old bonds, on the one hand, and establish the conditions for the learning of new and more desirable connections on the other. It is the specific character of stimulus–response bonds that lends to Action therapy a sometimes seemingly naive specificity of goals. But this same specificity serves to justify the position that the symptoms of disorder are the core of the therapeutic problem, not its periphery.

Another way of expressing the difference between the theories of the systems is now possible: Insight therapy, with its emphasis on motivations, is sometimes called "dynamic," and the "payoff" principle that describes motivation or drive theory (that is, the idea that overt behaviors are expressions of motives which serve to reduce their compelling quality) is called a reductionist or homeostatic principle. From the point of view of this theory, action is generally intelligible in terms of the drives it reduces or the motives it satisfies; it achieves meaning, in other words, from its effect on the motives from which it arose, as a by-product of its own reinforcement and habituation. In psychotherapy, cognition of either a deliberate or uncontrolled kind is the chief agency for the identification of motives. This is to say that cognition is used for the purpose of attaching meaning to action in the form of consciousness of motives, another cognition. This defines therapy.

Action therapy, by contrast, derives from a "structural" system whose main principle is that of "contiguity" or "association," which says that new behaviors are learned by chance associations with significant events which were previously irrelevant to them. From this vantage, the new behavior may have no meaning whatsoever; there is no underlying motive of any importance that it effects. In psychotherapy, any devices that are suitable are used to identify the stimulus–response connections that are the irreducible elements of the symptom under treatment, and very specific conditions established for the unlearning of old patterns of behavior and the establishment of more desirable new ones. Desired changes in patterns of activity define therapy.

The difference in the epithets I have used to name the two systems should now be quite plain: Insight defines the technical objective of all those psychotherapies that exploit cognitive processes for the establishment of meanings, the latter usually defined as consciousness of motives, but sometimes consciousness of self, or of existence. Action defines the technical objective of those therapies that manipulate stimulus–response connections in order deliberately to change specific behavior from one pattern of activity to another.

If the foregoing includes a general description of the main commonalities of the Action therapists, it fails to describe the specific techniques of any of them or the intramural differences in the ideas that guide their systems. There are two major kinds of Action therapy, one focused chiefly on changing old behavior and the other on shaping new behavior. The former is concerned with responses that are habitually and unfortunately made to noxious stimulation, and two approaches to this problem are described. The first, which might be called counterconditioning, is chiefly represented in the work of Joseph Wolpe. The second, which might be called extinction training, is the work of Thomas Stampfl. Both of these can be considered approaches to the problem of eliminating anxiety. The Action system concerned with shaping new behavior, that is, with constructing new response patterns to appropriate stimuli, is called operant or instrumental conditioning and is chiefly the work of students of B. F. Skinner.

Let us examine them individually to get some clear impression of their workings from which to judge their implications.

DISCARDING BAD HABITS:

THE PSYCHOTHERAPY OF JOSEPH WOLPE

It is not surprising that the most elaborate system of Action therapy should be developed and expounded by a clinical psychiatrist rather than an experimental physiologist or psychologist, for the demands of practice are more likely to call for the exercise of some therapeutic ingenuity than does the laboratory. Joseph Wolpe was a practicing psychiatrist of psychoanalytic orientation in 1944, according to his report, when he first became interested in work that led him to the general study of learning and the particular writings of Pavlov and Hull. It is to these men primarily that he credits the theoretical formulations from which he derived his therapy system, called "Psychotherapy by Reciprocal Inhibition." The term "reciprocal inhibition" is borrowed from physiology; it refers to the phenomenon in which one set of nervous or muscular activities functions antagonistically to another, so that they cannot both occur simultaneously. Wolpe applies this concept to psychotherapy by proposing a variety of techniques for antagonizing responses selected by the therapist to the symptomatic behaviors of the patient in a manner that will prevent the symptoms from being expressed. Wolpe assumes that the patient's symptoms are learned or conditioned habits; since the responses the therapist selects to suppress them may themselves be new habits to be learned or conditioned, it is appropriate to describe this form of psychotherapy as treatment by "counterconditioning."

It is Wolpe's belief that all neurotic behaviors, from phobias and compulsions to sexual impotence and pervasive discomfort in the presence of other people, are expressions of anxiety in one or another form. He further believes that there are numerous psychological states, both in humans and lower organisms, that are inherently antagonistic to anxiety, or as he would put it, reciprocally inhibitory of anxiety, so that when behaviors conducive to these states occur in the subject, he cannot experience anxiety along with them. If the therapist can discover, for any given symptom, precisely which anxiety-inhibiting response would serve to counterweigh it, and can then teach the patient to produce that response regularly enough, the symptom will gradually dissipate and may even be replaced altogether by its generally much pleasanter antagonist. The object of this procedure, however, is not to teach a preselected new pattern of behavior, but only to break the old pattern; where some particular stimulus once elicited an anxiety-laden response, the therapeutic procedure, by inhibiting the occurrence of that response, loosens its connection with the stimulus. Eventually, it is argued, that stimulus loses its power to confer anxiety, and the symptom does not appear at all. The new behavior that was originally used to inhibit anxiety is then no longer needed for that purpose, and may or may not be maintained for other reasons.

Over a period of years in which he has been making practical applications of these principles, Wolpe has selected a repertory of behaviors that he finds particularly suitable as anxiety inhibitors. Brief descriptions of a few of them should make his therapy perfectly clear.

Inhibitors of Anxiety

The prototype of anxiety-inhibiting behavior is the *feeding response*, which Mary Cover Jones first used therapeutically some forty years ago in order to eliminate children's fears. When a child who was very frightened of, for example, a rabbit, was also very hungry, Jones would feed him and present the rabbit at a "safe" distance while he was eating. This would be repeated often during the child's feeding periods with the rabbit closer each time. The soothing effect of eating evidently inhibited any fearful response to the rabbit—or so Wolpe quite reasonably interprets this experiment. Eventually, the rabbit failed altogether to arouse the child, even if the child was not eating when it appeared. Feeding had inhibited any anxious response long enough for the rabbit to have lost its stimulating value. Though Wolpe himself reports in a relatively early writing that he has never used food responses with his own patients, he sensibly proposes that they are very suitable for inhibiting anxiety; their great potential for use with children is especially noteworthy.

Wolpe's own clinical practice is with adults, one gathers, and the anxiety-inhibiting behaviors most characteristic in his own work are things such as: (1) "conditioned avoidance responses," including "anxiety-relief responses"; (2) sexual responses; (3) assertive responses; and (4) deep muscle relaxation, including "systematic desensitization."

Though not entirely clear from his writing, the order of presentation I have used here seems to me to rank the techniques Wolpe actually reports from those least often to those most frequently used in his own work.

1. *Conditioned avoidance responses*, particularly what Wolpe calls anxiety-relief responses, are not used very often, but they are good illustrations of how any stimulus and any response, including verbal ones, presumably may be attached to each other. The conditioned avoidance procedure is one in which the patient is continuously subjected to a harmless but painful electric shock; before shocking him, the therapist instructs him to say the word "calm" whenever the shocks become excessive. The instant he does say "calm," the shock goes off. Repeated many times, the word *calm* eventually becomes connected with the experience of relief from pain, so that whenever the patient says the word to himself in everyday situations, he finds his anxieties abate. Technically, of course, there is no reason why the word *calm* should elicit this response more effectively than does any other word, but its suitability to the desired effect goes without saying.

2. *Sexual responses* are used almost exclusively, it seems, for sexual problems, and apparently only for those such as impotence, in which the patient is inhibited and unable to have complete sexual relations. Wolpe's treatment consists of training the patient to attempt sex relations *only* when ". . . he has an unmistakable, positive desire to do so, for otherwise he may very well consolidate, or even extend his sexual inhibitions" (p. 130). The training necessarily requires that he learn to identify and avoid those situations in which sex may be anxiety-arousing, and that he learn also to seek out women who are clearly capable of arousing him "in a desirable way . . . and when in the company of one of them, to 'let himself go' as freely as the circumstances allow." If the pa-

tient already has a regular sex partner whose active cooperation can be enlisted to help him learn to make sex responses without becoming anxious, so much the better. At all events, "If he is able to act according to plan, he experiences a gradual increase in sexual responsiveness to the kind of situation of which he has made use . . . [and] the range of situations in which lovemaking may occur is thus progressively extended as the anxiety potentials of stimuli diminish . . ." (p. 131).

Surely no treatment could be more "symptom specific" than this in its objectives—the problem is the inhibition of sexuality, so the treatment is the disinhibition of sexuality. The therapeutic issue is a very limited one, and its description as a problem of exchanging one pattern of action for another is quite comprehensive. There is no concern here with insight, motive, or meaning except as these ideas may be usefully exploited to effect the patient's acts. Even the theory that anxiety is at the root of the problem, which Wolpe plainly believes, is relevant only because it is useful, not because it may be true; if nothing else, it provides the therapist with a rationale for the procedures he demands of the patient (p. 111–112), and it gives the patient reassurance and perhaps courage in attempting to comply.

It is doubtless plain by now that *assertive* and *relaxation* responses can be used as specifically as *sexual* ones. If the patient is excessively timid, deferential, shy, and easily made anxious by others, the treatment is to get him to assert himself more often and more forcefully; if he is characteristically tense and anxious, even in what seem to be unwarranted circumstances, the treatment is to get him to relax.

3. *The use of assertive responses* was elaborated by Salter some years before Wolpe, and Wolpe states that, despite differences in theory and language, his use of the technique is substantially the same as Salter's. Assertive responses are rarely employed by themselves, that is, as the sole technique of therapy, and they are most commonly used for problems of interpersonal relationships, particularly for those persons who become anxious in direct verbal dealings with others. His patients are typically victimized by others in these dealings, which may be the reason Wolpe uses the term *assertion* to mean one particular kind of aggression, the

expression of hostility and resentment. As before, the assumption is made that anxiety inhibits all kinds of appropriate interpersonal expression, and that such expression, in this case angry self-assertion, inhibits anxiety.

4. The use of *relaxation responses* has been extended from its original and obvious application to symptoms of tension into a highly developed technique that Wolpe uses for all those problems and situations ". . . that make irrelevant the use of direct action, such as assertion, on the part of the patient." This technique is called "systematic desensitization," and it works by means of the therapist getting the patient to vividly imagine increasingly frightening experiences while remaining deeply relaxed, sometimes hypnotized, on the therapeutic couch. Presumably, the relaxation inhibits the feelings of anxiety usually evoked by these images till the patient eventually becomes insensitive and unresponsive to them. This unresponsiveness then presumably generalizes from the imagined fears of the consulting room to the real ones of everyday life.

Initiating Treatment. In systematic desensitization, where no more activity is required of the patient than that he cooperate with the therapist by deeply relaxing and fantasizing what he is told, it is easy to see how the therapist conducts his operations. This is ". . . a method in which the therapist has complete control of the degree of approach that the patient makes to the feared object at any particular time." But in the case of sexual and assertive responses, where the patient must perform the significant curative action outside the consulting room, how does the therapist set the process in motion? How is therapy initiated?

"The Approach to the Patient" (Chapter 7 of Wolpe's book) appears very simple and straightforward indeed. Wolpe listens to his description of problems and symptoms, then takes a careful case history in which he attempts to identify all possibly related problems and symptoms that have occurred earlier or on other occasions.[1] This is the same procedure that a physician might

---

[1] "Taking a history" must not be interpreted as indicating an interest in history of the kind Insight therapists might have. Action therapists use historical materials to get clues for planning treatment, while Insight therapists of historical bent regard the excursion into history as the treatment itself.

follow in an initial examination. Following the history, Wolpe administers a psychological test which ostensibly measures neuroticism; he then proceeds to make a lengthy statement to the patient about how neuroses develop (by conditioned anxiety responses) and how they can be treated (by reciprocal inhibition). Using the information from the case history, he illustrates the origins of the patient's own problems and begins to discuss ". . . the formal use of particular responses that, through inhibiting anxiety . . . weaken neurotic habit" (p. 112). The stage is set. The rest is argument, persuasion, or whatever means the therapist can invoke to get the therapeutic action going outside his office. The rest of his task is the stimulation of the proper action and, once set in motion, its guidance and control.

Critique of Wolpe

Students of Wolpe's techniques, welcoming his exposition thus far, may be puzzled to find that he has practically nothing to say about the "method of choice" to set the proper system of action in motion. The minutely detailed rationale and description of which actions should be started is not accompanied by similar detail about the starting mechanism. On the contrary, Wolpe describes his preliminary hortatory lecture to the patient as if it were quite starter enough, and he even talks about the therapeutic benefits which derive from that very session. That the inducements to action are no problem for him may be a reflection of his great skill in the performance of his own therapy—the statistics of success he reports certainly support this possibility. But it may also be a result of the theoretical position from which he argues, namely that the therapeutic situation is one where the patient is simply freed from anxious responses to certain stimuli, rather than conditioned to give new responses. In that event, it would make little difference how one got started because it would not matter which actions he induced as long as they resulted in the reduction of anxiety in hitherto frightening situations.

This argument seems sensible enough as an explanation of the desensitization procedure, but it is just that procedure for which the mechanics of starting present no special problem; the action required of the patient is essentially passive there.

Over and above the technical lacuna, the question of how to induce the patient to undertake the very active procedures which are required for things like sexual and assertive responses reveals a difficulty in Wolpe's notion that his therapy simply frees the patient of anxiety. In these cases, Wolpe does not associate the frightening stimulus with any old anxiety-inhibiting response, such as feeding a man when he is sexually aroused or telling him to get aroused sexually when he is anxious in company—and it is well that he does not, for however much the expression of anger inhibits anxiety, there is some evidence that it inhibits sexual arousal as well; and a man who is afraid of his boss may be just as frightened of him across a lunch table as across a desk. Plainly enough, Wolpe recommends anxiety-inhibiting responses that are as specifically relevant as possible to the source of anxiety. In effect, by his own admission then, a large part of reciprocal inhibition therapy consists simply of getting people to do the very things they fear. To whatever degree this performance becomes habitual over time, an old response pattern has willy-nilly been exchanged for a new one, both to the same stimulus. This process is more familiarly known to students of learning as counterconditioning. And though one of its consequences, as intended, is indeed the dissipation of the anxiety-provoking aspect of some stimulus, another seems to involve some potential for novel behavior.

Significance of Wolpe's work

The importance of Wolpe's work rests in anything but the finality of the learning principles from which it was deduced. Desensitization does not have to be explained at all in terms of reciprocal inhibition, and while the concept has some descriptive value for the processes by which some forms of action become therapeutically effective, it is not really less speculative or better validated than the complicated motivational and cognitive systems that Insight therapists lay as the foundation of their structures. It is generally true, without doubt, that if you can get a person to do something of which he is needlessly frightened, the more so to do it regularly, his fears will tend to diminish—but it may be because of reciprocal inhibition, or counterconditioning, or because he learns to discriminate cues from which to anticipate where negative reinforcement will or will not occur, or because the positive reinforcement engendered by the argument in which you persuaded him to act was so powerful it inhibited anxiety responses even before the act occurred, or because the anxiety is extinguished for dearth of reinforcement—or for yet other reasons. The multiplicity of plausible explanations reduces the cogency of any one.

The great importance of Wolpe's formulation rests in the method of its construction, not in the accuracy of its contents. The accuracy of his contentions about the ways in which neuroses are learned or unlearned is less important, after all, than the fact that, having elaborated a theoretical conceit of this kind, he then developed a number of very specific procedures by which it could be implemented in the solution of psychological problems. Most of the details of his theory and therapy and the rather estimable body of empirical evidence that may be enlisted in their support are not suggested in this brief synopsis, but are contained in his single major work, *Psychotherapy by Reciprocal Inhibition*, an unusually readable technical book. The very fact that he describes a number of clearly discriminable therapeutic procedures to be applied individually to different clusters of specific symptoms makes his work important, even vital, in a field as much given to vagaries as this one. This is no less true even though a loose theory is proposed for all of them, and even if that theory is wrong. Therapeutic cookbooks are far less elegant intellectually than theoretically more integral approaches, but in medicine they have proved far more useful, and may yet do so in psychotherapy. Wolpe's status as a pioneer is thus quite secure regardless of his ultimate claim to operating space on the psychotherapeutic territory.

Symptom Return and Treatment Statistics

There are two other features of Wolpe's work that deserve citation, though neither lies at its core:

1. In some respects, he challenges Insight therapies, particularly psychoanalysis, more profoundly than he realizes.

2. He presents naive statistics of the successes and failures of his work.

1. The problems Wolpe finds most common in the "life situation" of his patients are essentially the same as those Freud considered primary—sex and aggression. Like Freud, moreover, Wolpe regards neurotic sexual and aggressive behaviors as the products of anxiety that has become attached to sexual and aggressive drives and inhibits their proper expression. Wolpe's learning theory derives most directly from Hull, whose theory of behavior places great importance on the concept of "drive." Hull's is a motivational theory, like Freud's instinct theory (cf. *trieb* and *drive*) and is, in fact, the basis for Dollard and Miller's translation of psychoanalytic theory into learning language in *Personality and Psychotherapy*. While Wolpe does not specify, particularly for assertive responses, why the actions he recommends can be maintained in the face of the anxiety which must be overcome, his theory demands the assumption that these behaviors have powerful drive-reducing properties. To this extent, Mowrer is entirely correct to identify the structure of Wolpe's theory, with respect to sex and assertion, as "thoroughly Freudian."

The vital difference between the therapies, once language differences are accounted for, is really methodological—Freud tries to expose the drive or motive system and the anxiety which attends it so that the behavior can then be disinhibited and expressed; Wolpe tries to produce the behavior so that the anxiety attending the drive will then dissipate. But both systems are clearly directed at the goal of freeing the behavior and reducing the anxiety that blocks it. The traditional argument of the psychoanalytically oriented has been that the disinhibition of the behavior, even if attended by an immediate reduction of anxiety, could bring no permanent relief without exposure of the motives (Insight) which, in inducing the behavior, also aroused anxiety; as new forests grow from old roots after fires and lumberjacks, so new symptomatic responses will presumably erupt from motives still nurtured in unconsciousness when old symptoms are excised. But Wolpe operates from what, translated into the language of learning, is much the same theoretical framework, and by and large, he finds that symptoms removed by his quite direct techniques tend *not* to be replaced by any new symptoms. If the motivational theory has validity then, Wolpe's work challenges the empirical necessity for "uncovering" or Insight psychotherapy much more strongly than it would were he operating from a radically different theoretical position.[2]

2. Finally, the matter of statistics. In each of his major writings, Wolpe includes either raw statistics or summary data about things like the number of cases he has seen, the presenting problems, the number of sessions of treatment, the extent of improvement shown, and the rate of relapse upon subsequent investigation. He is not a sophisticated statistician, and the information he presents may be criticised as inconclusive on many grounds. All such criticisms are trivial in proportion to what is, in the psychotherapy business, the overwhelming fact that he presents any statistical information at all. Psychoanalysis is the bête noire of Wolpe's writing, of course, but his prejudices are to some extent exonerated by the plain fact that almost seventy years of psychoanalytic work by many thousands of therapists has produced no great inclination on the part of analysts to submit their individual activities to the scrutiny of the scientific community. Even the rare corporate studies of psychotherapy results that analysts have conducted have been unduly restricted in circulation, if not actually suppressed, in a way that challenges the good name of the profession. This one man, on the other hand, working essentially alone, has invited the examination, not merely of an isolated sample of his work, but evidently of the results of his entire career as a therapeutic innovator. More important than any of the deficiencies in his report of results is the fact that Wolpe's willingness to expose his work to actuarial evaluation sets a model of intellectual good faith that all other pretenders to innovations in psychotherapy must finally emulate.

[2] It is possible, of course, that Wolpe's therapy involves much more facilitation of insight than he thinks, and that these inadvertent insights are the true agents of cure. Wolpe is especially fair game for this charge since he proposes that such cures as Insight therapies effect are really the results of reciprocal inhibitions accidentally introduced into treatment.

TEACHING FEARLESS BEHAVIOR: THE IMPLOSIVE
THERAPY OF THOMAS G. STAMPFL

This section must begin with a caveat.

None of the work discussed below has yet been published, so my remarks cannot be verified. Thomas G. Stampfl is a professor of psychology at John Carroll University, a distinguished Jesuit school in Cleveland, Ohio. In addition to teaching psychology courses, Dr. Stampfl conducts a clinical practice and does considerable animal research related to his psychotherapeutic system. Undeniably, he does not rush prematurely into print. When I first learned of his work, in the spring of 1961, his therapy system was barely four years old. Before and after that time, he has treated a wide variety of patients with a wide variety of problems, has run innumerable rats through increasingly elaborate refinements of the same fundamental experiment, has trained several students to use his therapy techniques, and has interested a number of psychologists both in his therapy and in the learning theory from which it is derived. This has all been done without ever publishing a single book, article, or note about it in any journal, magazine, or newspaper, which may indicate a talent for public relations as estimable as for psychology!

At all events, the reader has, to my knowledge, no way of independently studying Stampfl's therapy. My knowledge of this potentially important Action therapy is based entirely on access to two mimeographed papers entitled "Implosive Therapy: A Learning Theory Derived Psychodynamic Therapeutic Technique" (received May 1961), and "Avoidance Conditioning Reconsidered: An Extension of Mowrerian Theory" (received October 1961); attendance at a lecture of Stampfl's to the Psychology Department at the University of Illinois; a brief stay with him in Cleveland, which included several discussions with him and with his students and actual observation of one session of implosive therapy; repeated listening to tape recordings of three sessions of psychotherapy by this system; and maintaining correspondence and contact with him and his students. Dr. Stampfl must not be considered responsible for my remarks, therefore, except as quoted directly from his papers. Since much of my account is from memories of personal conversations, moreover, I shall make no special attempt to identify the separate sources, times, or places of each, trusting that the exposition which Stampfl will eventually publish under his own authorship will substantiate this one reasonably well.

A GENERAL LEARNING THEORY OF NEUROSIS
AND ITS VARIANTS

Stampfl's theory of neurosis is, in its inception, much like Wolpe's, both in that it is a learning theory, heavily indebted to Pavlov, Thorndike, *et al.*, and in that it is also an anxiety-centered theory, that is, one which assumes that neurotic behaviors and symptoms may be defined as expressions of, or reactions to, learned anxiety. Beyond this point, the similarity seems to end, for Stampfl's use of learning theory is much more complicated and sophisticated than that of Wolpe or any other Action therapist, while his technique of psychotherapy is vastly simpler.

The ideas from which *implosive therapy* derives are not credited so much to early experimental workers as to the current "two-factor" learning theory of O. H. Mowrer. The critical concepts of Mowrer's theory, for our purposes, try to explain how "avoidance responses," behaviors that reflect fearfulness or anxiety —are learned and maintained. It proposes, in the first place, that one learns to be fearful of otherwise innocent things by being accidentally confronted with them at the same time that some frightening event occurs. A classical illustration of this phenomenon is an experiment by Watson in which a child was taught to fear a once-loved rabbit by being startled by a sudden loud noise in the rabbit's presence. Thenceforth, the sight of the rabbit, or even of a furry object, would be enough by itself to frighten the child.

This learning of fear by contiguity follows the principle of "classical conditioning" discovered by Pavlov (and is the nominal basis for the idea of therapy by counterconditioning). But Mowrer, accepting the conditioning principle, goes on to observe that anxious or avoidant responses, once learned, tend to last almost indefinitely. In this, they differ from other conditioned responses, whose longevity depends upon their being periodically replenished or reinforced. In the Pavlovian scheme, reinforcement would take the characteristic form of repetition of the experience in which the innocent stimulus became associated with a frightening one. This recurrence of the original trauma is not necessary for the maintenance of anxious responses, however, for they seem to sustain themselves forever after even a single traumatic event that is never again repeated.

Mowrer's theory offers an ingenious explanation of this phenomenon by means of a principle originally discovered by Thorndike: that a behavior is most likely to be learned and sustained if it effects the solution to some problem. Mowrer proposes that anxiety is learned in the first place by contiguity, as suggested by Pavlov, but that the avoidant behaviors which result from it are maintained because they successfully reduce anxiety even though contiguity never again occurs! In other words, avoidant behaviors are self-reinforcing by virtue of their very success in escaping the source of anxiety.

If some of the terminology of clinical psychopathology is substituted in the previous paragraph, then we have, in the formal terms of learning theory, the basis of all anxiety-centered theories of neurosis, including Wolpe's, Stampfl's, and indeed, Freud's. Assuming that neurotic symptoms are reflections of anxiety, it says: An individual becomes neurotically anxious because of the accidental association of some innocent experience with a truly frightening one. A symptom is an avoidant behavior which, occurring in the context of the anxiety-provoking stimulus, tends to reduce the strength of that stimulus. By so doing, the symptom is reinforced and fixated in the behavioral repertoire of the individual. Though the symptom may itself cause pain or difficulty, it will persevere so long as it reduces more anxiety than it arouses pain. Plainly, the aspect of the symptom which defines it as neurotic is the fact that it aims to reduce anxiety which is not realistic in the first place because it is aroused by a stimulus which is actually harmless.

This theory is incomplete as an exposition either of Freud or Wolpe, but it is hardly inimical to either of them.

Translating into Freudian terms, it says that anxiety is the motive for the symptom in question, and the development of insight into the unrealistic character of the anxiety reduces its motivational or stimulating properties, so that the patient, freed of the source of fear, no longer needs his symptom for its relief. Stated more generally, and perhaps loosely, the anxiety is *meaningless*, that is, unrealistic, because of the *accidental* nature of its association with some harmless stimulus, and insight is nothing other than the recognition of which associations are meaningful and which are not.

No translation is needed for Wolpe, who uses this very model.

Stampfl's contribution can be best understood as it diverges from the uses that either Wolpe or traditional psychodynamic theorists make of this model; he claims to pursue its logical implications further, as does Mowrer, and to base his psychotherapy system more rigorously upon it.

Dissent from Counterconditioning

The principle argument Stampfl might make contra Wolpe, in this connection, is that all explanations of the *persistence* of neurotic behavior, including Mowrer's, are irrelevant to Wolpe's psychotherapy, but indispensable to his own. The requisite theoretical conditions for Wolpe's system are simply that neurotic behaviors are classically conditioned responses to anxiety, and that anxiety cannot occur simultaneously with certain other responses. As long as anxiety responses can be *inhibited*, it therefore matters little how they can be *reinforced*. Pavlov and Sherrington alone do well enough for Wolpe's methods. But Stampfl is not interested in the suppression or inhibition of neurotic responses, certainly not with the imputation this has for teaching new responses to replace the old ones. He is primarily interested in reducing the frightening character of the cues that arouse the old avoidance behavior rather than initiating or reinforcing new responses that are antagonistic to the behavior. In learning theory terms, this process is called *extinction*, and it is the antithesis of *reinforcement*. Just as the latter is the process that strengthens the occurrence of a learned behavior, the former is the process by which the behavior is weakened. His concern with the relationship between the processes separates Stampfl from Wolpe and connects him both with Mowrer and, almost perversely, the Insight therapists. The latter connection requires some further translation of therapy terms into learning ones.

A New View of Repression

Using the language of learning theory, it is apparent that Insight theorists, particularly psychoanalytic ones, are similarly interested in the extinction rather than the inhibition of neurosis, meaning that, from their vantage, they are more interested in freeing the patient from his old neurotic symptoms than in teaching him specific alternative behaviors to them. The translation of their ideas into learning terms is impeded, however, by the apparent lack of any parallel in learning theory to the concepts of "repression" and "insight" in dynamic personality theory. Dynamically, repression can be thought to prevent the extinction of neurotic behavior by preventing any interference between anxiety-provoking stimuli and the self-reinforcing symptomatic responses they evoke. Bringing repressed material to consciousness—obtaining insight—would make it possible presumably to interrupt those connections, weakening the reinforcing quality of the symptom by identifying its absurdity, its lack of meaning. Now it is a matter of common experience that the concept of "insight into the repressed"—(verbal) awareness of things previously unthought or forgotten—has general significance only for the behavior of human beings. Dynamic theorists who try to integrate their work with learning theory explain repression as the inhibition of verbal responses, and insight as the disinhibition of these responses. This formal usage still leaves these behaviors entirely and uniquely human, for no other organisms are known to use significant amounts of verbal behavior. If so, then the knowledge of the development of neurosis that can be gained from experiments on lower organisms is severely limited, for the concepts of repression and insight cannot be meaningfully applied to rats, cats, and the like. The domain of consciousness, as reflected in verbal awareness, is limited to our own species, and a suitable model of therapy must account for the unique property of this species; the procedural models of Insight therapy do just that. It is obvious that making insight the ideal antidote for repression makes such therapies too sophisticated for the solution of infrahuman problems.

It is precisely this uniquely human model that Stampfl rejects. Basing his argument on Mowrer, he has developed a theory of repression that fits rats as well as people and has no necessary relationship to verbal awareness. From this theory, he has devised an experiment in which he produces persistent "unrealistic" avoidance behavior in rats and treats this "neurosis" quite effectively without the use of insight. Applying the same paradigm to humans, he treats their psychological disorders without recourse to insight and apparently with great success.

Stampfl's own theory of neurosis may now be stated briefly as follows: Neurotic behavior is the learned avoidance of conditioned anxiety-provoking stimuli. Conditioned anxiety responses do not occur singly, but in a context where a whole series of hitherto innocent cues become connected with a single traumatic experience. As the avoidance behavior is learned, the organism becomes increasingly sensitized to many cues that were originally quite remote from the source of fear and unrelated to it; eventually some of these cues seem sufficiently frightening to produce avoidance, and the organism runs from them as if they were the true source of anxiety rather than innocent features of the context in which it first occurred. Since, in the ordinary course of events, conditioned stimuli always occur slightly earlier than the events to which they become related, neurotic anxiety is generally learned to a whole series of events, starting with the one that happens closest to the true trauma, whether in time, space, or degree of similarity, and working its way backwards to the elements that are furthest removed from it in the same context. Eventually, the avoidance responses are made to the more remote events even in the complete absence of the ones closer and more relevant to the initial source of fear. As long as these closer stimuli do not confront the organism, they never arouse anxiety; and they are not likely to confront the organism, for they usually occur in series only after more remote stimuli have already occurred and frightened the organism away. It then becomes quite reasonable to say that, for all practical purposes, *those anxiety-arousing stimuli are repressed!* Anxiety has been learned in connection with them, but they are literally out of awareness—and it is only because they are out of awareness that the organism is not made anxious by them. As soon as they are exposed to consciousness, so to speak, they elicit anxiety, and in even greater degree than do the merely symptomatic stimuli that have been producing the obvious avoidance behavior. But if they are not exposed, then they cannot be extinguished, and they retain their potential for eliciting anxiety and avoidance behavior in the future.

The parallel between Stampfl's theory and psychodynamic theory is intentional. Like dynamic theorists, Stampfl is arguing not only that anxiety lies at the core of neurosis, which Wolpe or other Actionists might heartily accept, but that repression is the great sustaining mechanism of neurosis, which Actionists would by and large contest. Along with psychoanalysts, Stampfl implies that true cures can be achieved only by the "lifting of repressions." But here the connection ends. Far from equating the lifting of repression with the achievement of insight into unconscious motives, Stampfl denies both the range or specificity of motives and the relevance of insight. His scheme of neurosis, instead of viewing symptoms as significant and meaningful expressions of hidden motives, treats them as meaningless gestures of escape from very complicated but meaningless accidents in which a person was hurt and badly frightened. His plan of therapy resembles dynamic therapy only in that it employs a single cure for all ills—but it allows the patient neither option nor responsibility in the conduct of the therapy, and instead of encouraging insight, it seeks only to elicit emotion—and only one emotion at that, namely anxiety. The thoroughly mechanistic character of this Action therapy becomes even more evident from a description of the therapy itself.

Implosive Psychotherapy

Avoiding unnecessary details, Stampfl claims that neurotic symptoms are avoidance responses to unrealistic fears; in other words, a psychological disturbance can be understood as a chronic fearful reaction a person makes to a situation in which he thinks, incorrectly, that he will be hurt. Although this erroneous impression is developed quite by accident, it is likely nevertheless to be a permanent one, for every time the person is confronted with the situation he wrongly thinks will be hurtful, he becomes frightened and runs away, either figuratively and ritually by the expression of his symptom, or perhaps literally. In either event, as long as he is able successfully to avoid confronting whatever frightens him, he is unable to learn that the frightening stimulus is harmless. The information that he is safe never reaches him, one might say, till *after* he has run away—and then he mistakenly concludes that his flight saved him, failing to realize that it was stimulated to begin with by an altogether foolish fear.

Under those circumstances, the general strategy of treatment is plain enough; a means must be found for teaching the victim that he need not be frightened. Whether one chooses the authority of Pavlov to argue that extinction is the most efficient means for eliminating conditioned responses or the homely wisdom which says that experience is the best teacher, he may sensibly conclude that no demonstration could be more convincing than one in which the person faced the source of his fears and discovered through his own experience that they were groundless. In the language of learning, if the person were exposed extensively to the conditioned anxiety-producing stimulus in situations where the anxiety was not reinforced, his response would extinguish, burn itself out, so to speak, for lack of fuel to replenish or strengthen it. The reason this does not occur in everyday experience is simply that once the person is frightened, he understandably removes himself from the source of fear with all deliberate speed. So the tactical problem is first one of arranging things so that the frightening stimulus will occur in circumstances where the subject cannot run away; he must then be continuously prevented from running and continuously exposed to the fearsome stimulus until it has lost all power to elicit anxiety.

Stampfl's therapeutic technique can be stated rather completely in a single sentence, which, in the context of the foregoing paragraphs, may now find the reader prepared to receive it with aplomb: *He uses every possible means to frighten patients as much as he can for as long as he can at a sitting*, taking care only to avoid hurting them physically in any way. He accomplishes this end by the general means of persuading them to imagine themselves realistically involved in situations he describes—and he describes, in copious detail, and with compelling urgency, the most thorough-going catalogue of horrors imaginable, perhaps as rich a collection of lore as was ever composed and narrated for the singular purpose of evoking nauseous terror from even the bravest men.

As implied by the theory, Stampfl considers the treatment most effective when he is able to frighten patients most thoroughly. He further believes that the effects of extinction generalize from stimuli of greater to stimuli of lesser anxiety-arousing potential, just as the anxiety which is initially learned to a stimulus close to the trauma becomes generalized to some which are more removed from it. This means, in effect, that if he can successfully assault the major sources of anxiety, the curative effects will spread auto-matically to the minor ones, whereas the opposite approach would have no such general impact from minor to major fears. With this in mind, Stampfl reasonably enough *tries to provoke maximum anxiety as rapidly as possible.* He does not want to soothe his pa-tient or gradually increase his tolerance for anxiety by giving it first in small doses, but to terrify him, to shock him, to produce an explosion of panic within him. Thus the name *Implosive Therapy,* treatment by inward explosion. The potential economy of this procedure is clear if its rationale is stated another way: Once anxiety is extinguished to a very frightening situation, there is no need to try to arouse and extinguish it to a less frightening one. If one learns to be unafraid of torches, he needs no special lessons to overcome a fear of matches.

Critique of Stampfl

The idea that anxiety arousal is the *only* necessary and suf-ficient technique of treatment, coupled with the hypothesis that the effects of extinction generalize, permits the Implosive therapist another significant economy—*he has no need for accurate informa-tion about the patient or his problem.* It is convenient to have some information, especially for the leads it may give about what kind of imagery will be most frightening to the patient, and Stampfl normally spends about two hours in diagnostic interview-

ing and testing before he starts the treatment. But convenience is
not necessity, and as long as the material presented is frightening
enough, even if it is wholly false and unrelated to the actual contents of the patient's life, the beneficial effects of extinction will
generalize to all other groundless sources of anxiety of equal or
less provocative stature. In this connection, it even makes no difference if repression makes it impossible for the patient to identify
the most significant real life stimuli of neurotic anxiety; as long as
their equivalents in strength are aroused and extinguished, they
will likewise disappear.

A peculiarity in Stampfl's system becomes evident at this
point. As discussed earlier, one of the most carefully reasoned and
technically difficult features of his theory concerns the development of a learning-theory view of repression which gives this concept a significant position in the learning and maintenance of
neurosis. He succeeds in articulating what is perhaps the best argument yet advanced to this end, and his ingenious animal experiments on rats offer a powerful heuristic support to his hypothesis.
Despite all this, the practice of implosive therapy completely dis-
regards the concept of repression and the hypothesis of generalization of extinction makes it into excess theoretical baggage! The
operations that define implosive therapy, in other words, can be
stated every bit as precisely as they are without even granting the
existence of repression; no part of the practice of this therapy requires the concept of repression as its rationale. If extinction of
anxiety generalizes, moreover, then repression is also irrelevant
even in theory to the neuroses both of rats and of people. The
serial context of conditioned anxiety becomes an interesting curiosity, and the experiments demonstrating it academically rigorous irrelevancies; neither has any real bearing on the extinction process,
where the strength of unreinforced anxiety is all that counts. The
insignificance of repression has little effect on the general validity
of Stampfl's therapy, but it has two important implications:

1. It suggests that Stampfl's position is considerably less
dynamic than he would like to admit, placing him further even in
theory from Insight therapists than he seems to wish and making
his therapy a more pure demonstration of an Action system than
might otherwise be true.

2. It raises the more general question, as with Wolpe, about the relevance of Stampfl's theory to his therapy technique. If the latter is not comprehensively rationalized by the former, and yet it works, then the explanation of effects becomes a problem in the public domain, and the wide range of explanatory notions now eligible for entry limits the predictable usefulness of the technique. This problem is a perennial plague on every new form of psychotherapy, and Stampfl does not escape it. Neither does anyone else, as we shall see.

Comparing Wolpe and Stampfl

Wolpe and Stampfl have very similar ideas about how psychological disorders are learned, but the techniques of treatment they use seem to differ enormously from each other—and both claim very great effectiveness. Wolpe applies his techniques almost exclusively to people whose problems are conventionally labeled neurotic by psychiatrists. He claims that 90 percent of patients have improved measurably in anything from one to more than two hundred sessions. The average is reasonably brief, however, compared to many psychotherapies; it is forty-three sessions, each generally less than an hour long.

Stampfl's claims are even more extravagant. He has used implosive therapy successfully, he says, on a great variety of problems, including psychoses, alcoholism, and other disorders that are often considered unlikely prospects for psychotherapy. He claims to have produced marked improvement in 100 percent of cases, with treatment sessions ranging from one to a maximum of fifteen, each about an hour long. Stampfl has not yet produced a statistical catalogue, however, as Wolpe has, and the statistics might not, in any case, be entirely comparable. Though they both use the same general criterion of cure—disappearance of anxious responses to critical cues, Wolpe does not specify very rigid criteria for deciding when this has occurred, while Stampfl terminates treatment as soon as it is no longer possible to elicit anxiety within the session. Proper statistical comparison requires that the same criteria and measurement procedures are systematically used by all parties to the comparison. The efficacy of Stampfl's and Wolpe's systems relative to each other is not much different, judging by their reports, and it is, at all events, less important than the fact that they both claim rates of success which, in terms both of percentage of persons treated and economy of time, are far prouder than the claims of any system of Insight therapy.

Though Wolpe and Stampfl both discount Insight, they differ in what they mean by therapeutic Action. In both cases, the therapist carefully directs the procedure, but for Wolpe, counter-conditioning occurs when the patient acts according to plan, while for Stampfl, extinction occurs with the patient a passive partici-pant (or victim) in the process. Both Wolpe and Stampfl would agree, however, that the activity of the therapist is intended en-tirely to produce specific patterns of action in the patient, and their extensive use of instructions in the one case and verbal imagery in the other has an altogether nonverbal aim. If Wolpe reasons with people, it is to persuade their effector systems, to prod their muscles into specific movements, not to convince their intellects. If Stampfl tells nasty stories, it is to elicit a specific activ-ity, anxiety, not to convey information. At their best, Stampfl's patients presumably *try to get scared*, and are indeed assigned this task as homework.

The very use of language by both Wolpe and Stampfl, in contrast to Insight therapists, can be seen as a necessary encum-brance that may confuse the students of their systems. Most of the behaviors that Wolpe counterconditions must be performed outside the consulting room, so he must rely on his own verbaliza-tions both to stimulate and to program the patient's response. Stampfl's extinction procedures take place mostly in the office, however, and are applied by the therapist. He freely admits that the same results should be available through the use of harmless anxiety-provoking gadgets as with frightening stories; insofar as a patient might be more frightened by seeing a garter snake thrust in his face than by hearing about it, in fact, the therapy should be still more effective. But until it is generally recognized as a legitimate method of treatment, the use of nonverbal implosive therapy might result in greater professional losses to the therapist than in personal gains to the patient.

In evaluating the two systems relative to each other, it is

well to recall that both therapy techniques are legitimate derivatives of the same general theoretical system. In other words, it is
entirely possible to eliminate some learned behaviors either by inhibitory means, as Wolpe does, or by extinction, as Stampfl does.
None of the theoretical differences between them would alter this
fact. By and large, the procedures of the two systems are not
contradictory, even though they are very different.

Desensitization and Implosion

There is one striking exception to the previous statement.
It occurs in comparing implosive therapy to Wolpe's systematic
desensitization. In both situations, as their authors describe them,
the therapist obtains some information in advance about what
frightens the patient. He determines which things are most and
which least frightening. He then has the patient lie down or lean
back in his chair, and instructs him to concentrate on the therapist's remarks and try to imagine the experiences he describes as
vividly and realistically as possible. The therapist then starts describing in the most compelling fashion possible the kinds of
situations that would provoke anxiety in the patient. But Stampfl
starts with the most frightening possible story, and when he gets
indications that the patient is anxious, he tries to make it even
more frightening, while Wolpe starts with the least frightening
situation, and when the patient gives any indication of anxiety, he
stops the session, only to start the next session with a set of images
he is sure will not arouse anxiety. Desensitization is supposedly a
counterconditioning technique in which relaxation provides a response that is incompatible with anxiety. Its success depends on
its antagonism to anxiety. Stampfl's extinction hypothesis, on the
other hand, says that the success of his technique depends on his
ability to produce anxiety. But the procedure is virtually the same
in both cases with respect to everything except the starting point
on the rank-order list of fears and the intentions of the therapist.
According to their theories, Stampfl must claim that Wolpe cannot get results if he is doing what he thinks he is doing (inhibiting anxiety), and Wolpe must extend Stampfl the same cour-
tesy!

The technical contradiction apparent here can be resolved eventually by controlled experimentation; while awaiting these results, however, it may be more fruitful to consider what the contradiction implies if real than to speculate about its possible falsehood. If both men are getting the results they claim under the circumstances outlined above, then it is apparent that the techniques they employ are not necessary derivatives of the theories they use.[3]

This may be true of all therapy techniques, but it is particularly critical for Action therapies because of their claim to specificity and precision. If their manipulations cannot produce rather thoroughly predictable outcomes, then they are indefensible in terms of the ultimate appeal of Action therapies for public attention: their scientific validity. Even if their predictions are successful, as long as their rationalizations are contradictory, they are very limited in the extent to which they can develop scientifically both in specificity and generality. If they cannot turn up good explanations of their work, then they lack a basis from which to develop it further. Scientifically, this forces them to be rude empiricists, which reduces their efficiency, and professionally it makes it very difficult to know where they can extend to new fields of treatment with a minimum risk to patients and maximum chances for success.

Conscience as content. Considering the similarity of their theories of neurosis, it is not at all surprising that Stampfl, like Freud and Wolpe, finds that sex and aggression are problem areas which elicit strong feelings of anxiety. What is perhaps surprising is that he has identified another area of human concern which he believes is far more anxiety-provoking than either sex or aggression. That is the area of "conscience" or general guilt feelings. Though he is able to evoke anxiety readily from his patients when he describes sexual and aggressive themes, Stampfl reports that still

[3] Professor Albert Bandura of Stanford University pointed out to me that extinction has been demonstrated to occur both in situations where subjects were gradually exposed to fearful cues and in situations where they were bombarded with them all at once. Thus there is experimental evidence which supports the respective observations both of Stampfl and Wolpe concerning the success of their methods. This fact has no bearing on the theoretical difference, however, except to indicate that neither theory accounts for the known facts of extinction.

more exaggerated feelings of anxiety are aroused in them by allegations of sinfulness, wickedness, or immorality, the constellation of behaviors or ideas by which people evaluate their "goodness." The implications of this finding will be discussed later on. For the moment, "conscience cues" must be treated as simply one more mechanism or technical implement that Stampfl uses to arouse anxiety.

Summary of Stampfl

To summarize Stampfl: His learning theory of neurotic anxiety provides a closer parallel to psychodynamic personality theory than any previously proposed. To the extent that it is valid it is therefore the most thoroughgoing negation of Insight therapy. The general structure of Stampfl's theory is much the same as Wolpe's, but the use of the principle of extinction as a model for therapy permits a uniquely simple technique to be applied to all disorders. In view of the impoverished results obtained so often in the psychotherapy business, Stampfl's claims of success are staggering, and many eyebrows will rise in response to them. His own are also raised, for he knows as well as anyone the unlikelihood of such splendid accomplishment in this field, and he is more concerned with the identification of truth than the propagation of any system of theory or treatment.

Churlish or witless critics of Stampfl's ideas find it hard to resist the temptation to question them ad hominem, exploding implosive therapy with the petard of desperate personal accusations of psychopathy, neurosis, or general insanity against its originator. Personal acquaintances of Thomas Stampfl know that, if anything, the opposite is true. Serious students of psychotherapy, like all persons of good sense and good will, of course will dismiss any personal evaluations as irrelevant, just as they will refrain from misjudging his system because of its apparently harsh assault upon people who are already overly prone to fearfulness. The effectiveness of Stampfl's techniques in alleviating symptoms must, when all is said and done, speak for itself, independent of its unhappy appearances, of the personal qualities of its originator, and finally, indeed, of the theory on which it is ostensibly based. No more or less is true of any psychotherapy.

SHAPING NEW BEHAVIOR: THE OPERANT
TECHNIQUES OF B. F. SKINNER

In some respects, it is improper to describe the work of B. F. Skinner as an illustration of Action therapy. In the first place, Skinner is not and has never been a psychotherapist. In the second place, those of his students who are psychotherapists have thus far developed neither a large collection of anecdotes and illustrations nor any statistics of success rates of the treatments based upon his ideas. However, despite the recent origin of this pursuit, they have successfully applied Skinner's principles to some specific psychotherapeutic problems. Partly for this reason, partly as a corollary of the general importance Skinner's work has had in psychology, and partly because Skinnerians tend to display their wares, advertise their accomplishments, and propagate their techniques with something like religious fervor, they are now beginning to attract serious attention from previously uncommitted psychotherapists. Thus far, the possibilities of Skinnerian therapy have been most apparent to therapists who work in institutional settings rather than clinics or offices; this is a rare and welcome form of evolution for a therapy system, for it is institutions such as mental hospitals that offer at once the most intractable therapeutic problems and the greatest opportunities for controlling the conditions of treatment.

The techniques which seem capable of deduction from Skinner's theories of learning may have such practical and theoretical importance, despite their relative lack of demonstrated effectiveness, that their significance does not depend entirely on their capacity to develop effectively in their present forms. Skinnerian therapists, more than any others, are models of what might be called an engineering approach to psychotherapy. Regardless of specific outcomes in any instance, their techniques of step-by-step functional analysis and empirical testing of their own predictions lends their treatment a constant experimental aura, and one that is perhaps freer of theoretical cant than any other system.

The practical importance of these techniques is the implication they have for shaping new patterns of behavior rather than merely erasing old ones, which is the aim of the anxiety-based theories of Wolpe and Stampfl. The theoretical importance of "operant" techniques, as they are called, comes from the fact that Skinner's theory represents an ultimate version of the kind of theoretical systems to which Action therapy is disposed; in this sense, it differs more radically from Insight therapies than does any other system.

The Basis of Behavior Shaping

Skinnerian psychotherapy takes as its basis two principles, the first of which was discovered by E. L. Thorndike, who named it the Law of Effect. It says simply that *an organism will learn to repeat a behavior for which it is rewarded and to avoid one for which it is ignored or punished.* The second principle, whose elaboration reflects Skinner's unique contribution to learning, says essentially that *complicated behavior patterns, particularly those that can be described as "skillful," are gradually learned in small steps that come progressively closer and closer to some optimal level of performance.*

A scheme of psychotherapy follows directly from these principles: all the therapist needs to know about an organism is what things it finds rewarding and what punishing. These can be identified by watching its overt acts and their consequences. When the result of an act is such that it causes the act to be repeated, that result is said to positively reinforce or reward the act. Conversely, when the result of an act is such that the act is then discarded or avoided, that result is said to negatively reinforce (fail to strengthen) or actively punish the act.[4] Since rewards and punishments are the sole bases of learning, and since they may be inferred entirely from the patterns of actions that are stimulated by things in the environment, it should presumably be possible to control what the organism learns by controlling the rewarding and punishing characteristics of the environment.

[4] Faithfulness to Skinnerian usage requires some treachery to the English language. In this system, the term *negative reinforcement* is used to mean *non*reinforcement, that is, ignoring the behavior which has just occurred. Others use "positive reinforcement" to mean rewarding a behavior and "negative reinforcement" to mean punishing it.

The implied operations of the Skinnerian psychotherapist then follow clearly.

1. He attempts, first of all, to analyze the nature of the interactions between the organism and the environment with respect to some specific set of problem behaviors.

2. He determines what features of the environment appear to be sustaining those actions and molding them through various positive and negative reinforcements. Then he decides what new pattern of behaviors he wishes to see developed by the organism.

3. He identifies some objects or situations that will function as positive and negative reinforcements for the individual and whose dispensation is completely in the therapist's control.

4. Finally, he manipulates the environment so that, whenever approximations of those desired behaviors occur, they are positively reinforced, whereas whenever behaviors occur that might interfere with the desired ones, they are negatively reinforced or punished.

Punishment, however, is a tricky technique, for unless it can be applied with great precision, its effects are somewhat unpredictable; they are likely to be more general than is desired. This is one reason why "aversive training," the application of punishing reinforcements, is used or recommended with relative infrequency for Skinnerian treatment. Perhaps more important, it is possible in general to reduce the frequency of undesirable behavior when it occurs by the simpler expedient of withholding positive reinforcement without resorting to punishment. In effect then, operant psychotherapy works by rewarding the occurrence of desired behavior (positive reinforcement) and ignoring or otherwise disregarding most undesirable behavior (negative reinforcement).

Still another way of describing this treatment might be to speak of it as the teaching of contingencies, that is, teaching the individual that the availability of rewards is contingent on the performance of certain behaviors.

The Potentialities of Operant Psychotherapy

Though the general sequence of operations, as indicated above, is simple enough for this kind of treatment, it is a far cry from a practical and workable psychotherapeutic formula. The environmental conditions that surround each individual differ somewhat, so do the patterns of behavior he has already learned or has available, and so do the consequences that have variously greater or less reinforcing effect on him. Each case must therefore be considered somewhat on its individual merits, and considerable ingenuity is required to develop a suitable treatment program, especially since the ideal conditions for the use of operant techniques are those where the therapist has maximum control over the environment of the patient. All these are reasons that explain, perhaps, why there has not yet appeared any single treatise describing operant therapy as a systematic psychotherapy and why there have been, till this time, fairly few case reports of its use as psychotherapy.

The potential for maximum control over the patient's environment is greatest, of course, in what Goffman calls "total" institutions, such as mental hospitals. It is therefore not surprising that most of the reports which have been made of successful therapy by operant techniques come from hospital situations. Some such accomplishments have been trivial, such as getting a mute psychotic patient to ask for chewing gum when he could not get it any other way. But Teodoro Ayllon and Jack Michael, in a paper titled "The Psychiatric Nurse as a Behavioral Engineer," also report an impressive instance of drastically reducing the use of psychotic language by one patient in a very short period. And Arthur Bachrach has told me of a case of anorexia nervosa he treated successfully by operant means in a patient whose previous extensive work in psychoanalytic therapy had apparently been of no help.

It is difficult to say with any confidence how great is the potential for developing a well-formulated scheme of operant psychotherapy for office practice, but in some respects this should not present excessive difficulties. Though a therapist is not likely himself to have much control over his patient's environment outside the office, there are many interested parties who do. Teachers and parents often control enough contingencies in the lives of children, and husbands and wives over each other, so that they can operate effectively as therapists if they have a proper understanding of the situations to control, the reinforcements to employ, and the schedule by which to administer them. In providing these, the professional therapist would be acting as a consultant to people who are concerned with the patient and in a better position to regulate the patient's behavior than he is. There is already considerable precedent for this consultant function in the office practice of psychotherapy, particularly among therapists whose speciality is the treatment of children. Increasingly, the trend develops towards treating parents simultaneously with their children, and what was once a *New Yorker* magazine caricature of a whole family on couches all at once in the same consulting room is becoming increasingly a reality in what is called "family group therapy." Most advocates of these practices do not accept or perhaps even know about operant principles, but their practices nevertheless reflect a concern to effect treatment by manipulating the reinforcement contingencies in the environment.

The potential usefulness of operant therapy in hospitals is even more significant than in office practice, especially since the very persons who are hospitalized for psychological disorders are considered, as a class, least amenable of anyone to any presently well known form of psychotherapy, including all Insight therapies. Perhaps even more to the point is the possibility that, if operant techniques prove as useful as their adherents claim, then the most effective way to treat most psychological disorders may eventually be to hospitalize the patient! Willard Mainord has developed a therapeutic scheme, largely along Skinnerian lines, that seems particularly suited to a wide variety of what are generally considered "neurotic" or other problems not now treated in hospitals. To be most effective, Mainord's techniques require the relatively complete control of environment that is possible in a hospital setting.

Skinner's own work also suggests obliquely that operant techniques cannot be used very efficiently in a free environment. His utopian novel, *Walden Two*, makes very clear his feeling that the best developments in man can only eventuate in a situation where the entire structure of society is regulated and experimentally manipulated by operant means for the welfare of all its inhabitants. By implication, this would be no less true of psychologically disturbed people, who must be manipulated into rapprochement with so-called normality, than with normal people who must learn to perform particular functions and roles within their societies.

The Implications of Skinner's "Anti-theory"

The relative lack of explicit formulas for treatment by operant means, as opposed, for example, to those of Wolpe or Stampfl, is partial evidence of its more explicitly experimental or empirical nature. The extent of Skinner's empirical orientation is even greater than that implied, however, for it is not merely free of the restrictions imposed by theory, but strongly biased in an antitheoretical direction. Until very recently, he was outspokenly concerned only with the operations that describe behavior, not with the assumptions about internal, unobservable events that may explain it. This kind of operationism writ large, with its implications for personality theory as well as practice, makes Skinner the purest of the Action therapy theorists; in effect, he takes as the total measure of man, the actions he can be observed to perform.

Action therapists, in their concern for alleviating symptomatic problems, are often accused of being superficial, of failing to cope with the internal source of overt difficulties. To some extent, Wolpe's and Stampfl's anxiety theories are directed against that allegation. They deny the necessity for insight, but concede in effect that anxiety is the internal motive of neurosis. Not so Skinner. Not only does he deny the necessity for insight and the significance of motives, which latter Wolpe and Stampfl in theory do not, but he questions their existence in any terms—and is no more loathe to question the existence of thoughts, ideas, and intentions as entities! He casually nods in recognition that there exist some elementary physiological drive states but he thinks it is generally a waste of time to study them. Very recently, he has conceded the utility of studying private behavior, but is deeply concerned to see that students of such behavior steer clear of the postulation of "mental way stations" in attempts to explain what they cannot truly describe. It is equally wasteful, he proposes, to construct psychological theories, the more so when they require inferences about conditions and events that cannot be observed. Finally, the ultimate paradigm for all Action therapy, as Skinner might state it: It serves no purpose to explain behavior, but only to learn how to control and modify it.

It is possible to interpret this extreme position as a reaction against the strictures of scientific theorizing and an implicit appeal for better experimental method and empirical probing of ideas. This may be historically true, but I believe it is irrelevant in understanding the most important implications of Skinner's work either for psychology in general or for psychotherapy in particular. For the latter, I believe this implication to be that the individual's problems, and indeed all those aspects of his existence which are therapeutically relevant, are of concern only insofar as they affect his relation to the external environment and not at all in relation to his hypothesized or expressed internal state. In that event, therapy may be defined as the deliberate adjustment of the relationship between the individual and his environment to elicit maximum net functioning of the entire system. What constitutes maximum net functioning is partly defined by the therapist and partly determined by experiment. More important, however, is the implication that the individual is always part of a system which includes more than himself and in which, at some choice points, he may not be granted, for any practical purpose, the possession of any self turned inwards. That this system posits a social character to all significant functions is plain enough from Walden Two. The point here is that it may allow no others.

Meanwhile, this problem is largely academic, for the empirical issue at hand is whether the techniques of operant training can be developed and systematically employed to shape the behavior of psychotics into what are plainly desirable directions, to make it possible for neurotics to work effectively, and so forth. If Skinnerians have little use for the internal states of men, their feelings or ideas or motives, there is still plenty enough overt behavior that needs prior shaping to permit the other issue, for the moment, to be laid aside. It will be enough for now if they can usefuly fulfill their own criteria for cure. This is not an easy matter, however, for operant psychotherapy has the vices of its virtues—the very specificity that functional analysis permits and behavior shaping demands may limit the variables that can be dealt with at once and require so much time for its implementation as to be practically useless. It is marvellous to induce psychotics to ask for gum after years of total silence, even if months of effort are required. But it is not clear exactly when or how or whether this kind of maneuver will equip them to leave a hospital and function again in society. And great as the promise of operant therapy is there, a Scotch verdict is still in order—not proven.

COMMON CRITIQUE OF ACTION THERAPY

SCIENCE AND ACTION THERAPY

Though they have none of the Skinnerian's disdain for theory, neither Wolpe nor Stampfl nor any other Action therapy theorist would rest the scientific claims of his system very heavily on the intellectual elegance of his theoretical formulations. Quite the contrary, the scientific pretensions of all systems are based primarily on the claim of practical consequences, specifically on their potency for symptom reduction. Under the circumstances, the scientific status of Action therapies is relatively easy to judge; either they remove symptoms or they do not. Their claim, accompanied by some evidence, is that, by and large, they do.

Insight therapists have long since proposed, however, that symptom removal without treatment of motives would eventuate in the development of new symptoms or return of the old ones. In some instances, this claim seems to be dramatically supported, but while such cases are certainly impressive, the weight of evidence suggests that they are hardly typical. The odds against harmful aftermaths of symptom removal are great enough, apparently, so that given the choice, most patients would be wise to take the risk of future troubles against the certainty of present ones. Whatever their other failings, the Action therapies are not very vulnerable to attack on the grounds either that their criteria are unclear or that they cannot be satisfied. How worthwhile their satisfaction is another question. Meanwhile, the limited claim to empirically testable results is itself sufficient to lend a scientific status to the Action therapies which Insight systems cannot so readily claim. Neither is their scientific status so great, however, as the

Action therapists themselves would like to claim, for there may be a great separation in fact, as we have seen, of their techniques of therapy from the theories that are supposed to underlie them. The fact that one deduces a therapy from a learning theory and then applies it successfully is no guarantee of either the validity of the theory or the necessity of the therapy. Plenty of nonsensical treatments deduced from all varieties of intellectual rubbish have undoubtedly effected genuine cures in some cases throughout the history of the healing arts. This phenomenon, which is not understood scientifically, is variously labeled "faith healing," "placebo effect," and the like, and the possibility of its operation in the case of psychological disorders may be even greater than in medical ones. There is a legend in the psychotherapy trade, at all events, that whatever is new and enthusiastically introduced and pursued seems, for a time, to work better than what previously did, whether or not it is more valid scientifically. Eventually, these novelties too join the Establishment of techniques and turn up nothing more than whatever went before. Perhaps there is more than idle fantasy in this idea—maybe the really critical factors in the accomplishments of psychotherapies have been more related to the persons of their adherents than to anything else. A distinguished psychoanalyst has observed that young, fresh psychoanalysts seem to get more cures than their more experienced colleagues; and Carl Rogers recently noted that client centered psychotherapy seems, after twenty years, not to have done much better than any other. On strictly scientific grounds, and by a strictly actuarial criterion, one wonders then if Action therapy systems can sustain their apparent effects, not against logical criticism or emotional denunciation, but against the pallor and flaccidity that may result from sympathetic acceptance and familiarity.

MORALS AND ACTION THERAPY

The primary moral problems engendered by Action therapy are those that presuppose its success rather than its failure; just as the fascination of the search for meaning in Insight therapy may cause the participants to overlook the question of whether symptoms are being cured, the relief from symptomatic pain in Action therapy may encourage its parties to disregard the cost or consequences of that relief.

The techniques of Insight therapy, for better or worse, vest both choice and control of behavior in the patient, which, as we have seen, has its own problems. But Action therapies do neither, assigning to the therapist, as far as possible, all options in the therapeutic scheme. Responsibility for the outcome thus rests more with him than with an Insight therapist, perhaps more with him in some sense than with his patient. But what is he responsible to do? The naive answer, entirely consistent with one moral tradition of Western man, is that he should remove pain. But for psychological disorders, the pain in question generally turns out to involve some disharmony between one's mental processes or feelings, on the one hand, and one's overt behavior on the other. The term symptom may refer either to internal or to overt processes so that the removal of symptoms may mean, in one instance, inducing changes in the way a person feels without effecting the way he acts, while in another case it may mean changing the way he acts to correspond with the way he feels. In either case, the Action therapies imply that the decision as to which is to be attempted lies within the proper domain of the therapist.

Now consider the situation in which a man comes to a psychotherapist to be treated, say, for homosexuality. The symptom may be defined either as the performance of this relatively unconventional behavior or as the anxiety the person experiences about it. In either case, his pain results from what Festinger would call the "dissonance" between these two aspects of his experience —and the pain would presumably disappear if harmony were reestablished between feeling and act. On the face of it, harmony could equally well result either from giving up homosexuality, thus escaping both guilt and social remonstrance, or from giving up the moral posture that condemns and abjures homosexuality. Which is the better choice? One answer is that the best choice is that which involves the line of least resistance; so, if the patient expresses the wish to stop being homosexual, the treatment should encourage that outcome, whereas if he wishes to remain homosexual but not be bothered by it, the best choice fosters that result. If the central issue is surcease of pain, argument from the line of least resistance seems most reasonable.

But pursued a little further, it may turn out that in cases such as this, the true line of least resistance is almost inevitably the one that eschews the prohibitive moral code rather than the prohibited behavior, for the former is bolstered and surrounded by a network of religious and legal inanities which weaken its claims to observance, while the latter is driven biologically, and the tensions it arouses are thus most easily reduced by being gratified. This is exactly Wolpe's position in a case he reports in which he cured a man's anxiety over homosexuality by persuading him to disavow the religious code that condemned this behavior.

In this instance, the patient entered therapy with the questionable behavior already established, and the therapist treated the unhappy feeling that went with it. Equally common, however, is the converse situation in which the therapist proposes a new behavior as the solution to the symptomatic feeling. The attack on *feeling* alone characterizes all of Stampfl's therapy, on *behavior* alone all Skinnerian therapy, and on either or both, one or another of the variety of techniques that Wolpe developed. At all events, the choice is always the therapist's. Wolpe does not hesitate to take responsibility for his decisions, and the Skinnerian position does not allow the possibility even that responsibility could rest anywhere else than with the therapist; Stampfl, operating more like Insight therapists, holds his breath as to the outcome, hoping that by eliminating the feeling of anxiety, he is not permitting more reprehensible, if painless, feelings to dictate the behavior of some men. Stampfl also rationalizes that arousing "conscience cues" implies self-civilizing possibilities that may have never had much chance before to work.

That the locus of control in therapy should reside in the therapist rather than the patient may seem reprehensible to some people who are accustomed to one or another Insight model of psychotherapy. But the Actionist may fairly claim, from within the framework of his assumptions, that he is doing much the same thing a physician does in the treatment of a symptom of physical illness. Viewed that way, the most reprehensible behavior of which

the Action therapist can be accused is that he uses his own judgment in the conduct of the treatment. The outcome of his treatment may radically alter the life of the patient, but that is no
argument one way or the other for attempting it. Surgery radically
alters people's lives, and so can the recommendation that they
move to another climate, take exercise, or stop smoking. It is perhaps less presumptuous of the doctor, when all is said and done,
to treat the symptom with some disdain for its role in the total life
of the patient, than to think too far ahead of its consequences.

THE LIMITATIONS OF ACTION

As long as he concerns himself exclusively with symptoms
in their narrow sense, the Action therapist can claim indifference
to much of his patient's life, just as the physician can. The restora-
tion of function is, on the face of it, a fairly mechanical job. And
in that event, he may not be attacked in terms of the social philosophy which is or is not implied by his therapy any more than a
mechanic can be blamed for fixing a car which subsequently has an
accident or a doctor for treating a criminal. Everybody cannot be
responsible for everything, and while the society is obviously em-
powered to curb its specialists in whatever ways seem best for it,
it hardly expects them to anticipate and legislate their own powers
or restraints. In this respect, the Actionist is not subject to the
same moral scrutiny as is the Insight therapist, who is, to begin
with, more broadly concerned with the patient's life.

But not all the problems that people bring to psychotherapists can be, with equal ease, identified as limited problems of
function, and even when they can, it is not always possible to restore functioning without radical changes in the patient's systems
of meaning. Phobias are good examples of clear-cut symptoms
where function is lost and may be directly restored, and we may
likewise grant that many other psychic troubles rest in learned anxieties, as Wolpe or Stampfl claim. But one cannot speak so glibly
of dysfunctions of husbands who are unhappy with their wives and
seek counsel, or of young people who, fearing an insecure and
shadowed future, fear to cast themselves into it in love and work
and seek to borrow courage, or the aging whose fear of what is

ahead commingles with regret at what is left behind, and seek both solace and repair. Nor is it easy to specify and circumscribe the ills of homosexuals and whores and hoods and gamblers and drunks and all that broad array of people whose malfunctioning defines their lives instead of merely staining them, and for whom the very definition of disorder is as likely imposed externally as felt within.

It is not obvious that the Action therapies are equipped to handle problems in the former category, for they would be hard put to identify general unhappiness or insecurity as problems of function rather than meaning. But it is not apparent, for the most part, how they would deal with the latter either, unless the patient who had ordered his life in some socially deviant pattern had some system of meaning to which he could refer changes in his life style or unless the therapist could offer him one. The very modesty which makes the Actionist limit his concern to symptom relief, simultaneously gives a powerful scientific impetus to his work, frees him of much moral concern—and perhaps forces him to drastically curtail the range of persons and problems he attacks. Courting specificity, the Actionist risks wedding triviality.

The only alternative to this self-restriction is to deliberately expand the definition of "symptom" to incorporate a wider and wider range of human troubles. This is apparently what many Action therapists have done. But the further this expansion goes, the more tenuous their effort becomes to define symptoms as malfunctions, and the more presumptuous becomes the definition, implied or explicit, of what good functioning is. In effect, this effort produces precisely the same progression of events through which Insight therapists passed, and which was described earlier. The only difference is that problems of general happiness, security, and so forth are now identified as problems of functioning rather than of meaning, and the definition of adequate "functioning" now becomes the property of the therapist.[5] Precisely this situation is anticipated by Skinner in his utopian novel, *Walden Two*. In that society, people are engineered to function perfectly in a fashion

---

[5] That might not be so different from Insight therapy either. Theory of patient options aside, the definition of meaning may also effectively rest with the therapist in any system which proposes that meanings may be symbolized, condensed, distorted, or otherwise hidden.

which blends the needs of society with those of the individual. A concern with freedom does not arise, for properly functioning organisms do not experience themselves as being denied any freedom. A concern with happiness and security does not arise, for adequate functioning in Skinner's human society, as among the ants in White's *Once and Future King*, obviates both unhappiness and insecurity. And the society itself is organized by planners whose power is experienced both by themselves and by their citizens as nothing more than another form of functioning within the society, one which serves it and the individual all at once.

Embarrassments of Action

The convergence of the concepts of functioning and meaning need not, in one sense, be an embarrassment to the Action therapist, for he may legitimately choose to define meaning as the subjective aspect of what may be seen objectively as functioning, much as feeling is defined as the subjective aspect of what is objectively emotion. His problem comes from the facts that:

1. the more broad the function he wishes to identify, the more tenuous it becomes scientifically;

2. the more control he retains over the definition of function, the greater his violence to the patient should his broad definition of function be wrong; and

3. the implications of what he proposes for the patient's life are just the same whether he chooses to call them meanings or functions.

When all is said and done then, the Action therapist is no more likely to escape the moralistic implications of his activity than is the Insight therapist, though he bids fair to enter into these difficulties with his eyes somewhat wider open, and perhaps he will get into them less often. No matter how much he specifies his goals, or limits his attack to the alleviation of clear-cut symptoms, the fact remains that some symptoms of dysfunction are sources of psychological distress precisely because they are rooted in what may equally well be seen as systems of meaning; and whenever this happens, an effective therapy is likely either to change behavior to satisfy a meaning system or change the system to justify a behavior. Even the fact that meaning can be described as a semantic imposition on reality, and that language, indeed thought itself, can be construed as a collection of conditioned responses so gross that they always involve some movement of the skeletal musculature has, finally, no bearing on the case.

CONCLUSION

Taken in the balance, the Action therapies can claim very striking advances over the Insight therapies, a fact that is slowly impinging itself upon graduate training facilities in the psychotherapeutic professions. Its relatively mechanistic techniques are more subject to direct scrutiny than the often esoteric-sounding Insight schemes, and they imply the use of more rigorous criteria for the evaluation of success and failure in therapy. Its relatively more systematic, thus scientific, theoretical formulation suggests direct lines of inquiry, exploration, and innovation in the field. For both of these, the gain in precision alone would have great value, let alone the apparently greater rate of therapeutic success. And the restriction of application to that which can be identified as individual malfunction may itself serve a social function that can be too easily qualified, even obviated, by an excessive concern with social philosophy or with the relation of meaning and function.

But the gains are not all clear cut. The range of techniques is terribly narrow at one extreme (Stampfl), and too broad to have yet been very practical at another (Skinner). The underlying theory must assume a very restricted basis for disturbance (anxiety) in the former case, and the broad concept of manipulability (operant learning) in the other seems to require something like an entire social order for its optimal fulfillment. Both theories, moreover, are content to treat human behavior as a rather straightforward arithmetic extension of two very simple principles of learning, which may be as much too neat a concept as that of meaning is too vague. Finally, the lack of overt concern with social philosophy or some hypothetical moral order does not free the Action therapist from any involvement in these issues. Indeed, the fact that he is so courageous (or stupid) as to himself assume responsibility for his work, must make him more alert to the implications it has for the social order and his own, as well as his patient's role in it. With the single exception of Krasner, Action therapists have either not yet recognized this problem or, like Wolpe, have committed themselves to much the same moral goals as the Insight therapist; substituting happiness for meaning as their aim, they are nonetheless still committed to the welfare of the individual patient. Like Insight therapies then, the more they seek to comprehend his welfare in terms of his total life rather than his symptomatic pain, the more they pose a moralistic end which is finally no less problematic or perplexing for all its scientific gains.

CHAPTER SIX

THE MULTIPLICITY OF MAN
INTEGRATING THE THERAPIES

If psychiatry is still the most backward branch of medicine, and psychotherapy continues to be a perennial embarrassment to scientific psychology, it is not for lack of diligent and intelligent students of these fields, but because knowledge still comes harder here than in other branches of these disciplines. The disease model of psychological disturbances gained ascendance over demons and dybbuks only in very modern times, as progress in man's thought is measured. And its own obsolescence, foreshadowed two centuries ago by Pinel's concept of "moral disorder," has not yet led to the demise of the term "mental illness," or its replacement by any more appropriate coinage which would imply disorders of learning, of behavior, or of meaning, any or all of which would represent still a further step forward in thinking on this theme.

At each stage in the development of this field, yesterday's

innovator is today's reactionary; the psychiatrists who championed the structural disease or defect model of psychological ailments in the nineteenth century opposed the relatively functional, non-organic model of disorder that got its greatest impetus from psychoanalysis; and the dynamic psychiatry born of the latter has hardly hesitated to disown the new technology that learning theory has spawned. Something like this took place within psychology too, where trends in personality theory may be less clear, but plainly follow Zeitgeists of their own.

Psychiatrists and clinical psychologists, the two groups who contribute most to new developments in psychotherapy, are both at relative disadvantages within their professions for gaining new knowledge—most of medicine and psychology deal with smaller units and more clearly isolable problems than do these specialties. Psychotherapists wish that they could too, and so it seems they try to ape their better-seated colleagues by clinging to each discovery that has some plausibility for explaining human beings and that suggests some body of technique from which to operate. Their subject matter really is enormously complex, and since the techniques of choice at any time are just effective enough to be reinforcing and sometimes very hard to come by, and lack many alternatives for replacement—they stick. Thus psychotherapists understandably have great difficulty rising above their professional origins, either to see the limits of the familiar or to explore the novel as it appears.

It is not surprising that this process in short order overtakes even the very proponents of novelty, who themselves, reinforced by sympathetic colleagues and the happy testimonials of erstwhile patients, crystallize novel orthodoxies with all due speed, and thus immured against new inquiry, equally disclaim too much the error-laden past from which they come and disregard the future's sure exposure of weaknesses they cannot foretell.

Precisely this development has come to pass, it seems, with Action therapists, whose reactive zeal against the Insight schools preceding them, has made them overlook some attributes of insight that may have merit.

Organized on the basis of their techniques, it is easy to see how psychotherapeutic systems can be described in terms of essential orientations in the direction of eliciting *insight* or *action*. What is sometimes hard to see from within either system is the limits of both, especially since the latter has addressed itself so polemically to the former. Each has severe limitations however, as well as significant merits, and it is only by means of some compromise formulations of insight and action that psychotherapy systems can be derived which adequately comprehend human behavior. This chapter discusses such a formulation and describes one serious effort in this direction.

THE LIMITS OF THE SYSTEMS

Although the historical debate between Insight and Action therapies was presented in terms of their different approaches to the problem of dealing with symptoms, the conflict between them goes considerably beyond that issue. The unprejudiced observer cannot escape the conclusion, I believe, that the Action therapies have a better case with respect to symptoms, and insofar as the removal of particular limited classes of symptoms is concerned, Insight therapies have no longer any *raison d'être*.

The fatal flaw of the Insight therapies, in this respect, was the notion that consciousness somehow inevitably moved behavior. It plainly does not, certainly not inevitably. Actuarial evaluations of the results of Insight therapy could have told us this long ago, and in a sense, did tell just that when they were done. But the doing was belated and sometimes half-hearted and ineffectual, and it was only the comparable statistics of antagonists like Wolpe and Eysenck that forced many people to take very seriously the issue of an empirical criterion of therapeutic results. Action therapy scores heavily on that account.

But there is a parallel error in the Action therapies, in this case one of omission rather than commission. Whereas the Insight systems make too much of consciousness, insight, and meaning, the Action systems make too little of them, both technically and theoretically. In their righteous rebuttal of the sanctity of consciousness and insight, they have tended, apparently somewhat unwittingly, to disregard entirely the efficacy of thinking as a means of controlling behavior. Hurrying to the animal laboratory

for simple and accurate models of learning that could be trans-
ferred effectively from cats and rats to human beings, their proper
eagerness to make use of the similarities between species made
them all too casual about the implications of the differences. The
most evident and important of these, at its most descriptive, measurable level, is that human beings can talk and other animals cannot. Complicating it only a little, humans can emit extensive reports concerning internal processes that are not identical either
with overt, gross responses of the skeletal musculature or with similar activities of smooth muscles or glands; they can talk about
thinking, imagining, and feeling. What is more, in this connection, and more signally specific to the human as opposed to other
species, they are apparently able to discriminate between these
very processes as they experience them; that is, they recognize a
distinction between cognitive and affective processes, on the one
hand, and overt muscular responses on the other. In general, the
Action theorists tend to disregard these human peculiarities in
their theories, though they may find them eminently useful in
practice. Limiting their sources of conjecture to behaviors which
can be derived from lower organisms, they produce a model both
of neurosis and of therapy which studiously disdains to notice that
the verbalisms of psychotherapists may have properties other than
the simple stimulus values attributed to them by analogy with rats
and cats, while the response capacities of patients include an enormous array of internal behaviors, such as pondering, remembering,
and mentally rehearsing, which are demonstrably species-specific.
In their attempts at psychological sophistication, their scientific
postures have led the Actionists not only to reject humanism, but
to overlook evolutionary biology, which might propose without
embarrassment that the behavior of men is signally different from
that of other animals.

It is apparent that a therapy system which tries to integrate
internal processes like thinking into the stimulus–response model
of *Action* therapy will be a more complicated one than any hitherto discussed, but it might also apply more realistically than others
to larger segments of human behavior. In one instance, at least,
that of the apparent contradiction between Wolpe and Stampfl,
the concept of "cognitive discrimination" indicated above may

offer some useful clue as to how it is possible for both therapists to elicit the same result by opposite procedures.

A Cognitive Theory of Action Therapy

Wolpe and Stampfl, you will recall, both propose true learning theories of psychoneurosis and psychotherapy, and both claim very great effectiveness for their practical applications of them. The singular difference in their presentations is that Wolpe says he is "desensitizing" people to anxiety by a technique that avoids anxiety insofar as possible, while Stampfl says that he is producing "extinction of anxiety responses" by eliciting it as much as possible. Even more remarkable is the great similarity in what they both describe as their essential therapeutic procedure: They create as vivid a mental image as they possibly can of all the different things that arouse anxiety in their patients. Wolpe says that the preliminary procedure of relaxation produces a response state which is incompatible with anxiety, so that patients unlearn anxiety responses, in effect by counterconditioning. Stampfl claims that he reproduces anxiety without reinforcing it, and it therefore reduces by simple extinction.

Neither considers, however, that a third possibility may exist, in which both counterconditioning and extinction responses are facilitated: The repeated elicitation of vivid imagery produces a discrimination set such that the patient increasingly learns to distinguish between the imaginative, cognitive, affective aspects of experience, and the sensory and overt muscular aspects. The very process of repeatedly inspiring imagination, in other words, may dispose the patient to discriminate between imaginary and "real"—between mental and physical experiences—more readily than any other means. Anxiety is reduced as he develops increasing ability to tolerate the imagery, which both Wolpe and Stampfl agree is necessary, and the ability to tolerate the imagery is progressively increased in turn as the patient makes an ever-finer discrimination between the impulsive, motivational, cognitive aspects of experience, and the sensory muscular ones. The closer the imagery comes to representing "real" experience of the most complete sort without being followed by the actual experience it stimulates, the more the patient's expectation of disastrous action, with its disastrous consequences, is reduced. By this means, he learns increasingly that the most intense thoughts, feelings, and motives do not impel him helplessly to perform those concrete acts whose punishment would realistically produce intense pain. Thus the patient learns control, so to speak; the differentiation process, as it becomes more efficient with repetition, creates a new response alternative to anxiety in the face of provoking stimulation; it might be labeled mediation. By this process, it becomes increasingly possible to think over the stimulus instead of automatically trying to escape it. Since by definition the threatening stimulus really is harmless, its discrimination becomes increasingly easy and unimportant at the same time, so that its stimulus value gradually decreases beneath the threshold of observation.

The principle of discrimination is hardly new to students of learning, and it is also thoroughly applicable to cats and rats. In this sense, its use does little violence to either Stampfl or Wolpe. But the variant I have termed *cognitive* discrimination has two functions in this paradigm that limit it more specifically to people:

1. It explains why speech on the therapist's part can be sufficient to arouse imagery that has no innate connection with the purely auditory aspects of the stimulus.

2. It suggests that the only critical issue in the stimulus input is its capacity to elicit imagery, not its success at either producing or avoiding anxiety. In that event, neither Wolpe's verbal brinkmanship nor Stampfl's verbal brutality count as much towards success as the skill they both have in vivid description, and perhaps the luck they have in patients whose imaginations can be so aroused.

The speculation above illustrates how the cognitive behavior of man can be incorporated into anxiety models of neurosis and therapy such as those some Action therapists use. But it may be even more to the point to observe that the anxiety model is itself a very limited one which fails to account for the wide variety of human anguish which cannot very well be represented as a mere extension of the reaction of a caged animal to an electrified floor. The anxiety model fails to countenance the fantastic capacity of humans to remember long past experiences and to plan distant future ones, attenuating reinforcements and maintaining stable behaviors at such length that no present stimulus–response theory of learning suffices to explain very refined and sustained adult behavior.

The Need for Meaningful Action

If a single generalization is in order in this connection, it might be this: The more complex the problem behavior in question, the less any pure Action model of psychotherapy seems applicable to its solution. Perhaps the failure of such models ultimately results, not from the inability of the therapist to identify mechanisms of action for the achievement of goals, but from the fact that, for complex issues, he is unable to specify very fruitful goals. When he does the latter, moreover, it may be argued that he only does so by establishing or supporting a meaning system to which the patient can refer his acts.

It may be demonstrated without doubt that a psychotherapy does not require a system of meaning in order to function within some limits and with some demonstrable effects. But in view of the history of the enterprise, as well as of the logic of the continuity of human experience from misery to other states, it is hard to see how it can avoid any implications of meaning. Granted that people come to therapy seeking comfort, not knowledge, and that they are entitled to surcease of pain without the inevitable imposition of self-consciousness, it still seems likely that they will finally seek the latter, once healed, if for no other reason than that, at their best, unchallenged by the distractions of personal suffering, men tend to see themselves as creatures of purpose.

If this is true, then pure Action therapies may be challenged even when represented at their best, not for being unable to accomplish their goals, but for an excess of modesty that limits them to all too demonstrable empiricisms. Ultimately, they beg all ultimate questions, which are necessarily questions of meaning.

But Insight therapies, whose only coin of worth is the facilitation of meaning, have not succeeded well enough in the prior, if less important, task of easing personal suffering, to take title to offer the profundities they claim to have. And it is possible that they could not, in their most common current forms, in any case effect some satisfactorily permanent amelioration in people's lives.

For their referent, by and large, is the individual himself, and the chances are good that most people cannot find their lives meaningful except in some context of experience which is greater than themselves. For most people, the most likely context would be a social one.

The significance of socialization has certainly not been overlooked by students of psychotherapy; relatively early in the development of this field Adler and Sullivan were very concerned with it. More recently, and more broadly, Fromm, whose orientation derives from an Insight system, and Skinner, the purest of Actionists, posit the necessity for sane societies of rather similar kinds, the one finding it truly meaningful, the other truly functional, both finding it of greatest value for the development of man. But in all these cases, the social interest is either academic and peripheral, from the therapeutic point of view, because it offers no counsel of value for individual therapists or patients, or it is ineffective, for it offers only insight, from which significant actions may or may not result. Neither speaking of "sick societies" nor of the need of individuals to have "real relationships" tells a man much that he can use to meaningfully relate his own life to a social order or the individuals who people it.

A comprehensive psychotherapy of the kind implied by this argument would be one that uses both insight and action to attack complex psychological problems. But insight, within this system, would no longer focus so much on motives as on those *behaviors*, present and historical, that produced disorder by violating one's relationship with the functional context that lends meaning to one's life. And its primary purpose, once achieved, would be to steer the development of a new action system, one which channels the individual's behavior in ways intended to restore his functioning within that context. And the context, the referent that makes the action system meaningful, would be neither the painful symptom, nor the wounded selfhood that may lie beneath it, but something external to the individual. For most such therapies, a social system, real or hypothesized, must provide that context.

There are many psychotherapeutic schemes that attempt some degree of integration of insight and action systems, but their formulations are sometimes vague and esoteric sounding, and needlessly encumbered with mystical concern, as in Jung's case. Even when very systematic, however, as in the therapy of George Kelly, they tend not to use the stimulus–response concepts that have usefully if narrowly guided the Action therapists. Formulations aside, moreover, most therapy schemes, including Jung's and Kelly's, are not so pretentious as to address the concepts of meaning and action all at once, and to posit a social order as the context of their fulfillment. To my knowledge, only one psychotherapist, O. H. Mowrer, has formulated such a system, and it is significant in this connection that his own professional experience for many years centered around both psychoanalytic personality theory and the study of learning. A description of Mowrer's work follows.

THE PRICE OF PERSONAL INTEGRITY:

AN INTERPRETATION OF O. H. MOWRER

It is sometimes the fate of radical theories that they must pass political as well as scientific tests before they become respectable objects of intellectual inquiry. When such theories, by design or otherwise, assault positions that are cherished by established institutions, they are likely to arouse controversy proportionate to the force with which they are presented. This suggests an extension of Newton's Third Law to human behavior, in which one useful index of the seminal quality of a new theory would be the extent to which it is publicly reviled. If so, then the theory of the origin and treatment of neurosis put forth by O. H. Mowrer may deserve more serious attention than any such theory since Sigmund Freud's psychoanalysis, for in the two generations that lie between them, no other mental health theorist has been subjected to such voluble and vituperative criticism.

The fault therein does not lie entirely with the critics, however; Mowrer's theory of disorder and treatment has not received very systematic treatment even in his own writing. *The Crisis in Psychiatry and Religion*, which contains most of his writing on this subject, is a potpourri of essays that collectively embody much of his thinking about therapy, but with at least two major faults, one scientific, the other political. For the first, none of the essays pretends to offer a logical, step-by-step presentation of his argument. The systematic thinker is thus compelled to wade through the entire collection before he can really capture its essence—and then he must compose the separate thoughts into an integrated whole on his own, which is not easy. And if it is difficult with respect to the theory, it is impossible with respect to the details of treatment, for this book contains no description of the therapeutic techniques that Mowrer has devised. A later work, to be called *The New Group Therapy*, has not yet appeared (December 1963). His critical arguments are available from *The Crisis*, however, and their relevance for the integration of insight and action can be seen there, once past some language barriers they seem to present.

These barriers relate to the political faults of the book, which are more amusing and more germane to some of the polemic that surrounds it. Mowrer seems to have a genius for sensing the rawest intellectual nerve of his audience and then addressing himself to it in a manner that incites to riot. Deliberately and lucidly, he employs conventional *theological* language to describe thoroughly *secular* concepts, and thus endeared to the clergy, then proceeds to assault choice parts of their theologies with gusto, wit, and venom.

However stimulating and provocative this technique, it is understandable that it arouses more antipathy then enjoyment in some people. Since the doctrinal persuasions of churchmen may dispose them in any case to judge the theory on the basis of its goodness of fit to their prior commitments, it is perhaps legitimate to tease or bait them in this way. But mental health scientists and craftsmen should be enabled to judge the theory on its scholarly merits in terms of its heuristic appeal, its logical cogency, and its susceptibility to empirical verification, and the unscientific sound of religious terms, offered without explanation or apology, unhappily may dissuade them from seeking and recognizing the technical position expressed in these writings. A presentation that permits scientific judgments must strip the argument of its theological overtones and circumscribe it with the qualifications that characterize scientific hypotheses. This essay attempts such a technical description and interpretation of Mowrer's theory.

The Guilt Theory of Neurosis

To begin with, Mowrer proposes that mental breakdowns in general and the so-called neuroses in particular refer to the chronic subjective distress which results from an objective breakdown in an individual's relationships with "significant others." The term "subjective distress" does not exclude observable symptoms, such as anxiety, depression, delusions, and hallucinations. The concept of "significant others," borrowed from George Herbert Mead, is used by Mowrer to mean either specific individuals, such as mother, spouse, and employer, or the abstractions that embody the principle of relationships, such as Community, Society, or God.

Three categories are required to describe the occurrence of mental breakdowns: (1) the Subjects, (2) the Sequence, and (3) the Symptoms.

1. *Subjects.* According to Mowrer, breakdowns occur only in individuals who have previously experienced some unspecified modicum of socialization, meaning that they have previously learned to attach enough importance to relationships with others, and to make sufficiently great emotional investments in them, for them to suffer distress over their violation. The system of variables that describes this capacity is called "conscience." The basis of the capacity is unspecified by Mowrer in *The Crisis*, but he has discussed it at some length in an earlier work (*Learning Theory and Personality Dynamics*). A related attempt to describe its origins is contained in Eysenck's discussion of a personality factor called "Introversion."

The theory thus allows that there is a difference between some kinds of psychological *disorders* and any kinds of psychological *breakdowns*. By definition, it is inapplicable to certain known clinical groups, such as Cleckley's psychopaths, who have never been properly socialized, or the rejected children described by Spitz and Ribble, who, having never been mothered in infancy, either died or became so damaged as to prevent socialization processes from having much effect. It is addressed, moreover, only to those functional disorders believed to be, by and large, learned.

2. *Sequence*. The theory proposes as a second significant condition that breakdowns are both self-initiated and actively initiated, in other words, that an individual experiences a mental breakdown as a result of a sequence of specific behaviors he performs. The sequence operates as follows:

a. The individual makes positive, drive-reducing responses to primary or secondary impulses in a context where he has previously learned, as part of socialization training, to inhibit those impulses.

b. The absence of punishment in this situation itself stimulates anxiety, or at least the recognition of a breach of sociality created by the behavior stimulates anxiety, and conflict is induced by the simultaneous fear of the negative effects that revelation of the behavior might engender. The most obvious, and perhaps most significant, negative effect is the loss of social esteem, but it may be any form of punishment that is feared.

c. By not revealing the behavior to significant others—by maintaining secrecy—the individual facilitates and enhances his conflict, which is reinforced still further by the continued operation of the impulses whose expression got him in trouble to begin with.

d. Thus trapped between his revulsion over his behavior, on the one hand, and his reluctance to pay for it or be done with it, on the other, the individual may be overwhelmed with conflict and break down.

3. *Symptoms*. The third condition is that breakdowns are symptomatized by guilt, anxiety, and depression, or their correlates. The most significant and prognostically favorable of these is guilt.

The foregoing propositions do not, I believe, sound much different from the classical drive-reduction theory of adjustment, and structurally Mowrer's theory is indeed a straightforward adjustment theory. But there are three critical points at which it differs in content from other theories of breakdown, whether dynamic reinforcement theories or associationist theories, and whether oriented towards Insight or Action.

1. Without denying the initial significance of primary

drives, it proposes that, once these drives have achieved a modicum of gratification, they become functionally less significant than secondary drives, particularly those secondary drives which are critical in human relationships. This position capitalizes on some oddities of behavior that are embarrassing both to adjustment theories and to common knowledge, for example, that under particularly adverse circumstances, people have been known to inhibit the gratification of primary drives for the fulfillment of secondary ones, even with the foreknowledge that death would result.

2. Mowrer hypothesizes a direct and positive relation between the conflict leading to breakdown and overt behavior, whereas other theories give greater credence to purely mental phenomena as effective sources of conflict. In other words, Mowrer proposes that when a person feels guilty, he has done something to arouse this feeling, though not necessarily the precise thing about which he reports guilt. Most theories allow that, when he feels guilty, he may simply have felt or thought some impulse to evoke this guilt. Mowrer may assume a capacity for discrimination between impulse and overt action that mitigates the anxiety-arousing potential of impulse alone, but this is not made explicit in his writing.

3. The third great difference from other theories is more subtle but equally important. Mowrer's theory allows the existence of all the "ego defenses" postulated and elaborated by Sigmund and Anna Freud, but it denies the centrality of repression and lays heavy emphasis on suppression as the central defense involved in the development of neurosis. It is significant in this respect that experimental studies of repression have not established its centrality in mental illness and show no special signs of doing so in the future, though this mechanism may still have some significant functions in behavior. Mowrer's theory offers no vital place for repression in the development of conflict, as does Freud's, and current research seems to be demonstrating quite adequately that conflict behavior in humans, including experimental neurosis, has no special relation to unconsciousness. Though this argument seems to parallel Wolpe on repression, it does not really do so— for Wolpe's theory has no more room for *suppression* than *repres-*

sion. The concept of ego (self), let alone ego defenses, is foreign to Wolpe.

Before proceeding to the theory of therapy that Mowrer derives from the foregoing, a brief glossary of some of his terms may be in order.

God is used to mean the idealized objective of the socialization process.

Sin is used to mean the overt behavior that violates sociality, that is transgression.

Guilt is used to mean what it means in law: the objective existence of transgression or sin, as well as the subjective state that describes the recognition of such behavior. Mowrer insistently argues that guilt is always real, by which he means simply that the subjective feeling of transgression has, as a referent, directly or indirectly, some overt transgressive behavior vis-à-vis some social context. His theory logically allows, however, for the existence of neurotic guilt, which would mean about the same thing Freud means by it: guilty feelings whose referents are entirely limited to ideas, thoughts, and feelings that have not gained expression in action. Mowrer does not specify the existence of this phenomenon, despite its logical plausibility, both because he believes all such experiences have some referent in real guilt and because he believes that did they not have such a referent, they would have no great importance in conflict behavior.

The Theory of Cure

If breakdowns occur as a result of the active disordering of one's relationships with significant others, it is reasonable that cures may result from the active reordering of those relationships. This is precisely Mowrer's theory, and he proposes that this cure may be implemented through the use of two techniques, (1) publicity and (2) work. He calls the former confession and the latter expiation or restitution.

Publicity, the less essential of the two, is a procedure that derives directly from the theory of neurosis. If one part of the conflict leading to breakdown is enhanced by the maintenance of secrecy, then the publicizing of one's secret will, by itself, start to reduce the conflict. But the other part of the conflict results from the continued operation of troublesome impulses. Since these impulses are socially unacceptable, they will probably operate most forcibly in the context of secrecy. Mowrer proposes, in effect, that their publication also acts as a check against the force of their operation instead of increasing it, and this tends to relieve the contribution of the impulse to the conflict.

However valuable publicity may be in reducing conflict, however, its curative role is still minimal, essentially because people have long and detailed memories. While it may have been conflict that produced breakdown, it was the violation of sociality that produced the conflict in the first place. The publicizing of secrets does nothing at all by itself to abrogate the social consequences of the original transgression, and unless this occurs in some way, the person's sociality is not restored. By itself alone, publicity may actually reflect a further violation of sociality, a kind of paean of guilt that reinforces a continued differentiation and separation between self and society.

Cure occurs only when the individual, already relieved of conflict, recognizes the source of his trouble in his overt acts and recommits himself to the society he has foregone, healing his original violations directly or, if this is impossible (as it often is), paying in kind, that is, compensating for his behavior with new overt behaviors which facilitate sociality instead of violating it.

This positive commitment must be a continuous one, representing a process rather than an isolated fact, much as physical health is a process and not an isolated fact. For cure, in this theory, represents a state rather than an event. And just as positive commitment is curative, it is also self-reinforcing, for the society, broadly conceived, must be taken as the primary source that provides the individual with necessary life goals and with some of the means by which he can channelize and control the expression of his individual impulses. It is sociality which gives the meaning to his acts.

Critique of Mowrer

The foregoing material provides, I believe, a fairly comprehensive technical statement of the theories of psychopathology and psychotherapy that Mowrer has proposed. An evaluation of their effectiveness at the present time must be somewhat limited, though Mowrer apparently has had more successful applications of his techniques than have the Skinnerians of theirs, partly perhaps because his efforts have been directed at broader applications in the first place. Like the Skinnerians, however, he has not yet published any statistical reports of success rates or comparisons with other treatment methods.

It is important to bear in mind, in all attempts at empirical verification, that the test of one part of the theory is not necessarily contributory to an evaluation of another part, nor does the validation of technique necessarily illuminate theory. It is entirely possible, as we have seen, that therapeutic schemes can demonstrate their worth while the theories which underlie them are nonetheless untrue. In Mowrer's case, socialization techniques conceivably could cure troubled people even if they had not experienced breakdown as a result of violating their sociality. And should the therapy be unsuccessful, there is no logical basis for argument therefrom that the theory of neurosis is invalid. Where a therapy works, moreover, it is still necessary to isolate those variables that may be irrelevant to the specific theoretical propositions that are being tested, such as the personal characteristics of the therapist. My own clinical experience with a variant of Mowrer's therapy suggests that this is an extremely promising position, holding hope for relatively rapid, very dramatic, and quite lasting cures of a variety of complex psychological problems. His experience with these techniques is similarly favorable. But the returns are not really in yet, and the optimism of a system's sponsor and sympathetic prejudices of an observer are not good bases for passing final judgments.

Freud and Mowrer

Mowrer's radicalism is most easily contrasted with Freudian theory, which largely represents the psychotherapeutic orthodoxy of our day, but there are significant parallels in the development of these rather antagonistic positions that are striking enough to be worth a brief digression. Both Freud and Mowrer developed their theories relatively late in their professional careers, after having built solid scientific reputations in more orthodox fields of inquiry. Much of the content of both theories can be traced to problems generated in their laboratory work, Freud's in the study of neurology, Mowrer's in the study of the learning process. But both theories have more immediate and idiosyncratic personal origins, Freud's in the exploration of his own dreams and neurotic symptoms, Mowrer's in the analysis of his own misbehavior and depression. Both theories attracted favorable attention and some sympathetic misinterpretation from other professions before they made very much impact on the mental health professions to which they were initially addressed. Freud was lionized in literary and artistic circles, Mowrer in clerical and religious ones. And there are yet other similarities.

Significance of Mowrer's Work

Viewed in the spectrum of other theories of psychotherapy, Mowrer's relative position cannot be established with any ease. Like Insight theories, his is an ego psychology in which self-esteem is a most critical element in establishing and maintaining mental balance. Like Sullivan, he treats self-esteem as a proper function of reputation, but he idealizes reputation, making it more contingent on individual behavior and personal ethics than on the actual fact of social consensus. In Sullivan's view, moreover, self-esteem is a product of early experience, while Mowrer treats it as a continuously renewable product even of adult experience. On the other hand, Mowrer rejects the mechanism of both Freud and the Action therapists. He believes that insight, as an agent of cure, has value only insofar as it provides a basis for action, and it is action, not insight, that is ultimately curative. But in contrast to Stampfl, Wolpe, or other advocates of "behaviorist" therapy, he takes action to be meaningful only when it is deliberately initiated by the sufferer rather than when the patient is subjected to conditioning techniques, and when its referent is specifically towards social integrity rather than freedom from anxiety. In his concern with life styles and life goals, he is more like Adler than any other single psychotherapy theorist, especially in his insistence that the most significant life goals are those which involve social commitment. But he arrives at this conclusion from premises and with techniques so different from those of Adler that the similarity of goals must be seen as somewhat coincidental. He rejects out of hand the naive Rousseauianism of Rogers and Maslow, as of all existential therapists, denying the inherent goodness of man with the same force, if not at the same length, that he rejects the Christian or Freudian views of innate evil.

Mowrer did not develop his theory, of course, with specific reference to the modes of psychotherapy proposed here, but his technical position attempts an integration of insight and action, of meaning and function in psychotherapy. His techniques of confession and expiation, together comprising his entire therapy, are indeed the operational equivalents of insight and action. But in both instances, they are given a somewhat specialized interpretation—for these techniques of therapy only count towards cure, in Mowrer's view, when they are directed towards relating the individual's behavior to society.

But what does society itself represent? To Mowrer, society is partly a symbolic term, this time referring to a hypothetical normative moral order. It is because he implicitly believes that man's ability to achieve finally meaningful and stable personal states is hinged to his ability to formulate viable moral systems that Mowrer verbalizes his theory of neurosis in terms of "guilt" rather than "anxiety," as most Actionists do. For what is "guilt" but "moral anxiety," as Freud observed? One need hardly ask then what are the moral implications of Mowrer's therapy, for the warp and woof of his system is the relation between the behavior of man and his moral condition. And it is precisely for their lack of concern with morals that Mowrer eschews the Actionists as angrily as he does the Insight therapists.

From the vantage of its social implications, it is vital to recognize that Mowrer's concept of community is not an entirely consensual or cultural relativistic one. The commitment he demands as the price of mental health is not merely commitment to an existing group of men nor to an existing society; by implication, at least, it is commitment to an ideal group, to a potential society motivated towards its members by some hypothetical good, by an optimum, not just a norm. He labels this ideal the Judeo-Christian ethic; others might call it Humanistic, and there must be still other names available. The point is that the demand for an ideal as well as a real group to which men must be able to commit themselves is a psychological exoneration for characteristics which have been classically avoided by adjustment theorists and not very strongly preached by psychotherapists of any ilk—courage, altruism, self-sacrifice. In Mowrer's system, these attributes become potential indicators of the highest level of integration and adjustment rather than essentially defensive operations of a largely pathological system. And if this demand exonerates heroic virtues for individuals in relation to each other, it does at least as much for their relations to society, legitimizing dissent, altercation, and revolution as potentially legitimate commitments to a society that may not, at any given time, exist. What is demanded of men for the fullest exercise of their liberties is openness of objectives and earnest commitment.

Important theories of mental health always have implications for the nature of man and the structure of society as well as for the specific problems to which they are addressed. It is not necessarily the responsibility of the theorist to recognize all these implications or to state them explicitly, which is well for Mowrer, who does not always do so. By virtue of its attempt to integrate therapy modes in a system of meaning (morals), it seems to me that Mowrer's theory may be the groundwork for the most important such theory since Freud's, and that it is perhaps in its present form already more critically relevant to some of the knowledge slowly accruing to the many sciences of man. It implies neither the biological instinctivism or metapsychology of Freud nor the paeans to individual cultures of the neo-Freudian revisionists. It is essentially a biosocial view which proposes that man is biologically constituted as a social animal, an evolutionary advance over the gregariousness which has, as its first phyletic glimmer, the sexual reproduction of species. Incorporating the almost certain knowledge that man has never lived outside of organized groups, it proposes that he never can and therefore never should.

But allowing the significance of culture, it further comprehends that some cultures are more viable than others, and that man's responsiveness to his culture may be a function of ideal psychological goals as well as of the adequacy with which his primary needs are met by his immediate group. It permits us to understand that the Alorese and Kwakiutls and many other groups may be miserably unhappy even when they are well adjusted to their cultures, and it entitles us to treat the suicides and psychoses of Nazi soldiers in *Einsatzgruppen* as something other than a pathological withdrawal from their society. Without arguing a teleology, it implies a kind of Messianic drive in man, leading to no certain salvation, and it warns that he will fulfill any such drive in company with other men or not at all. Without certainty of what goodness is, it proposes that men must try to be good, striving for an ideal which may not require definition to achieve fulfill-ment. Without a doubt, this is a thoroughly pretentious theory. But perhaps any theory that pretends to less than this risks deny-ing man both cherished and valid parts of his humanity.

_____ PART THREE

THE SAVING GUILD

CHAPTER SEVEN

THE SALVATION OF SECULAR MAN

Most guilds, trade unions, and professional organizations, medieval or modern, are more concerned with preventing other people from trespassing on their territory than they are worried that they might be infringing on someone else's. This form of self-righteous group behavior serves at least three purposes.

1. It keeps the economic frontiers of the guildsman fluid, simultaneously limiting competition.

2. It aggrandizes the guild in the public mind, implying that others cannot do its highly complex and specialized work, while simultaneously restraining itself from any declaration of incompetence with respect to someone else's work.

3. Insofar as the allegation of complex expertise is valid, it also protects the public against rogues, charlatans and, less effectively, incompetents, some of whom are sometimes found within the guild itself.

If, moreover, the performance of the guild craft really does require very extensive training and demonstrable *expertise*, as is obviously true, for example, in the case of medical practice, then it almost always involves a large enough body of poorly understood but well-known expressions, some true but technical (such as "resistance to infection"), some false but usefully connotative (such as "nervous breakdowns"), some false and useless but still hanging around (such as "tired blood"), so that pretentious and unscrupulous guildsmen can use them for leverage to propel themselves, apparently justly, into areas they know nothing about. Organized medicine repeatedly demonstrates this tendency, in its current panic over who will pay whose doctor bills, by pious prattle about the dangers of interfering with a delicately balanced vagary called "the doctor-patient relationship."

The same thing happens in other guilds whose work is marked less by the need for training to develop true *expertise*, as in medicine, as by the complexity of the job to be done; this may be so great that it is hard to be sure what *expertise* is or how it should be developed or used, as in education. Thus, professional educators, not so much for immediate economic reasons as to buttress their very claim to *expertise*, sometimes portray themselves as possessors of a technology which has little more substance than its titles ("rounded education"), and claim that it satisfies goals which cannot be reduced to operations but surely imply something more grand than teaching children to read, write, brush their teeth, do arithmetic, and play amicably with each other ("developing the whole self").

The use of medicine and education as illustrations of guild behavior is not intended as idle slander (no judgment is intended of who should pay the doctor bills, and education is rapidly developing a true technology), nor even a casual reflection on these professions as, respectively, the wealthiest and largest in America; it is for their relevance to psychotherapy that they are of interest here.

Like doctors and teachers, psychotherapists display a number of guild characteristics, and it is useful to an understanding of this discipline to compare it with others as a guild. Historically, the profession of psychotherapy originated as a subspecialty both

of medicine, in psychiatry, and of education, in remedial and re-
habilitative counseling and instruction, and it often retains those
affiliations today—so some of the parallels are more homologous
than analogous.

PSYCHOTHERAPY AS A SERVICE GUILD

A service guild is an organization of skilled persons who certify each other's ability to perform, decide what kind of training
and apprenticeship are prerequisite to satisfactory performance,
and restrict candidacy and membership to a limited number of
persons who satisfy their requirements. If the guild, once opera-
tive, cannot prevent competition by limiting training, which keeps
the number of practitioners small, or if the craft the guild practices
is so vague or easy that competition comes from sources which do
not even try to affiliate with the guild, then it is likely to sustain
itself by seeking formal social sanctions.[1]

The nature of the bargain struck is that the society restricts
title or function of the craft in question to individuals who, in
effect, are either members of the guild or approved by it; in so
doing, it extends de facto permission to those approved persons to
accept gainful employment and collect fees for the hire of their
services in that craft. In return, the guild guarantees the society
that it will perform its service faithfully (by implication asserting
that it has a valuable service to dispense) and that it will police
or oversee the activities of its members in this connection. These
arrangements are generally formalized as *Licensing* or *Certification*
Laws in the United States. The former is intended to restrict the
practice of a craft, and therefore must undertake to define precisely what the craft entails; the latter purports only to restrict the
title of the craftsman, thereby limiting the way he advertises him-

---

[1] It is theoretically possible to control jobs as airplane or ship pilots,
for example, by restricting training, for nobody will employ a pilot who has
not been trained and certified by somebody who has already proved himself
in this capacity. Mark Twain, in *Life on the Mississippi*, gives a compelling
description of how a guild of river pilots gained complete control over the industry by such resorts, without ever invoking the authority of society. On the
other hand, many jobs can be done by almost anyone without reference to
their participation in any formal brotherhood—the concept of the closed shop
is intended precisely to prevent this free marketing of work.

self. Presumably, certification is more restrictive to charlatans than to bona fide guildsmen who, qualified to call themselves by the restricted title, are also qualified to exercise some function in connection with it.

For some years now, psychotherapists in this country have been seeking the passage of legislation that will either incorporate psychotherapy under existing Medical Practices Acts, in the case of psychiatrists, or that will license or certify psychologists. The efforts of each professional group are partly attempts to gain competitive advantage over the other, and the area of almost complete professional overlap, therefore of competition, is psychotherapy. Some psychiatrists would like to obtain a monopoly on the psychotherapy business by having it declared a branch of medicine, thus squeezing out psychologists who, for the most part, engage in the same business but are not physicians. Some psychologists would like to improve their competitive position vis-à-vis psychiatrists by having themselves legally sanctioned, either as practitioners of psychotherapy (licensed), or at least as a specialized profession to which there is only limited access (certification).[2]

For both professions, the chief issue involved concerns the practice of psychotherapy. Despite the different motives in each case (psychiatrists rationalize their greed for the whole pie and psychologists their need for a more open market in which to get a slice of it both in terms of somewhat different public interests), both groups are acting as guilds when they appeal to the society. However much they may be eager to protect an ignorant public from the trauma of psychic snake oil salesmen, they are also asking for economic protection for their own interests, much as electricians or bicycle makers do. But whatever good or harm the latter do society by seeking special favor, it is at least clear what electricians and bicycle makers want protection for—what it is they do

[2] Social workers, who do more psychotherapy than psychiatrists and psychologists put together, do not participate in this debate or any scandal relevant to it for two reasons: (1) The issues mostly effect private practice, and few social workers are in private practice. (2) Social work is traditionally the handmaiden of psychiatry, and most social workers are content to function under the supervision of psychiatrists. They had as well be, for membership in the National Association of Social Workers apparently demands that any clinics in which they work be directed by psychiatrists.

in the first place that they want to prevent others from doing on the same terms. But what do psychotherapists do? Here the comparison to doctors and teachers becomes more immediate; and it goes a good deal further than the fact that, like doctors, therapists claim to provide a service requiring tremendous *expertise;* like teachers, they claim the job to be done is terribly complex.

Psychotherapy, Medicine, and Education

Those psychotherapists whose training and orientation make them see themselves as "doctors of the mind," so to speak, think of the disorders they treat as "mental illnesses," and their "patients" as "sick, sick, sick." Psychotherapy is for them a branch of medical practice that cures people of sickness. This description sometimes upsets psychologist psychotherapists of this very medical orientation, for their conflict with psychiatrists forces them to abjure this medical usage even when they believe it. In fact, however, their quite reasonable position is not that psychotherapy does not involve illness and cure, but rather that medical training and license is largely irrelevant to its proper practice, much as is the case in optometry. The latter, professionally, is a proper subtrade of physics; the former, of psychology. Neither requires a physician for its practice, though both are medical enterprises.

Psychotherapists trained and oriented in the direction of education are more likely to see themselves as "counselors" or "special educators," to think of the disorders they treat as "problems" rather than illnesses, and to see the subjects of these problems as "clients" rather than patients; in short, these therapists are teachers.

In historical terms, all these usages are quite intelligible, but in fact, they are all of limited accuracy and sometimes tend to be misleading. Psychotherapists are not really doctors because the people they treat are not really sick, for one thing. The analogy between psychic disorders and disease is being tested and found wanting both by psychiatrists, such as Thomas Szasz, in *The Myth of Mental Illness,* and clinical psychologists, such as Albert Bandura and Richard Walters, in *Social Learning and Personality Development.*

But the disease analogy for the patient is itself no weaker

than the medical analogy for the doctor; physicians can define their craft entirely by two skills: (1) their ability to diagnose trouble only in terms of specific and limited anatomical and physiological properties of the body, and (2) their ability to attack these troubles primarily by chemical or physical means. Even little children have a pretty good idea of how to play doctor. How would they play psychotherapist? Finally, the entire claim to expertise in medicine is based on the technical skills just mentioned, and the need for years of training and apprenticeship for guild membership can be justified by them. The need for expertise in psychotherapy, however real, is protean, for there are few reliable means of judging what is wrong, or when it is righted, and no way to refer to the antiseptic judgment of either X-ray or microscope.

The historical development of psychotherapy out of medicine is well known, and the maintenance of the myth of medical parallel is, in that sense, easy to understand. But it is also known how surgeons started as barbers, and we are admittedly well shed of any equivalent myth of tonsorial parallel.

As professionals, psychotherapists are not much more like teachers than like doctors. Classically, teaching revolves largely around informational subject matter, infusion of which relieves ignorance. Psychotherapy deals primarily with behavior patterns rather than information, however, and sometimes more with identifying and shifting already established ones than with establishing and affirming brand new ones. It is certainly true that psychotherapy partakes more of education than of medicine, but its recipients are, to begin with, troubled and disordered, while those of education, for the most part, are empty and perhaps hungry, but not in pain.

As technicians, moreover, most educators, even in remedial capacities, can define their work in terms of some concrete contents and measure their success in more or less concrete ways. But what are the contents of psychotherapy, and what tests one's mastery of them? In terms of expertise, finally, educators can at least argue that they need to know some subject in order to teach it and need to develop a technology in order to teach it well. Their grand goals, moreover, may be defined by the contents they supply; a well-rounded education, for example, may be defined as one which includes contents a,b,c, . . . n. Such concreteness may be impossible for psychotherapists, both for relative lack of standard contents, lack of agreement for implementing them, and lack of instruments and criteria for measuring their effects. If the job of teachers seems complex, that of therapists seems abstruse.

The historical roots of psychotherapy in education come from the creation of remedial psycho-educational clinics near the turn of the century as well as from the early use of psychological testing for educational and selective purposes, the latter including psychodiagnosis. Though the relationship to education in its broadest sense is very real, that with the profession of education is much less so.

Now if these doctors are not quite doctors and teachers not quite teachers because they do not know how to do very well what it is not quite clear they are trying to do in the first place, their title to guild status seems equivocal, to say the least! Indeed, this proposition is plainly implied in Victor Raimy's summary of a wry statement by a participant at a conference on the therapeutic training of clinical psychologists: *Psychotherapy is an undefined technique applied to unspecified cases with unpredictable results. For this technique, rigorous training is required.* A similar notion is unwittingly and unwittily implied by the policy adopted by the American Psychoanalytic Association to the effect that medical training is an indispensable prerequisite for the practice of psychoanalysis except for those people who were trained in Vienna before 1937. These included Anna Freud and Theodore Reik, together with some others it would have been embarrassing to exclude—and it was adopted only after Sigmund Freud's demise; he regarded analysis as a nonmedical business, and favored training "lay" analysts.

THE PROPER USES OF PSYCHOTHERAPY

All this may seem to some a deprecation of the therapeutic craft, but it is meant as introduction to the proposition that, with half-true labels erased from psychotherapy, and more precise descriptions of it made, it is possible to see its true proportions as a craft. And doing so can, in turn, clarify its promise and its limitations and facilitate its proper growth or meet curtailment as a discipline. I do not anticipate the latter, partly because it is doubtful that the people who think it has helped them are all fools (though their explanations of that help contain many errors of observation), but more because I think the uses of psychotherapy can be suitably described and defined so that it achieves some realistic status as a guild, not necessarily in an economic sense, but in a conceptual one.

Psychotherapists have, I believe, two distinctive functions, a *scientific* and a *moralistic* one. Their scientific function is explicit, their moralistic one often only implied. The latter is, moreover, often corollary to the former rather than independent of it.

1. The scientific function of psychotherapists is that of *manipulators of behavior.*

2. Their moralistic function is that of a *secular priesthood.*

Many psychotherapists will object to such descriptions of their functions; Insight therapists in particular might take umbrage at the idea that their proper scientific role is that of manipulators, while both Insight and Action therapists may object to the statement that their proper moralistic role is somehow sacerdotal. But I believe it can be argued reasonably that these two concepts are valid to describe the potentialities of psychotherapy and that they are equally salient to all major variants of therapeutic technique.

THE MANIPULATION OF BEHAVIOR

In evaluating the different modes of psychotherapy thus far, I have indicated that the Action therapies appear more effective than do Insight therapies as scientific schemes, but that they are also apparently more limited in scope. Action therapies seem less equipped to cope with large issues, but Insight therapies, on the other hand, lack very satisfactory answers to them. Action therapies do not even pretend to have scientific prescriptions for very complex problems, but Insight therapies offer "meanings" for those problems that either are no basis for action to begin with or for which action satisfies too narrow a context of experience to be meaningful.

Mowrer's position represents an attempt to compromise between these technical systems, though it also contains some theoretical novelty. Mowrer advocates the use of *insight* in psychotherapy, but it is insight into man's overt behavior and his need for sociality that is more important, not his impulses or anxieties. The identification of the loss of sociality with loss of meaning is then the basis for taking *action* to restore it.

While it is the Action therapies that make most explicit the manipulative or control function of psychotherapy, the other systems also must assume its possibility. The difference between them in this case revolves solely around questions of fact concerning *control*, such as how much control and of what kind *is it possible* for therapists to exert, and questions of *propriety*, such as how much control and of what kind *should* therapists exert. The latter obviously depends, in the first instance, on the former, for one certainly *should* exert no more control than he *can*. The same limits apply to kind as to intensity.

In general, the Insight therapies are inclined to exert a modicum of control, and that only over cognitive and ideational processes. While this procedure is rationalized in a number of ways, common to all the Insight therapies is the immediate interest of the therapist in the manipulation of insight alone, not of action. His means of control over insight or ideation may be oblique, as in free association or reflection, but it is nevertheless real.

Action therapists are inclined to more direct control of overt behavior, as would be expected from their interests.

Mowrer proposes the manipulation of both insight and action.

There cannot be any reasonable question but that psychotherapists of all kinds wish to control behavior in some respects; it is obvious that they do, and only incredible stupidity, innocence, or malice would make them say otherwise. As with extent, the efficacy of the controls of one or another system is, of course, also in question, and the scientific disputes among systems are addressed mainly to this issue. But the manipulative character of psychotherapy can no longer be in serious doubt either logically or empirically, as Krasner has effectively argued. Some of the language current among therapists seems to suggest the opposite, it is true. Terms like "permissiveness," "spontaneity," and "warmth," seem to convey the aura of a benevolent laissez-faire arrangement; but as Krasner says, ". . . apparent spontaneity on the therapist's part may very well be the most effective means of manipulating behavior. The therapist is an individual programmed by his training into a fairly effective behavior control machine. Most likely the machine is most effective when it least appears like a machine."

The therapist's scientific job, from any viewpoint, begins with his gaining information that he can then use to manipulate, direct, or channel behavior, whether the behavior in question is the discovery of hidden motives, a change in habits, or a realignment with society.

The Propriety of Control

The real problem of control comes neither from the assumption of its possibility nor from the economics of its implementation. These are finally questions of fact that can be settled without reference to any but scientific standards. A central problem of psychotherapy that will not be solved by recourse to some technical position is the propriety of control, the ends it serves, the evaluative schemes it addresses. For this is finally a moral question, and its character is such that techniques of therapy must themselves finally address it for their justification. There is no such thing as a deliberate action without some end, and the end it satisfies can be taken as its meaning. Nor is there any meaning without intent in fact, in other words, that is not the basis for some act, and the act may therefore be judged as the measure of its intent. The acts of humans are, to themselves at least, significant of some meanings, capable of some valuations—and meaning gets its meaning from the action it sponsors. Thus therapists of either kind inevitably confront a dilemma—seeking the means of controlling some segments of behavior for quite limited purposes, they cannot honestly escape the issue of how men ought to live.

Insight therapists have tried to escape the dilemma by offering understanding as their only coin, thus avoiding the accusation that they tell their patients how to live. But insofar as they actually meet their claim, they seem to paralyze themselves so that they heal no wounds.

Actionists try to escape by restricting their functions to demonstrably limited problems, the very ones indeed that insight fails to help. But limiting themselves enough would limit them to trivia.

It is not possible for a psychotherapy to be comprehensive unless it can cope with this problem, and to do so it must incorporate an action system that avoids both triviality and bestiality by being rooted or justified in some system of meaning—and by a meaning system that is not paralyzed by endless cogitations without outlets in action, but one tested, revised, and fulfilled by its consequences in behavior. This is as much as saying that a comprehensive psychotherapy will be one which fosters both a pattern of behavior and a moral system which rationalizes and makes it meaningful.

The Function of a Comprehensive Psychotherapy

Such a scheme may not really be possible, and if it is possible, some aspects of it are potentially quite undesirable, but it is, in any case, not always necessary. There is no reason for a comprehensive psychotherapy to deal with circumscribed symptoms like phobias and anxiety attacks. For these, pure Action therapy seems quite enough, and the control the therapist exerts in such cases need not be tempered very much with thoughts of anything but what will serve to decondition, shape, extinguish, and remove the trouble.

It might appear that there is also no need for a comprehensive therapy in connection with unhappiness, ennui, and that whole class of problems which can be looked upon as pure problems of meaning, for where pure meaning is the issue, Insight therapy ought to be appropriate to it. This is more questionable, however, for it is possible that the need for meaning cannot be satisfied outside the context of some action system. In that event, a really pure Insight therapy would be as inapplicable to such problems as a pure Action system would be irrelevant.

The need for a comprehensive therapy is most evident for that middle group of problems which contain the classical character disorders, but which also may have more bearing on the lives of more people than either of the other two categories. This category includes all those instances where the problem is a function both of a faulty behavior pattern and of an underlying value system that is inadequate to make it meaningful.

For problems in the first group, people need a doctor. But for the third group, they need a priest, or someone at least who can fill that same function for which, in another generation, they would have sought a priest. In the middle group, they seem to need some of both, for the experience of people in that group, and this probably includes most people, is that their problems are *moral* ones in the most literal sense; that is, they do not know how they ought to behave. Then they need both to be told, in whatever way, some end that can help make their lives meaningful, and to be taught, by whatever means, how to pursue such ends.

At this point, when the therapist recognizes the possibility of his functioning in this comprehensive capacity, he adds to his tactical manipulative role a more crucial strategic one; at this juncture, he becomes an arbiter of morality.

THE SECULAR PRIESTHOOD

Life would be easier for psychotherapists if they were able to contain their role entirely within the bounds of something called "breakdown." In that event, they could identify themselves as repairmen, and the only standard of repair they would have to meet would be that of making people function as well as they did or should have done at some previous time. Theirs would then be a reconstructive job, and they could successfully dodge the issue of how people ought best to live in the same way that a physician can provide an invaluable service to man without ever facing it. But this is not possible, because human behavior is enormously variable, complex, and differentiated, so that people's problems refuse to stay in neat, clear categories, and because the culture in which we live and the subculture to which psychotherapy is chiefly addressed is becoming constantly and increasingly sophisticated in a way which makes it less and less subject to trivial or isolated problems and more and more to global, existential ones. The concept of psychotherapeutic repair of breakdown is essentially retrospective and as such is fairly amenable to concrete description and solution. But the problem of concern here is prospective, concerning a future that is always vague, and that is therefore hard to address wisely. Those human problems that concern the individual's past, and that once constituted the whole of the subject matter of psychotherapy, are problems of rehabilitation, remedy, or cure. But those that address the future can perhaps be described best and most simply as problems of *salvation*, even though the future of concern in any given discourse may be quite immediate. The acts which solve or compound those problems will gain or lose that salvation, insofar as it is subject to individual control; and the rationales which are used to explain, justify, and evaluate those acts, taken together, total to a moral code. Once psychotherapists choose to address such behaviors, they implicitly choose thereby to arbitrate and mediate those codes. How? By what schemes? According to what values?

The Moral Schemes Implied by Psychotherapies

The three technical systems of therapy that have been presented here each implies, I believe, a different principle of valuation, one that is, in each case, an intrinsic property of the technicalities involved: Insight therapy implies a moral scheme that is essentially the patient's own, and that may, in the extreme, even be opposed to that of the therapist. Action therapy implies a scheme that is the therapist's own, and that may, conversely, be opposed to that of the patient. Mowrer's combination of insight and action is one which implies that neither patient nor therapist is a fit judge of the proper ends of therapy—he posits a good life possible only in society. As such, Mowrer's is a normative system.

Each of these systems has its own difficulties and is given to contradictions and vagaries of a sort that prevents anyone from adhering very religiously to it, and that requires therapists of different sorts to borrow from each other's schemata.

The trouble with letting people identify their own goals, desirable as it may be in other respects, is like the trouble with letting children learn some things by experience: they are patently incompetent to judge either the stability of their aspirations or the consequences of their experiments. For troubled people, moreover, the very nature of the trouble may disqualify them from making judgments of the kind that the absence of the trouble would permit. Finally, the world goes round on more than the satisfaction of their needs, and their personal demands of it must somehow take account of its demands on them.

A therapist who acts in scrupulous keeping with this principle mediates a morality of individual liberty writ large; his priesthood, in that event, entirely dedicated to serving the ends of the patient, would incorporate the possibility that the patient will destroy himself, and would demand that the therapist loyally accompany this destruction. It must also logically overlook the fact that the patient's troubles are themselves motivators which sap some goals and pervert others, for to act on this idea would be to replace the patient's observable goals with the therapist's own, merely rationalizing that they are the patient's latent ones. Ultimately, it demands that the therapist permit the patient to violate the social order in any way he wishes, though the therapist himself obtains sanction from that social order for the ostensible purpose of somehow restoring people to it.

The trouble with a normative system of morals which refers to society for its norms is that a society such as ours is largely ambiguous, so it either lacks norms for many important things or they are not clear. But in that case, does it really make sense to say that all actions must be rationalized in terms of some society? If so, then the legitimacy of the behavior becomes a function of the rationalistic skill of the patient. On the other hand, that may be precisely true, at least inasmuch as it permits him to maintain some functional integrity. What is more, it is probably more realistic ultimately to base a system of goals on the assumption of a social code than of an individual one, even though it risks advocating a culture of conformity which could ultimately stifle that very society. The problem is that, in so doing, we will have substituted a stifling constrictiveness for wild libertarianism.

Suppose, in the third place, that the therapist does decide what is good for the patient. On the face of it, this might seem like an arrogant and ill-considered idea, but may it not be argued that he does this anyway? Are not all such relationships structured by him, even if he seeks their rationale in the patient's individual needs, or in his social ones? Then suppose he were to make virtue of necessity, and ask himself how, since his technical capacities imply a moral role, he could exercise that role most wisely.

Then he would fulfill a role more like that of a priest than of any other professional, but he would be a secular priest, whose justifications are not in a theology revealed from heaven, but one discovered or intimated in the laboratory. The genesis of his consideration would then be the nature of man, and his gospel the fulfillment of that nature, its decalogue the medium of behavior—and all preached from the altar of science.

For psychotherapists must finally appeal to science to justify their activity, just as ministers appeal to revelation. Even then, the possibilities of a scientifically viable moral order are only limited, for whatever potential science may have for identifying ever-more accurately the nature of man, it always has less for deciding the goals toward which that nature should be steered.

This problem has no final resolution, for the psychotherapist cannot take his function entirely from the social order, as do educators or lawyers, nor refer it to the physiological norms or optima that justify medicine, any more than he can parallel the certainty of clergymen that their keys to salvation are real. If, indeed, there is a natural law, it renders no easy judgments he can use. Yet without any of these groundings, he must confront individuals whose troubles demand solutions in terms of some moral order that will allow them to conduct their lives effectively and meaningfully. How can his science make him wise?

A New Scholasticism

The answer, however partial, may be that the position of the psychotherapist in an age of competing ideas is no worse than that of the religionist, though the sources of his pronouncements are a good deal less dramatic. The morality of religion assumes a cosmic order governed by God into which man fits teleologically; that is, it assumes there is some divine purpose for man which incorporates his individual purposes—and it further assumes that the nature of man, from which his individual purposes are formed, is itself a part of that teleological scheme. The moral order that religion advocates then becomes, by implication, natural law, a scheme of behavior whose completion according to prescription fulfills the destiny the behavior was created to serve in the first place. Now the religionist, in advocating such a system, uses his knowledge of the moral order as a means of discovering the nature of man. In other words, since his revelation has demonstrated with certainty how he ought to live, its very certainty should provide him with a reliable means for finding out what he is. Knowing what ought to be, he may deduce what is, for the potentialities of the former are limited by the actualities of the latter. The deduction will not be entirely comprehensive, but it does not have to be; at least it will comprehend that it is within man's natural capacity to follow the moral order, and it can then devote itself to the discovery of techniques to facilitate the growth of that capacity. Thus religious men, with no doubts as to right morals, borrow their science from the moral order, for the nature of man, like all questions of fact, is a scientific problem.

But is not the problem of the psychotherapist just the opposite, and part of its solution too? Just as the religionist used his moral certainty as the basis for postulates from which to deduce his scientific views, cannot the psychotherapist use the kinds of certainty that science can afford to induce some hints or clues to plausible morality? Can he not start off by addressing himself to the nature of man and use the information he can get about it as a means of calculating how he ought to live? He could not do so very comprehensively, but he does not need to be comprehensive; the very extent to which he can discover some limits to man's capacity and some parameters of it itself establishes some limits on his moral schemes, for one cannot be asked to live in ways that violate his nature.

In plain language, the above argues that finding out what men are like will go a long way towards determining for us what we should try to make them be like. To that extent, the moral wisdom of the psychotherapist will depend on his willingness to accept the dictates of his science. But since the dicta of science themselves depend on its progressive success in gathering and systematizing information, this implies both that the moral certainty of therapists should increase with time and that their goals should change!

The Changing Scientific Order

That the content of the sciences of man has immediate implications for the morals of psychotherapy as well as for its technicalities is logically apparent to the degree that morals are implied by techniques, but the fact that their underlying theories of personality are also subject to revision or abandonment has equally immediate implications which increase as our knowledge increases.

Science incorporates system as well as content, and the assumptions upon which scientific method is based are no more violable than are those of religion, and are just as effective in determining the contents to which they are applied. In religion, for example, the basic assumption of historical revelation dictates a hierarchial system of moral prescriptions, whose upshot is that those directions which are most revealed command authority. In science, the basic assumption about facts is that things which exist, exist in some quantity, and are therefore ultimately measurable; the assumption about the relationships between facts is that they are incapable of logical contradiction. These assumptions dictate the contents of science, and inasmuch as the science of man is to be used to establish some moral order, they dictate that some problems commonly considered of great moral significance are not even subject to discussion.

If this argument is valid, it follows that a psychotherapeutic system which is dependent on the state of the behavioral sciences when it is formulated, will inevitably become inadequate as a technical and as a moral system with the passage of time and increase of knowledge in the science. This seems to be the case with classical psychoanalysis, the oldest of current psychotherapies. Originally formulated as a "psychic pain killer" rather than a "soul saver," it seems actually to have accomplished neither for many people. The most sympathetic test of its technical efficacy was made by the American Psychoanalytic Association, whose somewhat disappointing results were withheld from publication. A tacit, if stupid, admission of the limited effectiveness of this system comes, however, in the increasing retrenchment of classical psychoanalysts into the argument that analysis is primarily "a research device for exploring personality rather than treating it." Presumably, nobody gives this information to the patients before they start treatment.

The moral order implied by classical psychoanalysis, moreover, was one based on scientific assumptions now generally considered obsolete. One of these is that the ultimate goal of organisms is quiescence or entropy, from which derived the notion of instinctual aggression. Another such assumption, that sexuality is a prepotent force in children, gave rise to the intricacies of the Oedipal complex and the emphasis on the role of repression, particularly of Id impulses, in the creation of neuroses; the latter suggested sexual and aggressive libertarianism as their cure. The most important of all such assumptions, however, was probably that of the compelling nature of unconsciousness, which intimated that nobody was responsible for anything. These ideas, along with a biological orientation that was relatively inattentive to a person's ability to function constructively within society, gave psychoanalysis a distinctive moral cast. It seemed to propose that men were entitled to live individualistically and irresponsibly, gratifying their needs as possible, evaluating the alternatives for action entirely in terms of the satisfactions they could afford. It made no difference whether or not psychoanalysts actually preached this doctrine (some did), for the personality theory that informed it was public property, and the moral of the theory was self-evident from its content.

It was also wrong—for none of the propositions cited are scientifically demonstrated truths, and increasingly marshalled evidence suggests that some, such as the repression theory, are false.

The Action therapies, subject to their own limitations of scientific content, contain a smaller number of scientific errors, and thus dictate a more effective therapy, and perhaps a more defensible morality, partly by virtue of their relative youth, which makes them the products of a more sophisticated era. The conditioning model of behavior, for example, can only be accused, at its worst, of disregarding the subjective experience of personal responsibility, not of arguing the patient out of it. On the other hand, ignoring responsibility does not encourage people to assume it, and the net effect may be the same as in Insight therapy.

Operationism and Existentialism

The contribution of scientific method, particularly of operationism, to the development of psychotherapeutic morals, is most evident when contrasted with the moralistic implications of some of the declared objectives of existential psychotherapy. This school describes the psychological condition of man as one of "aloneness," and posits that his natural goals are "self-actualization," "fulfillment," or "self-realization"; these objectives are achieved by developing consciousness of, and functioning in accord with, one's "real self." In whatever small measure these terms permit stable operational definitions, they suggest that the objective of psychotherapy is the satisfaction of some subjective state of value to the patient. This implies an individualistic moral even more radical than the Freudian, for the latter limits gratification to a biological value, while Existential therapy seems to legitimize any behavior that the individual himself prizes. What is more, the concept of "real self" implies that some selves are false, in turn suggesting that an individual's assumption of responsibility for his behavior depends on his willingness to be identified with it! This moral is explicitly reported by Abraham Maslow, who characterizes existential psychology as denying the significance of all values outside the self.

But the operational attack on morals need not be limited to systematic psychotherapies alone. For what moral is implied, if any, by touting such vagaries as "love," "sincerity," "integrity," "spontaneity," or other such homemade therapeutic goodies? To have scientific status, they must have ultimately measurable properties; otherwise, they have no place in a scientifically based morality, and their exposition is then a mask concealing some other moral or else it has no bearing on how men ought to live.

NEW THEORIES OF HUMAN NATURE

Scientific psychologists have been reluctant to address themselves in very comprehensive terms to the nature of man. This has not been from fear of its moral connotations, but from trepidation at the size of the question and the absolute certainty that, whatever their answers, progress in the behavior sciences would sometime show the fallacy of their speculations. Gardner Murphy has attempted just this, however, in his recent book, *Human Potentialities*, and at least two of the aspects of human nature he posits are sufficiently novel to warrant attention from therapists, most of whom have never tried to formally incorporate such notions in their systems.

1. In discussing the biological character of human nature, Murphy describes the trait of "simian sociality," arguing that social relations are a biological property of simian species, including man. To the extent that this is true, it suggests that an adequate psychotherapy must orient its goals towards the relationship between the individual and his society. While this does not argue for anything like the precise therapeutic formulation of Mowrer, it certainly does propose that scientifically viable therapeutic morals must be concerned with some kind of dynamic balance between what C. Wright Mills called "individual troubles" and "social issues."

2. Murphy further argues for the recognition of another aspect of human nature, one which might best be called aspirational. Basing his conjecture on a general description of human development in infancy and childhood as well as the specific experimental work of investigators like Berlyne on what might be called a curiosity drive, Murphy speculates that, once the basic biological drives of man are satisfied, and once he has formed a viable relationship with his culture, his nature impels him to aspire to the creation of new things. In this way, he suggests that science and the arts alike are intrinsic to man's natural development. But in any case, if it is true that the curiosity drive gives rise to a permanent state of aspiration, then another reasonable objective of therapy would be the facilitation of such drives.

Neither of these notions of Murphy's are formally incorporated in therapy systems, but this is less important than the fact that he has formulated them as scientific, not moralistic propositions; still, they serve as obvious foundations for a scientifically based morality.

There are other developments in the behavior sciences that hold promise for discovering valid rules of human conduct: The use of high-speed electronic computers for simulating many cognitive processes seems on the verge of causing scientific breakthroughs in the study of personality. One reason is that a number of artistically creative processes, like musical composition, and destructive ones, like neurotic defenses, seem to be truly reducible to computer processes; another is that the very attempt to simulate behavior forces investigators into closely detailed logical analyses of their ideas. The operation of these machines and their apparent capacity for truly novel, organized behavior, challenges stimulus–response models of psychology, suggesting that cognitive, emotive, and other internal processes which we generally describe as subjective experience, have some properties which are not reducible to S–R models, and which organize, plan, remember, and create. New developments in the study of conditioning, particularly in the Soviet Union, point toward new knowledge of the relations between the action systems of the body and its perceptual and sensory characteristics. New work in personality measurement seems about to demonstrate empirically a network of stable psychological structures which differ from one person to another in degree and which help determine responses to a variety of experiences.

A Proposed Model of Man

The upshot is that as work progresses, we come closer and closer to an understanding of the nature of man, always assured that, as our propositions gain accuracy, they differ somewhat from their forerunners and will be revised yet again by later, better tests. And each refinement in the total scheme of fact and theory suggests a new dimension of objectives. Even now, we might scientifically describe man as follows.

He is a complex biochemical mechanism, powered by a self-contained combustion system, which energizes a maintenance system, a transportation system, and very efficient digital and analogue computers with prodigious storage facilities for retaining encoded information and undisclosed capacity for integrating information, developing new programs for data analysis, and directing the gross operations of the other systems.

Far from belying a concern with how men ought to live, this description is intimately related to it. Considering, for example, Sherrington's idea that the subjective experience of free will is intrinsic to humans, as well as the notions of Murphy discussed above, we might add that, in some unspecified measure, the ability of this machine to function optimally depends upon its disregarding part of the above description, and operating in terms of two principles:

1. It is apparently indispensable to the human condition that man see himself as possessing control over his behavior, that he refuse to regard himself as the *victim* of circumstances, and that he deny that his operations are imposed from outside some self-contained self. His first requirement is control. As Sherrington says, this sense of freedom of will is as surely a part of man's nature as is the fact that he does not have it. It is self-operating, and one might propose, as a scientifically testable hypothesis, that there is some correlation between the extent to which a man sees himself as victimized and the extent to which he objectively malfunctions physically, mentally, and socially.

2. But as surely as man must *envision* his own machinery as controlled from within, he cannot *function* effectively unless the object of that machine's operations is external. This says, in other words, that man must experience not only control, but aspirations, external goals, and the need to strive towards the achievement of some perhaps inchoate ends, which he may define as the equivalents of goodness. It is these external goals that permit man to define some image of himself, and it is only the definition of some such image that enables him to experience control. The two mechanisms are thus mutually reinforcing.

As a corollary of the hypothesis that man requires aspirations, I submit that his aspirations are effective in defining an image only when they involve specific actions. This denies, in other words, that man may have significant aspirations "to be" or to identify some "essence of being," and it asserts that these aspirations, to be effective, must be aspirations "to do." Being is thus defined by doing, belief defined by practice, creed by deed. If so, then the verbalizations that men make about themselves, their faiths, and their aspirations, in some cases may not be meaningful criteria at all. It is not clear to me precisely what role such statements of belief may play other than a mildly facilitating one, but it is apparent that religious systems, insofar as they have encouraged the verbalization of creeds rather than the performance of acts, have not served the aspirations of man very well.

Nothing can be clearer, I believe, than that it is possible to use the scientific study of man as a basis for formulating the morals of psychotherapy. Their consequences cannot be predicted very well, and in that sense, their adequacy is indeterminate, but this is no worse for psychotherapy than for any other moral scheme. Their consequences are indeterminate in another sense as well—in terms of the impact of psychotherapy on the public. On the one hand, relatively few persons seek it, or perhaps ever will so long as it is primarily and appropriately associated with the solution of problems in living rather than the dispensation of patterns for it. On the other hand, the psychotherapeutic enterprise is addressed almost entirely to a particularly educated, sophisticated, and presumably influential segment of the population, and its influence may therefore be felt, for better or worse, considerably beyond the immediate range of its application.

The Secular Moral Order

As they are likely to become increasingly concerned with fostering sociality, aspiration, and individual responsibility, I suspect that psychotherapy morals will come increasingly to correspond with the rather general, nondenominational, liberal American interpretation of the Judeo-Christian ethic. If so, and if this occurs as a consequence of developments in the behavior sciences rather than as an artifact of sloppiness or thoughtlessness within the discipline, it can hardly be objectionable. But in that event, it seems, ironically enough, that psychotherapists, from their thoroughgoing secular positions, would be able to argue the merits and the defects of this ethic much more cogently than would the clergy, its traditional representatives. The same might be true of any other moral scheme that can be based upon a scientific description of man; this raises the final question in this connection, namely the right of psychotherapists to arbitrate morality.

There is nothing wrong, on the face of it, with psychotherapists trying to fill a moral vacuum in the lives of modern men, a third force in the areas once dominated by philosophy and religion.

Philosophy traditionally demands more intellectual commitment, if not ability, than most people, however educated, are prepared to give it. And religion, in most of its modern institutional forms, is so unimpassioned in objectives and impoverished in ideology as to have little current claim to the loyalties of good minds and men. Science is our sacred cow, and psychotherapists, with their apparent roots in scientific knowledge and method, can lay their claims to preach whatever codes they do, not merely on the grounds of great truth, or on the assurances across guilds that they will not compete for the same pulpits, but also on the apparent facts that the clergy have tended to abdicate their claim to moral competence in favor of psychology and that the congregations have, by and large, resigned from their clergy.

Were this a religious era, many of the problems raised here could not arise, and psychotherapists would not be faced with moral problems, but only technical ones. For they would know, or their patients would, or their patient's ministers would, how people ought to live, and their only problem would be to relieve the pain that interfered with their living that way. It is the very secular character of our time, however, that fosters the problem, by divorcing Christians from the naiveté of faith, hope, and charity, and Jews from the functional simplicity of fulfilling their commandments, both of them knowing what the meanings of their lives are, or knowing where to find out, or knowing that God knows, so that they need not be concerned about it.

Traditionally, a man's ultimate referent for morals was God. This is no longer possible, however, even for many religious people, for it is not readily translatable into sets of concrete propositions for how to conduct one's business, or career, or sex life. But the absence of some compelling religious system does not leave the secularist any less concerned with his salvation than the religionist, only more aware of the lack of clear-cut means to get it. And these are not provided by the society, nor can they be by a free society, which in some sense serves man best by involving him least. Psychotherapists, offering a secular morality, leading to a secular salvation that consists of ways to live that are full of meaning, with only a modicum of pain, seem in so doing to recast God as Science. While this may not be their intent, they cannot legitimately be concerned at the upset it may cause some people, especially clergy-men. The forms of religious systems are not their concern, and the contents they must approach from their own ground.

Psychotherapists have an important job to do, and it looks as if they will learn to do it well. As their ability to control and manipulate behavior improves, the moral character of their enter-prise will become more visible, and more embarrassing. But at the same time, their knowledge of man should also improve, and their moral stand thus become more defensible. When that happens, their title to guild status will be free and clear, and their ability to serve men, individually and in society, precious.

_____ PART FOUR

COMMENTARY

Values in Social Science. The virtues of moral detachment in scientific investigation received their most severe shock with the explosion of the first atomic bomb, and physical scientists ever since have been reconsidering the extent to which they can decently disregard the consequences of their work.

Since the social sciences have had the more serious problem, till recently, of ascertaining that they have _any_ consequentiality, they have been able to escape the moral issue even longer.

They are no longer able to do so; the challenge to the validity of this widely accepted idea now comes from several different sources. Writing from the perspective of political science, Dennis Wrong states that social scientists need ". . . more sensitive awareness of the inevitable interaction between factual knowledge and values."

Wrong, D. H. Political bias and the social sciences. *Columbia University Forum*, 1959, 2, 28–33.

It is important for them to recognize, he claims, that political beliefs are moral ones, and are not scientific in origin.

Alvin Gouldner pursues this notion still further in a brilliant essay entitled

Anti-Minotaur: The myth of a value-free sociology. *Social Problems*, 1962, 9, 199–213.

Gouldner argues that it is

. . . a myth created by . . . Max Weber . . . that social science should and could be value-free. Like Berkeley's argument for solipsism, Weber's brief for a value-free sociology is a tight one and, some say, logically unassailable. Yet it is also absurd. For both arguments appeal to reason but ignore experience.

He goes on to allege that sociology is not a value-free discipline and that it is impossible for sociologists to exclude their values and beliefs from their scientific work. The multiple grounds on which the value-free myth appears absurd are identified in a series of questions:

Does the belief in a value-free sociology mean that sociologists cannot, do not, or should not make value judgments concerning things outside their sphere of technical competence? . . . If technical competence does provide a warrant for making value judgments, then there is nothing to prohibit sociologists from making them within the area of their expertise. If . . . technical competence provides no warrant for making value judgments, then at least sociologists are as *free* to do so as anyone else; then their value judgments are at least as good as . . . say, a twelve year old child's. And, by the way, if technical competence provides no warrant for making value judgments, then what does?

Does the belief in a value free sociology mean that sociologists are or should be indifferent to the moral implications of their work? . . . Does it mean that sociologists cannot logically deduce values from facts? . . . Does it mean that sociologists should never take the initiative in asserting that some beliefs that laymen hold, such as the belief in the inherent inferiority of certain races, are false even when known to be contradicted by the facts of their discipline? Does it mean that social scientists should never speak out, or speak out only when invited, about the probable outcome of a public course of action concerning which they are professionally knowledgeable? . . . Does the belief in a value-free sociology mean that sociologists, either as teachers or researchers, have a right to covertly and unwittingly express their values but have no right to do so overtly and deliberately?

One of the consequences of the "internalization of the value-free principle," Gouldner points out, has been "a temporary suspension of the moralizing reflexes built into the sociologist by his own society," and this suspension has been useful in sociology, just as it proves useful in the development of medicine, psychotherapy, or any other scientific endeavor which has consequences for the public welfare. As Gouldner puts it, the notion of a

. . . value-free discipline provided a foundation for the development of more reliable knowledge about men and, also, established a breathing space within which moral reactions could be less mechanical and in which morality could be reinvigorated. . . . Doubtless there were some who did use the opportunity thus presented; but there were also many who used the value-free postulate as an excuse for pursuing their private impulses to the neglect of their public responsibility and who, far from becoming more morally sensitive, became morally jaded. Insofar as the value-free doctrine failed to realize its potentialities it did so because its deepest impulses were . . . dualistic; it invited men to stress the separation and not the mutual connectedness of facts and values: it had the vice of its virtues.

The unfortunate effects of this on the sociological profession do not appear to have been much different from what they have been, in some instances, on the psychotherapeutic disciplines:

On the negative side, it may be noted that the value-free doctrine is useful both to those who want to escape *from* the world
and to those who want to escape *into* it. It is useful to those
young men, or not so young men, who live off sociology rather
than for it, and who think of sociology as a way of getting
ahead in the world by providing them with neutral techniques
that may be sold on the open market to any buyer. The belief
that it is not the business of a sociologist to make value judgments is taken by some to mean that the market on which they
vend their skills is unlimited. From such a standpoint, there is
no reason why one cannot sell his knowledge to spread disease
just as freely as he can to fight it. Indeed, some sociologists have
had no hesitation about doing market research designed to sell
more cigarettes, although well aware of the implications of recent cancer research. In brief, the value-free doctrine of social
science was sometimes used to justify the sale of one's talents
to the highest bidder and is, far from new, a contemporary version of the most ancient sophistry.

There has been increasing recognition among psychologists
too, of the relevance of moral issues to the pursuit of their discipline. Perhaps the most complete statement of the evaluative implications of different orientations within psychology is that of Marshall Lowe, in

Value orientations: An ethical dilemma. *American Psychologist,* 1959, *14,* 687–693.

M. Brewster Smith takes a position not unlike Gouldner's
concerning the place of values in psychology. In an essay titled

Mental health reconsidered: A special case of the problems
of values in psychology. *American Psychologist,* 1961, *16,*
299–306

he proposes that psychologists have both a right and an obligation
to deal with values even to the extent of positing and promoting
value orientations. In doing so, however, he points out that they
have a scientific responsibility to examine critically and understand value effects.

A discussion of the problem of values in connection with

mental health is contained under the heading, "The value dilemma" (pp. 76–80), in Marie Jahoda's

> *Current concepts of positive mental health.* New York: Basic, 1958.

The quotation of Jahoda on page 6 is taken from page 77 of this book.

Several authors have been specifically concerned with the problem of morals and values in psychotherapy, though such concerns are quite atypical of the literature on this subject. Two earlier articles present ideas similar to those contained in the first chapter above. They are:

> Watson, G. Moral issues in psychotherapy. *American Psychologist*, 1958, 13, 574–575. This essay has also been anthologized in *Clinical psychology in transition*, compiled by J. R. Braun, Cleveland: Howard Allen, Inc., 1961

> Jessor, R. Social values in psychotherapy. *Journal of Consulting Psychology*, 1956, 20, 264–266

Jessor's essay is reviewed in some detail by Julian B. Rotter
in

> Analysis of trends in clinical psychology. In Koch, S. (Ed.), *Psychology: A study of a science.* Vol. 5. New York: McGraw-Hill, 1963

In a section titled "Psychotherapy and the clinical psychologist's values," Rotter presents a description of the value problem much the same as that given here. He emphasizes that most psychologists have avoided defining their own values, and have instead relied on the disease concept of psychological disorders, with its apparently objective standards of practice. He describes in some detail three value concepts, one or another of which Jessor believes are implicit in all therapy practice.

1. The *conformity* approach, which is nothing but the use of adjustment in the absence of other explicit value concepts as a criterion of therapeutic success. Few admit to this approach.

2. The *self-centered* approach, characteristic of psychoana-

lytic and client-centered therapies and, in my exposition, of all Insight therapies.

3. The *social-centered* approach, which seems to be Jessor's version of what might be called Integrative therapies. This approach characterizes Adler's concept of "social interest," Sullivan's advocacy of the development of ability to love others, and Mowrer's notion of social responsibility.

Rotter concludes this section as follows:

> Although these value concepts are more frequently complementary than incompatible, as good social scientists, clinical psychologists will need to explore more thoroughly both their own value systems and the implications of these value systems for the practice of psychotherapy.

A few books have also appeared which are explicitly concerned with problems in this area. Stanley W. Standal and Raymond J. Corsini have edited

Critical incidents in psychotherapy. Englewood Cliffs, N.J.: Prentice-Hall, 1959.

This book contains samples of twenty-three problems from the actual experience of psychotherapists; experts of different psychological and therapeutic orientations make evaluative comments on the incidents.

Because it is taken directly from experience, the work is necessarily unsystematic, but it is very useful for observing the differences between therapy orientations in the context of real clinical events. Not surprising, since the events are real, is the general concern of different commentators and practitioners with the evaluative implications, in the moralistic rather than predictive sense, of therapist or client behavior.

A related book, edited by Jules Masserman, is

Psychoanalysis and human values. New York: Grune & Stratton, 1960.

The most recent contribution to this field is a lengthy monograph by Charlotte Buhler,

Values in psychotherapy. New York: Free Press, 1962.

In this work, Dr. Buhler attempts to deal both with the problem of the technical importance of values in psychotherapeutic procedures and the more general one of how the values which guide the individual lives of therapist and patient influence their interactions in psychotherapy. The work developed directly out of discussions between Buhler and several colleagues on this subject, so its presentation is necessarily somewhat unsystematic. Many of the issues dealt with are the same as those presented here.

Morals and therapy training. It is true that training programs in psychotherapy tend to be unconcerned with introducing students to the moral implications of therapy, but it is not clear why this is so. One possibility, of course, is that the homogeneity of therapists and patients in the American culture is so great as to make the problem a relatively minor one. Wherever value-consensus exists, all therapy problems do indeed become entirely technical ones. There is some evidence, on the other hand, that psychotherapists as a group represent an extreme heterodoxy within the American culture, which would make the homogeneity hypothesis somewhat unlikely. Paul Verden, of the Institute for the Study of Human Problems at Stanford University, and Archer L. Michael, then of Cedars of Lebanon Hospital, Los Angeles, presented a report of their research in this area at the Annual Meeting of the California Psychological Association in December 1962. Their paper, entitled "Cultural unorthodoxy among a group of American psychotherapists," compares the "cultural orthodoxy scores" of thirty psychotherapists attending a workshop of the American Academy of Psychotherapists with the scores of members of eight other subcultural groups on a scale of the authors' own devising. The other groups included

a Fundamentalist Bible Class, Student Nurses, Teenagers, Jesuit Priests, Bohemians, Suburbanites, College Undergraduates, and Medical Students. Results indicate that the therapist sample, while not as homogeneous in attitude as some of the other groups, *is less orthodox than all samples examined except the Bohemians.* Subsequent comparisons of additional medical and non-medical therapist samples suggest that the American Academy of Psychotherapists group is not atypical with respect to psychotherapist unorthodoxy (authors' italics).

The authors summarize the implications of their findings as follows:

> These results challenge previous conceptions about the middle class value orientations of psychotherapists. Perhaps more significantly, they also raise questions concerning the utility of the class concept in social psychiatry, the nature of professional socialization in the training of psychotherapists, and about the relationship between the therapists' values and behavior. While not bearing directly on the part played by values in the psychotherapeutic situation, these findings serve as a warning that any attempt to investigate this area must attend to therapist as well as patient value positions.

A more detailed presentation of some of this research as well as a review of the literature in this area is contained in an unpublished paper by Verden entitled

> *Value assessment and American psychotherapy.*

Therapy Contracts. The concept of psychotherapy as a contractual relationship is developed by Karl Menninger in

> *Theory of psychoanalytic technique.* Menninger Clinic Monograph Series No. 12. New York: Basic, 1958.

MORALS AS TECHNICALITIES

The technical concern of psychotherapists for freeing their clients of unrealistic conflicts (p. 7) has often caused them either to overlook or disparage moral involvement in these conflicts. This tradition, among psychoanalytic therapists, is at least as old as Freud's work. Benjamin Wolman summarizes this position in his book,

> *Contemporary theories and systems in psychology.* New York: Harper, 1960.

> Freud seemingly avoided ethical and philosophical problems but he could not evade them. He suggested that the psychoanalytic therapist remain neutral and noncommittal on ethical

issues. It would not be proper for a psychoanalyst to impose his moral standards on his patients or to offer them a definite set of values. Psychoanalytic therapy aims at helping the individual to overcome infantile fixations and regressions and to become a mature adult. Moralizing would not help (p. 273).

Buhler points out that the foregoing neutralist position was not unequivocal on Freud's part, but became dominant among his younger psychoanalytic colleagues. It is carefully sustained among contemporary analysts such as Trygve Braatoy, whose book,

> Fundamentals of psychoanalytic technique. New York: Wiley, 1954,

deals realistically with the problems of morals in psychotherapy on the one hand and is oriented towards a consistently neutralist position on the other. Braatoy quotes Freud's dictum that "happiness here coincides with health, unhappiness with neurosis," quotes Helen L. Witmer's *Psychiatric Interviewing with Children*, to the effect ". . . that moral judgments are carefully avoided," and speaks of the conduct of "amoralistic analysis."

The Agent of Conflict Resolution. The precise means by which psychotherapists are able to function as the agents of conflict resolution is not clear to anybody. The possibility that this may happen by virtue of personal characteristics or unwitting attitudes and behaviors of the therapist rather than of his deliberate technical activities presents a challenge of some importance to all claims of all psychotherapies. As indicated in Chapter 5, in connection with Action therapies, the question gains currency as the therapy system does. Some therapists have been more prone to recognize it than others, however. Among the former are Franz Alexander. In

> The scope of psychoanalysis: 1921–1961. Selected papers of Franz Alexander. New York: Basic, 1961,

Alexander states:

Another powerful . . . neglected therapeutic factor which is present to some degree in all psychoanalytic treatment, consists in the patient's positive expectations, in his trust in the healing power of the procedure and in that of the therapist. Recently, French in his most careful studies demonstrated the cardinal significance of hope, which increases the integrative capacity of the ego. In an equally thoughtful paper, Jerome D. Frank convincingly explained the healing function of faith, and reviewed the literature devoted to this subject ("Psychoanalytic education for practice," 1961, p. 581).

For a very detailed discourse concerned entirely with this subject, see Jerome Frank's

Persuasion and healing: A comparative study of psychotherapy. Baltimore, Md.: Johns Hopkins Press, 1961.

Despite the generally greater concern of Action therapists with the scientific validation of their position, there has been relatively less discussion among them than among Insight therapists concerning the influence of such contaminating variables as faith, hope, and clarity in the cures they achieve. Although it is not clear why, the reason may well be that, since the theories of Action therapists tend to be rather neat and precise, they are more likely than are Insight therapists to think that they know what they are doing in the therapy session. If so, this would demonstrate how theory construction is sometimes as useful for impairing scientific inquiry as for directing it.

MORALS AS GENERALITIES

The inevitability of the moral agency of psychotherapists, which we have proposed, raises serious doubt that the therapist can avoid the imposition of his own value system in one or another form even if he wishes to remain scrupulously neutral. The attempt to remain neutral is nevertheless strongly ingrained in psychotherapists. Buhler reviews some of the literature on this phenomenon, including a survey of British psychoanalysts conducted by E. Glover and reported in

The technique of psychoanalysis. New York: International Universities, 1958.

Glover found that the majority of his respondents expressed themselves against the therapist's conscious expression of opinions, while some did not, and still others admitted that their views might be communicated "by implication."

Psychotherapy as Reciprocal Interaction. The concept of psychotherapy as a reciprocal interaction receives experimental support, at least as far as it involves interview techniques, in a very carefully designed study by Kenneth Heller, R. A. Myers, and Linda V. Kline,

> Interviewer behavior as a function of standard client roles. *Journal of Consulting Psychology,* 1963, 27, 117-122.

Their experiment is based on a hypothesis of Leary to the effect that each instance of interpersonal behavior tends to "pull" or provoke specific counterresponses from the individual who is the "target" of specific client behaviors. They used student actors as clients; the actors portrayed roles specified in advance in the course of interviews with thirty-four interviewers in training. The latter, of course, did not know they were seeing actors. A judge observed the entire interview proceedings through a one-way vision screen, a device which is commonly used in the training of interviewers and which would not, therefore, arouse the interviewers' suspicions that they were being subjected to a fake interview situation. In general, the ratings of the judges indicated that the actors were correctly performing the roles to which they had been assigned.

The authors made four correct predictions, two concerning control and two about affect. For the former, they correctly predicted that dominant behavior on the part of the client would evoke dependent behavior on the part of the interviewer and, reciprocally, that dependent behavior on the client's part would elicit dominant behavior from the interviewer. Concerning affects, they correctly predicted that hostile behavior from the client would evoke hostility from the interviewer and that friendly behavior by the client would elicit friendly interviewer behavior. They also predicted that hostility from the client would make interviewers anxious, but this was not true.

The authors conclude that psychotherapy should be viewed as a "reciprocally contingent interaction," following Jones and Thibaut.

The exchange relationship is said to make the therapist's moral agency inevitable for several reasons. First, the client necessarily interprets the therapist's response to his moral concerns. Alexander and French recognize this fact in

Psychoanalytic therapy. New York: Ronald, 1946.

In making interpretations, we often set up for ourselves the ideal neither to praise nor condemn the motives that have activated the patient's behavior. We deceive ourselves, however, if we hope thereby to keep the patient from reading praise or blame into our interpretations (p. 94).

Second, the ethical codes that professional psychotherapeutic societies promulgate serve to restrict the activities of the therapist himself. For psychologists, the American Psychological Association has published a code titled

Ethical standards of psychologists. Washington, D.C.: American Psychological Association, 1953.

This 170-page document, which was revised in 1959, is the initial publication of this organization on ethics. It is essentially a collection of general principles of ethical conduct in professional work together with illustrative true incidents from which the general principles were formulated. Some of the topics covered are: Ethical standards and public responsibilities of the Psychologist. Relationship of practicing psychologists to legal authorities. Personal responsibilities for maintaining high standards. Responsibility for ethical standards and professional competence of others. Representing psychological services accurately and responsibly to the public.

Though the topics covered are not limited to the practice of psychotherapy, a large number are especially relevant to it. Most of these go under the heading, "Standards in client relationships." Included are: Recognizing limitations of techniques; Defining the individual or agency to which the psychologist is responsible;

Respecting the integrity of the client in the clinical relationship; Protecting the confidential nature of clinical relationships; Fees in clinical work; and Malpractice in clinical psychology, such as offering inferior services, misusing techniques, violating social codes, conventions, and moral expectations, and practicing outside the professional field.

The code is now out of print, but a description of it is presented by Erasmus L. Hoch under the title, "The character of the controls operating on psychologists" in an essay titled

> Psychology and the public. In Wilse B. Webb (Ed.), *The profession of psychology*. New York: Holt, 1962 (pp. 257–265).

A succinct description of the same code and the circumstances surrounding its composition is given by Robert I. Watson in

> *Psychology as a profession. Doubleday papers in psychology*. New York: Doubleday, 1954 (pp. 20–24).

The third reason that the exchange character of the therapy situation forces a moral agency on the therapist is that he has a personal value system which, one way or another, becomes communicated to his patient. That this idea is not mere conjecture is demonstrated by the empirical work of Rosenthal and of Parloff. In the former, titled

> Changes in some moral values following psychotherapy. *Journal of Consulting Psychology*, 1955, 19, 431–436,

Rosenthal found that patients who improved in therapy tended to revise certain of their moral values in the direction of their therapist's values. Similarly, Parloff found that

> . . . the therapist who perceived a patient as approximating his Ideal Patient concept more closely created the better relationship with that patient.

> Parloff, Morris B. Some factors affecting the quality of therapeutic relationships. *Journal of Abnormal and Social Psychology*, 1956, 52, 5–10.

The means by which this communication takes place is unclear, as indicated by Albert Ellis in

> Requisite conditions for basic personality change. *Journal of Consulting Psychology*, 1959, 23, 538–540.

Ellis describes several theoretical notions of the prerequisite conditions for personality change, including his own, and suggests that none are adequate. He concludes that change does involve changes of ideology and values, but how it takes place is not identifiable.

Some such exchange of values does take place, at all events, and it is probably more appropriate to ask what to do with it than how to prevent it. This is cogently stated in a comment by O. H. Mowrer in Standal and Corsini's *Critical Incidents in Psychotherapy* (*op. cit.*):

> . . . many psychotherapists are careful not to impose their own values upon their patients. Yet, as recent studies show, this cannot be entirely avoided in practice; and it may be that we will soon recognize, even in theory, its desirability and necessity. The two imponderable questions that will then arise are: What values can we most legitimately offer to others in exchange for their old ones? And how can we make these alternative values acceptable and attractive to them? (p. 97)

IMPLICATIONS

Therapists as Committed Social Agents. The morals of psychotherapy are largely a result of the social responsibilities of therapists and of the social character of the therapy situation and of many of the problems that bring people to it. In functioning as social agents, however, therapists would not necessarily be protagonists of society as it now stands. Abraham Maslow, for example, who is a leading exponent of existential psychotherapy, not only espouses a libertarian position, but states that morality itself is an epiphenomenon of nonacceptance or dissatisfaction of the individual with himself. In

> *Motivation and personality.* New York: Harper, 1954

Maslow takes this stand on the social committment of therapists:

. . . good society is synonymous with psychologically healthy
society, while bad society would be synonymous with psychologically sick society, which in turn means basic-need gratifying
basic-need thwarting respectively . . . (p. 322).

Maslow talks at some length about sick societies, and quite
explicitly proposes that psychotherapists should, as necessary, see
themselves as opponents of the society in whatever respects it may
be sick.

Successfully Influencing Behavior. The very existence of psychotherapy as a legitimate business, as well as the many problems
which accompany its practice, are ultimately contingent on the
ability of psychotherapists to make good the claim that they can
influence people's behavior. Peculiarly enough, this claim is not
easily established scientifically, nor is it altogether clear what the
best means are to go about validating or infirming it. Two general
approaches are available. The first is the conduct of what are technically called "outcome studies" of psychotherapy. It is very difficult to do such studies well, however, because of enormous difficulties in the establishment of acceptable criteria for successful or
unsuccessful outcomes, the difficulty of establishing base rates of
spontaneous recovery, and the difficulty of comparing subject and
experimenter, or treatment and therapist populations.

More important than any of the above perhaps is the fact
that outcome studies, by their very nature, cannot be definitive.
This is no excuse for not doing them, and few indeed have been
done, but it is an inevitable limit on their usefulness.

A more basic approach is to examine the problem of influencing behavior in the experimental laboratory. Simulations of
therapeutic situations in the laboratory are necessarily limited
also, but it is at least possible there to ascertain precisely what
processes are available to exert precisely what degree of control
over the behavior of experimental subjects.

Since the psychotherapeutic situation is, by and large, an
interview, a basic approach to the problem of influence concerns
the influencing of verbal behavior by different combinations of
verbal and nonverbal means at the experimenter's disposal.

A very large experimental literature now exists on this subject, and cannot appropriately be reviewed here. The paradigm for these experiments was devised by Lloyd G. Humphreys, now of the University of Illinois, in an article titled

> Acquisition and extinction of verbal expectations in a situation analogous to conditioning. *Journal of Experimental Psychology*, 1939, 25, 294–301.

This work lay dormant for some time, however, until it was followed by some better-known experiments by J. Greenspoon and W. S. Verplanck; their work wakened people's attention to the implications of this area, now generally called *verbal operant conditioning*, for psychotherapy. An abstract of Greenspoon's original experiment, which was his doctoral dissertation at the University of Iowa in 1951, appeared as

> The effect of two nonverbal stimuli on the frequency of members of two verbal response classes. *American Psychologist*, 1954, 9, 384.

A more detailed report of his research appeared subsequently as

> The reinforcing effect of two spoken sounds on the frequency of two responses. *American Journal of Psychology*, 1955, 68, 409–416.

A rather recent review of work in this area was written by Greenspoon as a chapter entitled

> Verbal conditioning and clinical psychology. In A. J. Bachrach (Ed.), *Experimental Foundations of Clinical Psychology*. New York: Basic, 1962 (pp. 510–553).

The major works of Verplanck in this area are reported as

> The control of the content of conversation: Reinforcement of statements of opinion. *Journal of Abnormal and Social Psychology*, 1955, 51, 668–676

> The operant conditioning of human motor behavior. *Psychological Bulletin*, 1956, 53, 70–83.

A comprehensive review of related work was made by Leonard Krasner, who found that most of thirty-one studies reported success in attempts to manipulate interview responses by means of very simple interviewer reinforcements. In this article, titled

Studies of the conditioning of verbal behavior. *Psychological Bulletin,* 1958, 55, 148–170,

Krasner summarizes the implications of these studies for psychotherapy:

If future results in this area confirm the indicated trends, it might be concluded that all psychotherapy is to some extent directive in nature. The therapist uses cues, often without his own awareness, to modify, control, guide, or manipulate the patient's verbal behavior. This mode of subtle communication can probably be offered as a means of understanding how the therapist's own theoretical explanation of the dynamics of personality and of psychotherapy are transmitted to the patient.

A more recent review of the research in this area, especially as it relates to personality and psychotherapy, is contained in an essay by London and Rosenhan titled

Personality dynamics. In Paul Farnsworth (Ed.), *Annual review of psychology,* Vol. 15. Palo Alto, Calif.: Annual Reviews, 1964.

The upshot of such studies is that, without any doubt, it is possible to influence significantly a wide variety of verbal behaviors of many individuals by essentially simple verbal or nonverbal means. The extent to which such manipulations can actually be taken to account for changes which people undergo in psychotherapy or the extent to which they can be used as a basis for the development of psychotherapeutic techniques à la Skinner is another story —but in principle, at least, the case is thoroughly established.

Social Control and Responsibility. Once therapists claim to influence people, they must certainly take some responsibility for the nature of that influence. This may seem like a truism, but the idea has received remarkably little attention in the psychotherapeutic literature. A welcome exception is a recent essay by Leonard Krasner,

> Behavior control and social responsibility. *American Psychologist*, 1962, 17, 199–204.

Defining Health and Illness. It may seem spurious or superficial to define health as the absence of illness and illness as the presence of symptoms, but another definition may prove even more unsatisfactory. By any definition other than that rendered above, the term "health" actually implies a value more than a fact. Illness, on the other hand, is simply a subsumptive label for symptoms, which are entities.

The theoretical issue is much less relevant, at all events, than is the empirical one. An empirical definition of illness has never been very difficult to establish in medicine but is very hard to come by for psychological disorders. The difference is one of criteria, which are inevitably more concrete and measurable, and generally more predictable, if not lethal in effects, in medicine than in psychiatry. The criterion problem has been an endless source of frustration in attempts to evaluate the effects of psychotherapy, and failure to cope with it has sometimes wrecked evaluation studies which would otherwise have made signal contributions to knowledge.

A description of one sophisticated attack upon this problem is given by Jerome D. Frank in

> Problems of controls in psychotherapy as exemplified by the psychotherapy research of the Phipps Psychiatric Clinic. In E. A. Rubenstein and M. B. Parloff (Eds.), *Research in psychotherapy*, 1959, Washington, D.C.: American Psychological Association (pp. 10–26).

The response variables were changes in the patient's subjective discomfort and his social ineffectiveness. These were chosen as representing the least common denominator of the aims of all the healing arts, including psychotherapy. However else a patient may change under treatment, unless he becomes more comfortable and more effective, it is hard to maintain that he has improved. Discomfort was defined in terms of 41 symptoms or feelings which the patient reported as distressing. Ineffectiveness was defined in terms of fifteen types of behavior, generally recognized as socially ineffective, rated by interviewers on the basis of information obtained from the patient and an informant. We attempted to measure decrease in discomfort and ineffectiveness rather than increase in comfort and effectiveness, because it proved much easier to define degrees of malfunctioning than of succesful functioning. It is easier to define illness than health.

Another excellent summary of the criterion issue is presented by Harold H. Mosak in

> Problems in the definition and measurement of success in psychotherapy. In W. Wolff and J. A. Precker (Eds.), *Success in psychotherapy*. New York: Grune & Stratton, 1952.

SCIENCE AND MORALITY

The idea that science is defined by facts and their interactions while values are excluded from it is central to this entire work, but it is hardly the unanimous view of psychologists. The failure to dichotomize them which is lamented here is actually celebrated by Franz Alexander in *The scope of psychoanalysis* (*op. cit.*)

> The dichotomy between "facts and values" is a pseudodistinction and the problem of whether values belong to a realm which is beyond the reach of scientific methods is a pseudoproblem (p. 532).

Just how values might be within the reach of scientific methods is the subject of a volume edited by Abraham Maslow,

New knowledge in human values. New York: Harper, 1959,

a collection of papers from a symposium sponsored by the Research Society for Creative Altruism. One of its objects was to explore the notion that a science of values is possible.

Walter Weisskopf, commenting on the papers (pp. 199–223), observes that there are three images of man on which different approaches to values are based, i.e. the naturalist, the humanist, and the ontological. The psychologists in the symposium, Gordon Allport, Erich Fromm, Kurt Goldstein, and Abraham Maslow, are all identified as humanists with naturalistic traits. Weisskopf proposes that the naturalist approach makes it difficult to establish a relation between science and values.

> The conception of such a unity seems to be impossible to antinomic naturalist thought, with its self-chosen confinement to the instruments of factual observation and logic (p. 209–10).

Using Weisskopf's terminology, my position is a naturalistic one with humanist traits. It argues that a unity of science and values is quite impossible, and that the most critical problem of psychotherapy is that these two independent dimensions must both receive attention and consideration without any comfortable assumption that an easy reconciliation between them is possible.

Scientific Evaluation. Evaluation in science is factual, not moralistic; it is concerned only with the induction of unknown facts from known ones. Isaac Asimov discusses this idea in "What is Science," the first chapter of

> *The intelligent man's guide to science.* New York: Basic, 1960.

> Galileo's general viewpoint was just the reverse of the Greeks'. . . . No amount of inductive testing could render a generalization completely and absolutely valid. . . . And no matter how many times a theory meets its tests successfully, there can be no certainty that it will not be overthrown by the next observation.
> . . . The inductive method cannot make generalizations about what it cannot observe, and since the nature of the human soul, for example, is not observable by any direct means yet known, this subject lies outside the realm of the inductive method.
> The new natural philosophy came in time to be called "science" (from the Latin word meaning "to know"). It is generally taken to mean specifically the inductive method (p. 17).

THE MEANING OF NORMAL

However abusive history's use of the term may have been, there is no doubt that one connotation of normality which is most firmly established today is that of a relatively satisfactory, if not optimal, condition. In psychology, the optimal state implied is generally labeled "personality integration." Several essays that attempt to describe such states have attracted the attention of psychologists in recent years. Three of these, all anthologized in

> J. R. Braun (Ed.). *Clinical psychology in transition.* Cleveland: Howard Allen, Inc., 1961,

are

> Shoben, E. J., Jr. Toward a concept of the normal personality. *American Psychologist*, 1957, *12*, 183–189.

> Lynn, D. B. A model man for applied psychology. *American Psychologist*, 1959, *14*, 630–633.

Seeman, J., Toward a concept of personality integration. *American Psychologist*, 1959, *14*, 633–637.

PROFESSIONAL CONFUSIONS

The public could hardly be more confused in its thinking about psychotherapy than are some of its professional representatives, who should know better. Nowhere is this confusion better illustrated than in a hilarious and appropriately bitter essay by Alexander W. Astin (also anthologized by Braun),

The functional autonomy of psychotherapy. *American Psychologist*, 1961, *16*, 75–78.

The Reactionaries. Despite this surge of productive activity, certain reactionaries within the field attempted to lead psychotherapy back to the Dark Ages. Notable among these was Eysenck (1952) who claimed that nowhere in the scientific literature was there any good evidence psychotherapy worked. In a crushing attack on Eysenck's position, Rosensweig (1954) pointed out that neither was there any good evidence that psychotherapy hurt anybody. Eysenck (1955) agreed. Now that everyone agreed that the evidence was no good, psychotherapy had been vindicated. Eysenck tried again (1954) to promote his position. This time his claim was that to squabble over who should do psychotherapy before its efficacy had been demonstrated is, in essence, to put the cart before the horse. Eysenck was answered by Raush (1954) as follows: "It is not the point to discuss the efficacy or lack of efficacy of psychotherapy here . . . psychotherapy is a method for studying the human psyche . . . whether it is a good or bad method is not at issue" (p. 588). Thus, without the bothersome business of first knowing if, how, or under what conditions psychotherapy might work, we could still engage in controversies about who should perform it and also use it to "study the psyche." Who could doubt now that psychotherapy had indeed become functionally autonomous?

More Ethics. A serious ethical objection lodged by the practitioners against "outcome" research centered around the necessity for using controls in such investigations. . . . In a desperate counterargument, some reactionaries suggested that psychotherapy might conceivably be deterimental under certain conditions, and that ethical considerations really demanded that controlled outcome studies be done in order to evaluate at least these possibilities.

"*The Experts.* Perhaps the most up-to-date picture of outcome's waning popularity is available in a recent monograph, *Research in Psychotherapy* (Rubenstein and Parloff, 1959) which is based on an interdisciplinary conference of 27 experts in the field. In summarizing the main biases and points of view of these experts, the editors conclude: "as if by some tacit agreement, the issue of outcome was skirted by the conference." [1]

The difficulties of the criterion problem are the major obstacle in the way of outcome studies, but these do not excuse the absence of such studies. Astin goes on to review the reviews of psychotherapy in the research literature, and concludes that "Outcome's Outcome" is, if anything, a trend further away from the performance of these needed studies.

Despite the understandable bitterness of Astin's remarks, his pessimistic conclusions concerning outcome studies may be unjustified. George Frank briefly reviews the development of organized research on psychotherapy and comes to the conclusion that it is progressing despite difficulties in the achievement of adequate research methodology. This is reported in

On the history of the objective investigation of the process of psychotherapy. *Journal of Psychology*, 1961, *51*, 89–95.

The Profusion of Schools and Doctrines. Since psychotherapy has always been a scientifically pretentious craft, it is somewhat surprising that its students have been so given to forming schools of thought and practice rather than open-mindedly entertaining and investigating the facts of disorder and its relief. Psychoanalysts have probably been somewhat more guilty of this than others, though Skinnerian Action therapists parallel them rather well. A striking exception to the former is found in the work of Kenneth Mark Colby, particularly in his most recent book,

[1] Reprinted by permission of the American Psychological Association.

A *skeptical psychoanalyst.* New York: Ronald, 1958.

This is an altogether delightful, entirely unsystematic collection of essays criticizing psychoanalytic professional practices, literature, and in minor ways, technique. The first essay, "Letter to a young psychoanalyst," is particularly relevant to the issues of orthodoxy and doctrinaire practice as opposed to open minded empiricism; it also discusses apprenticeship.

An ironic comment which is worth noting here is that Colby is considered not merely maverick, but heretic, in some psychoanalytic circles, which have more or less officially castigated him for having truck with dissidents. Such procedures are more familiar in the excommunicative rites of churches and secret societies than in scientific bodies.

Jones' life of Freud, referred to on page 24, is

Jones, E. *The life and work of Sigmund Freud.* New York: Basic, 1953–1957.

The Quest for Historical Context. Insight therapists in general, and psychoanalytic ones in particular, have apparently been so enamored of the therapeutic value of tracing the history of personal ailments that they sometimes insist on applying the same techniques to the process of understanding the treatments! The history of a system of therapeutics has no bearing on its effectiveness, of course, nor is it necessarily even heuristically valuable for understanding its content. The excursion into history is not treated merely as a matter of interest, however, by some therapists, but as a sine qua non of understanding. Leopold Bellak exemplifies this view in

Psychoanalytic theory of personality: Notes toward a systematic textbook of psychoanalysis. In J. L. McCary (Ed.), *Psychology of personality.* New York: Grove, 1956 (pp. 1–62).

. . . at best one can learn psychoanalysis only if one traces the development of its concepts historically, and only he who knows all of it knows anything about it at all, because concepts are defined—insofar as this had been done—differently in different papers, or even inconsistently within one publication.

THE COMPONENTS OF THERAPY SYSTEMS

Personality Theory. Very many books have been written on Personality, but by far the most important volume which surveys theory in this discipline is the quite comprehensive and readable work by Calvin S. Hall and Gardner Lindzey,

Theories of personality. New York: Wiley, 1957.

The descriptions of personality theory in the present book have been heavily influenced by theirs, though the distinctions between Insight and Action therapy schools cut across several formal theories. This emphasizes that these technical orientations must be carefully distinguished from the various theories which may be invoked to justify them.

Freudian psychoanalysis, for example, is quite pure Insight therapy, but Freudian personality theory can be taken as a basis for Action therapy quite as readily as for Insight therapy (their Chapter II); this is more obviously the case with stimulus–response theory (Chapter XI). Jung's analytic theory (Chapter III), moreover, plainly has little logically necessary connection with the largely Action orientation of Jungian analysis. The same could probably be said of any very comprehensive personality theory, perhaps because the level of inference of such theories is so far removed from the known facts of behavior that their range of applicability seems (spuriously) endless.

Organismic theory (Chapter VIII), and Roger's self theory (Chapter XII), are among the most popular formal theories employed by modern Insight therapists, especially among existential analysts.

The Therapeutic Muddle. The dimensional analysis of psychotherapy is proposed here as the most systematic possible one, but even a molecular analysis which classifies its component parts would be more systematic than what is usually attempted. At this writing, there are apparently only two major works which survey the most prominent therapies at the respective poles of the technical dimension. For Action therapies, Hans Eysenck has edited a mildly systematic casebook,

Behaviour therapy and neuroses. New York: Pergamon, 1960.

For a major segment of Insight schools, Ruth Monroe produced a thoroughly scholarly critical work titled

Schools of psychoanalytic thought. New York: Holt, 1955.

Even these works, however, are limited in scope, and neither attempts to dimensionalize psychotherapy.

Patrick Mullahy has also written a distinguished review of psychoanalytic Insight therapies, using their different views of the Oedipus complex as his point of departure:

Oedipus myth and complex: A review of psychoanalytic theory. New York: Hermitage, 1948.

The modal presentation in the literature, however, is still less taxonomic, sometimes consisting of nothing but the juxtaposition of schools and case studies. The extreme of this procedure is illustrated in a work edited by James L. McCary and Daniel E. Sheer,

Six approaches to psychotherapy. New York: Holt, 1955.

However valuable the "approaches" in their own right, one is struck by the very dearth of effort to conceptualize them in relation to each other. The editors' introduction states:

This book is not a systematic, integrated investigation of the approaches in psychotherapy. There is no special system of presentation . . . Neither preference nor judgment is implied in the sequence of the chapters . . . it is not feasible to expect uniformity of either terminology or organization of material.

The works referred to on page 27 are:

Greenwald, Harold. *Great cases in psychoanalysis.* New York: Ballantine, 1959.

Fenichel, Otto. *Psychoanalytic theory of the neuroses.* New York: Norton, 1945.

Salter, Andrew. *Conditioned reflex therapy: The direct approach to the reconstruction of personality.* New York: Capricorn Books-Putnam, 1961 (original edition, 1949).

Wolberg, Lewis R. *The techniques of psychotherapy.* New York: Grune & Stratton, 1954.

Fromm, Erich. *Man for himself.* New York: Holt, 1947.

Prescientific Psychoanalysis. The defensive argument that only members of an inner circle, elected by sympathetic participation in the movement, could really understand psychoanalysis or properly criticize it, represents a position which is no longer characteristic of leading thinkers within psychoanalysis. A more current and more sensible position comes in

> *Psychoanalysis as science: The Hixon Lectures on the scientific status of psychoanalysis.* New York: Basic, 1952.

This book presents lectures by Ernest R. Hilgard, Lawrence S. Kubie, and E. Pumpian-Mindlin, sponsored by the California Institute of Technology. In his Introduction, Pumpian-Mindlin, who edited the book, states:

> It is my hope that the reader who is not trained in psychoanalysis will find in this series of five lectures an attempt to

discuss basic problems of observation, methodology, validation, and theory as they have been applied in psychoanalysis. In addition, I hope there has been a sufficient presentation of the raw data of psychoanalytic observation to enable him to form an independent and considered judgment of his own (vi–vii).

A similar view, which explicitly disavows the earlier position, is presented by Franz Alexander in "A review of two decades" in

The scope of psychoanalysis: 1921–1961. New York: Basic, 1962.

The most pertinent and penetrating questions, however, are asked by our scientific confreres in other fields of knowledge, concerning the precision and validity of our formulations and the nature of our evidence. The time is past when you could retort with the once-valid formula: "You are asking all these questions because of your emotional resistances." Today we must answer these sincere and pertinent questions in good faith . . . This is the moment when our field, which was a combination of a nucleus of a new science with a new creed, begins to change into a rigorous science which has to accept universal standards of validation in research and to adopt academic standards of teaching established by tradition in all other fields of knowledge (p. 540).

PUBLIC CONFUSIONS

Popular Works on Therapy. Popular interest in psychotherapy is reflected in a steadily growing number of popular works which variously endeavor to explain it, describe personal experiences with it, and offer personal advice about when to get it and from whom. Qualifications for expertise in any of these efforts are somewhat uncertain; some entertainers, for example, have written magazine articles about their psychoanalyses. Some such confessions have also appeared in book form, including

Knight, J. *The story of my psychoanalysis.* New York: Pocket Books, 1952 (Original edition: New York: McGraw-Hill, 1950.)

Freeman, Lucy. *Fight against fears*. New York: Crown, 1951.

Miss Freeman's account of her personal experiences was followed by a more general effort to advise people on the nature of emotional disorders and how they can be effectively treated,

Search for love. New York: Avon, 1957.

The book is a collection of letters written to her and answers to them. It includes careful advice on avoiding charlatans and the like, and hopeful misinformation about the efficacy of psychotherapy.

Another work in the same genre, by Rudolph Wittenberg, is

Common sense about psychoanalysis. New York: Dell, 1963.

Dr. Wittenberg is a well-known psychoanalyst, which lends some authority to the limited position he describes.

The foregoing are all paperback books, itself indicative of their wide distribution. National magazines are nothing loathe to deal with this subject also, as illustrated by

Solving emotional problems, Special Project #4, August, 1961, by the Editors of *Coronet*, pp. 105–128.

Beware of psycho-quacks, *Changing Times*, August, 1957, pp. 11–13, by the Staff of Changing Times (The Kiplinger Magazine).

By far the best popular work on this subject is a paperback by June Bingham, compiled under the direction of Fritz Redlich and with the collaboration of Jacob Levine,

The inside story: Psychiatry and everyday life. New York: Vintage Books (Knopf), 1953.

All the popular works in this area are written from the vantage of Insight therapy. In part, this reflects a psychoanalytic orientation which is more or less common to all of them, but it is equally a reflection of the relative novelty of Action therapies as far as the public is concerned.

The Multiplicity of Schools. The quotation from Robert A. Harper is taken from the preface to

Psychoanalysis and psychotherapy: 36 systems. Englewood Cliffs, N.J.: Prentice-Hall, 1959.

Dr. Harper describes his work as intended to give

> . . . Wide and brief coverage of the many systems . . . not the details and refinements of any one system . . . what is lost in fine and mystical detail is more than compensated for by clarity of general perspective . . . this book offers a more complete survey of contemporary systems of psychotherapy than has been previously presented in a single volume. Such a presentation should be of particular interest to students of the behavioral and social sciences as well as to the intelligent layman who has heretofore looked in vain for an understandable map of the therapeutic maze.

Apologia for Technique. It is hard to explain the relative dearth of books which are concerned primarily—much less exclusively—with psychotherapeutic technique. One reason which may be quite important, though incidental to the main thesis of this work, is that there has been a considerable inclination among practitioners to view the practice of psychotherapy as an art rather than a scientific or technical skill. Though theirs is not a very common opinion, some therapists consider the discipline essentially unteachable. More common is the idea that the limits of teachability of psychotherapy are lower than of most professional activities, in which case it would not be terribly important to concentrate much effort on technical textbook writing.

Whatever the theoretical merits of this position, and however much some people may be better practitioners because of inclinations and skills that are unrelated to their training, the position is not very fruitful, since most therapists try to train people to perform the craft anyhow.

Two works of some importance on techniques of individual Insight therapy have been available for some years.

Wolberg, L. R. *The technique of psychotherapy.* New York: Grune & Stratton, 1954.

Colby, K. M. *A primer for psychotherapists.* New York: Ronald, 1951.

The latter is a manual for the beginning pyschotherapist, intended essentially as a technical aid to the conduct of treatment. It is a pioneering work, and I have seen nothing quite like it since. There has been considerable discussion of technique in other writing about therapy, but little else has been written of a deliberately and specifically "how to" nature. Even Karl Menninger's book on analytic technique is limited, as its title implies, to *theory* of psychoanalytic technique.

Some change seems to be taking place, however. Haim G. Ginott has only recently written a book titled

Group psychotherapy with children. New York: McGraw-Hill, 1961.

Though subtitled "The theory and practice of play therapy," its orientation is, from the very first, much more toward practice than toward theory. As Ginott says:

> The purpose of this book is to give clear descriptions of play-therapy techniques and of the rationales which support them. It is a practical book . . . The need for such a book became apparent in a series of play-therapy workshops . . . [where] . . . A number of the participants evinced greater knowledge of theory than of practice. They knew about Oedipus and Electra, but were puzzled when confronted with children's incestuous approaches; they knew about transference and resistance, but had difficulty transferring a resisting child from the waiting room to the playroom (p. ix).

THE HANDLING OF SYMPTOMS

The position of Insight therapists regarding symptoms is ably stated by Franz Alexander in "Psychoanalysis revised," in

The scope of psychoanalysis: 1921–1961. New York: Basic, 1961.

> The inadequacy of symptoms to resolve emotional tensions lies just in their regressive nature, in the fact that they represent solutions which were adequate in the past but are no longer so. Clinical experience shows that they usually represent a very

early behavior pattern of childhood . . . A neurotic symptom
is a foreign body embedded in the texture of rational behavior.
In order to grasp its significance, one must first (as Horney
validly requires) understand in all detail the actual emotional
situation. Yet without knowing the past emotional patterns
which it repeats, the symptom remains unintelligible (pp. 149–
150).

The distinction of Insight and Action therapies in terms of
symptom orientation is not unique to the present work. E. L. Phillips and C. U. Mattoon make a similar distinction in

Interference versus extinction as learning models for psychotherapy. *Journal of Psychology*, 1961, 51, 399–403.

The authors further propose that the difference in orientation as
to means of control of behavior is similarly characteristic of the
two positions. Insight—full knowledge of the source of difficulties
—means direct control over them, while behavior manipulation
(action) without full knowledge implies indirect control.

THE LIMITS OF THE SYSTEMS

For better and for worse, practitioners cannot take their
theoretical commitments too seriously if they realize both that
these positions are not altogether validated and that they do not
entirely comprehend the range of human problems in any case.
The leavening effect this has on all but the most ruthless dog-
matists is described by E. Lowell Kelly in a way that parallels the
description given here:

Clinical psychology: the postwar decade. In *Current trends
in psychological theory.* Pittsburgh: Pittsburgh Univer. Press,
1961, pp. 31–49.

. . . continually confronted with service problems for which
there are as yet no scientifically derived solutions of known
validity. Intelligent people, confronted with complex problems,
inevitably prefer to view them in the light of some set of organ-
izing principles—and it is hardly surprising that each clinician
adopts that set of principles which to *him* makes the best sense

out of what would otherwise be an incoherent mass of clinical case materials. Similarly, in the absence of diagnostic and prognostic techniques of proved validity, each clinician confronted with the necessity of making professional decisions of critical importance in the life of a patient is understandably likely to rely on that technique or group of techniques which yield information which can be most readily integrated with his theoretical formulation of the case. And finally, in the absence of any conclusive evidence for the effectiveness of any therapeutic technique, one can hardly blame a clinician for utilizing whatever therapeutic approach he finds most comfortable in his effort to help a person with problems (p. 45).

Rival Camps within Insight Therapy. The disputations that go on among psychotherapists vary in type from scholarly debates of an impersonal kind, which contribute a good deal to the development of understanding, to hysterical condemnations of heresy. The latter are probably less common than the former, but far from extinct, as witness Maxwell Gitelson, recent president of the International Psychoanalytical Association, in

> Communication from the president about the neoanalytic movement. *Journal of the International Psycho-analytical Association,* January 1962, 373–375.

Dr. Gitelson attacks Neo-Freudians for their misguided revisionism, and is especially incensed at their claim

> . . . that such developments indicate that the scientific place of psycho-analysis is now assured. In fact all we can be certain

of is the survival of the name, which is being increasingly used for its derivatives and applications . . . there is now a galaxy of diluted and distorted improvisations . . .

Dr. Gitelson goes on to propose a means of dealing with these dissidents that will preserve his colleagues' wholeness, and finally proposes a re-examination of self within his own ranks to explore the dangerous softness there towards dissidence:

> So it would seem that the wisest procedure would be to avoid outright debate or other open encounter with the organized proponents of so-called "liberalism." But this does not absolve us from the task of dealing with the problems which their existence calls to our attention in ourselves and in our organizations.
>
> . . . what may be at the root of such dissidence . . . answers bearing . . . on those qualities of the training analysis . . . which eventuate in failure of resolution of pathological narcissism, in survival of narcissistic identification in the transference and the counter-transferences, and in the persistence of the transference neurosis itself. Our failure to be uncompromising in the application of our psycho-analytic insight into our authoritarian roles as teachers and educators may have something to do with the fact that at least some of our colleagues and students find solace for narcissistic injury in alliance as dissident coteries . . . our functions as members of groups which are responsible for passing on the torch of self-knowledge which we received from Freud.

Commonality among Insight Schools. The fundamental commonality which continues to unite Insight schools, as seen here, is the insistence that the achievement of insight is the critical goal of psychotherapy. The cardinal source of contention between the schools is over the question, "insight into what?" Among classical and revisionist psychoanalytic schools, the dispute has generally centered around the relative influences of biological and cutural factors in the development of personality. In

Psychoanalysis revised. In *The scope of psychoanalysis.* New York: Basic, 1961,

Alexander describes Horney's entire critique of classical psychoanalysis in just these terms. Similarly, Ruth Monroe, in

Schools of psychoanalytic thought. New York: Holt, 1955,

treats the essential difference between the Freudian and Neo-Freudian systems in terms of the emphasis which the former places on instinct gratification (reduction of biological motives), compared to the emphasis on the self-system in the latter (concern with satisfaction of culturally derived motives). It is the source of the dynamism that differentiates the schools.

This makes clear, on the one hand, why these schools should be in conflict with each other, and why they should nevertheless continue to be classified as one: because their therapeutic objectives in all cases remain the production of insight. Though there may be differences in the implied actions that result from insight into instinct and insight into self system, neither of these are as different from each other as is either of them from a system designed to elicit action in the first place.

Carl R. Rogers. Though his writings have been prolific and have covered a wide range of topics relevant to psychotherapy, three books in particular represent Rogers' position on psychotherapy at different points in his own intellectual development. The book which originally made him the center of extensive controversy in American Psychology, and which first presented the "nondirective" approach to psychotherapy, is

Counseling and psychotherapy. Boston: Houghton Mifflin, 1942.

The position was extended and elaborated, together with a theory of personality in its support, almost ten years later in

Client-centered therapy: Its current practice, implications, and theory. Boston: Houghton Mifflin, 1951.

His most recent book-length statement,

On becoming a person. Boston: Houghton Mifflin, 1961,

continues to develop the thesis of Rogers' therapy, but focuses much more sharply than have his previous works on the personal characteristics of the therapist, demanding explicit understanding of his own values and transparent presentation of his true self in relationship to others, and encouraging full functioning in the client by virtue of being one's own real self. This eventuates in a frankly existentialist position, with which Rogers is presently publicly identified.

Existential Analysis. The foremost representative of existential psychotherapy among American psychologists is probably Rollo May, who has also been identified with the Sullivanian group because of his affiliation with The William Alanson White School of Psychiatry, Psychology, and Psychoanalysis in New York City. May's first full-length work presenting an existentialist approach to malady and treatment is titled:

Man's search for himself. New York: Norton, 1953.

He views anxiety as the central problem of psychological disorder and sees the loss of individual values, of the self, and of the feeling of interpersonal relatedness as the chief source of anxiety. The solution comes in the rediscovery of selfhood and the achievement of consciousness, permitting the individual to gain the strength which freedom of choice confers. The "struggle to be" results in "integration," which is expressed in freedom of choice, creative conscience, courage, and maturity.

A more recent work, and one usually considered a more definitive statement of the existential position, is jointly edited by May, E. Angel, and H. F. Ellenberger,

Existence: A new dimension in psychiatry and psychology. New York: Basic, 1958.

A brief and particularly useful introduction to this field is contained in a paperback,

R. May (Ed.) *Existential psychology.* New York: Random, 1961,

a collection of papers originally presented at a symposium on existential psychology of the American Psychological Association in 1959. It contains papers by May, Maslow, Feifel, Rogers, and G. Allport, all of whom are explicitly identified with this position.

Even more important, an extensive bibliography has been compiled by Joseph Lyons (pp. 101–126); titled "A bibliographic introduction to phenomenology and existentialism," it has been selected from an annotated bibliography on the same subject in *Psychological Reports*, 1959, 5, 613–631.

As is commonly the case with relatively unfamiliar or novel systems, existential analysts have been at some pains to emphasize their many differences from classical psychoanalysts. That they nevertheless are very much within the mainstream of Insight therapies in general, is indicated both in their own writings and in critical evaluations of them. Rollo May says, for example,

> The "unconscious" . . . [is] *those potentialities for knowing and experiencing that the individual cannot or will not actualize.* . . . every mechanism or dynamism, every force or drive, presupposes an underlying structure that is infinitely greater than the mechanism, drive, or force itself . . . it is the underlying structure from which they derive their meaning (*Existential psychology*, pp. 24 ff., italics in original).

Abraham Maslow, also an ardent existentialist, begins a discussion of psychotherapy by carefully distinguishing Insight therapy from what he considers a preferable treatment, "need gratifying therapy"; he ends the discussion, however, by uniting them:

> The final step would be to realize that there was no difference between organismic insight, organismic emotion, and organismic conation except the angle of approach of the student, and the original dichotomies would be clearly seen to be artifacts of a too atomistic approach to the subject.
>
> *Motivation and personality.* New York: Harper, 1954 (p. 331).

In his critical evaluation of trends in clinical psychology, Rotter devotes some space to an evaluation of existential psychotherapy:

> The general orientation has much in common with phenomenological approaches, although many variants deal with the un-

conscious life and use historical techniques . . . It is difficult to determine . . . what many of these methods have in common—each borrows from different aspects of different writers —and most of the theoretical justification for the approach is obscure and laden with value terms. Perhaps the common ground for these approaches is the primary emphasis on the inner experiencing of the patient and a rejection of stereotyped approaches, "canned" interpretations, and psychiatric labels (p. 816).

Analysis of trends in clinical psychology. In S. Koch (Ed.), *Psychology: A study of a science.* Vol. 5. New York: Mc-Graw-Hill, 1963.

A critical essay by Franz Alexander gives a somewhat different view. Titled "Existential analysis: Impressions from the 4th International Congress of Psychotherapy (1959)" (in *The scope of psychoanalysis, op. cit.,* pp. 548–557), it clearly argues that the existential point of view, though representing a "general orientation" of some value to psychoanalysis, does not involve any radical departures either in theory or technique.

The Rules of Insight Therapy. The use of talking as the single instrument of therapy in Insight systems has a historical as well as a logical basis. Freud was one of those therapists who never took notes, and he even wrote a paper in which he said the analyst should not do so because it would interfere with his ability to draw on his own unconscious responses to the patient's associations. Freud also never lectured from notes, as Jones and others have observed, and was generally possessed of an astonishing memory.

A more recent and thoroughly rationalized variant of the same position is argued by Lawrence Kubie, who comes to the somewhat astonishing conclusion that "the written word (is) literally useless as an instrument of record." He reports in an essay entitled

Problems and techniques of psychoanalytical validation and progress. In *Psychoanalysis as science.* New York: Basic, 1952,

Over a period of many months, daily observation of a process which waxes and wanes continually by just perceptible increments and decrements gradually dulls the perception of even the keenest observer, paralyzes the memory through the monotony of repetition, and renders the written word literally useless as an instrument of record. After a time, the observer can no longer differentiate clearly and surely what the patient has said from what he himself has said, or which came first. To this I would add that since the process of analysis makes use of the free associations of the analyst as well as those of the patient, the memories of both must be subject to selective influences in an identical way, if not to the same degree.

Hence, it is impossible for the analyst to make adequate records of what transpires between himself and his patient merely by writing notes either during or after each session . . . tying himself down to his pencil would inevitably limit the flexibility of the analyst's associative responses (p. 116).

A considerable number of technical rules have always characterized the practice of psychoanalysis. These are listed by Thomas French in his introduction to Alexander's selected papers: *The scope of psychoanalysis* (*op. cit.*). They include such dicta as that the patient should lie on a couch and the analyst sit behind him out of sight, that the patient should free associate and the analyst limit his activity to interpretations of these associations, that the analyst should avoid giving advice about decisions which the patient faces in real life, that the patient should be seen no less than five days a week, and that the analyst should avoid social and other contacts with the patient outside the analytic session. French goes on to report that Alexander pioneered a number of revisions in these standard analytical practices, but he emphasizes that a conservative bias towards these variations is in order. When in doubt, even Alexander and his colleagues advocate rather strict adherence to the traditional rules for the conduct of therapy sessions.

The Similarity of Psychotherapists. The studies of F. E. Fiedler that demonstrate the similarity among different Insight therapists are:

The concept of an ideal therapeutic relationship. *Journal of Consulting Psychology*, 1950, *14*, 239–245.

A comparison of therapeutic relationships in psychoanalytic, non-directive, and Adlerian therapy. *Journal of Consulting Psychology*, 1950, *14*, 436–445.

Factor analyses of psychoanalytic, non-directive, and Adlerian therapeutic relationships. *Journal of Consulting Psychology*, 1951, *15*, 32–38.

A method of objective quantification of certain countertransference attitudes. *Journal of Clinical Psychology*, 1951, *7*, 101–107.

These studies are summarized and evaluated by Hans Strupp in

Patient-doctor relationships: The psychotherapist in the therapeutic process. In A. J. Bachrach, *Experimental foundations of clinical psychology*. New York: Basic, 1962.

A pioneer effort was a series of widely quoted studies by Fiedler which, unfortunately, have not been replicated or expanded. The measuring instrument was a Q-sort consisting of 75 statements describing the therapeutic relationship in terms of communication, emotional distance, and the role which the therapist maintained toward his patient. The items read, for example, "The therapist is well able to understand the patient's feelings," "The therapist is hostile toward the patient," "The therapist maintains a friendly, neutral attitude throughout," etc. Fiedler found that trained therapists as well as untrained judges agreed on the desiderata of a good therapeutic relationship. He then asked judges to rate, by means of the same Q-sort, early interviews conducted by ten therapists representing the psychoanalytic, the client-centered, and the Adlerian orientations. Within each group of therapists, half were nationally recognized experts, half beginners. Factor analyses of the ratings showed that therapeutic relationships created by experts, regardless of theoretical orientation, were more alike (more "ideal") than the relationships created by novices. From these findings and those of related studies, it was concluded that the quality of the therapeutic relationship is more basic to therapeutic sucess than the therapist's specific methods and techniques" (p. 599).

Since the material in this section was written, however, some work has been called to my attention which may require the revision or abandonment of the hitherto unchallenged conclusions of Fiedler. Donald Sundland and Edwin Barker have devised a Therapist Orientation Questionnaire which may be more refined and reliable than the Fiedler measure, and hence more sensitive to differences among therapists. Their study is reported as

> The orientations of psychotherapists. *Journal of Consulting Psychology*, 1962, 26, 201–212.

> The 16 subtests yielded 6 factors and a general factor labelled Analytic vs. Experiential. The subtests were used to characterize the methods and attitudes of the sample. The three major psychotherapy orientations held by psychologist-therapists were described. Analyses were made of the relationship between experience and therapy attitudes and it was found, contrary to the widely quoted conclusion of Fiedler, that experienced therapists are more similar to inexperienced therapists of their own orientation than they are to other experienced therapists.

PSYCHOANALYSIS AND CLIENT-CENTERED THERAPY

It has been proposed that the distinction between interpretation and reflection is less critical than either Rogerians or Freudians claim because each technique serves precisely the same function for the therapy system in which it is used. Strupp, in the chapter in Bachrach's *Experimental foundations of clinical psychology* cited previously, actually presents empirical evidence, however, that the differences in usage are in fact smaller than Rogerians in particular might be inclined to believe.

> The present writer (1955a) compared Rogerian and psychoanalytically oriented therapists, using their responses to a series of patient statements, presented to them on cards, and analyzing the data by means of Bales' (1950) system of interaction process analysis. As might be expected, Rogerians showed a strong predilection for reflection-of-feeling responses, whereas the second group preferred exploratory questions. In this sample,

experienced Rogerians, as opposed to inexperienced Rogerians, showed a significant decline in reflection-of-feeling responses, with a concomitant increase in other response categories (p. 596).

Importance of History. The notion that Rogerian de-emphasis on history is a matter of therapeutic parsimony rather than principle has also been implied by Rotter:

> Rotter, J. B. Analysis of trends in clinical psychology. In S. Koch (Ed.), *Psychology: A study of a science.* Vol. 5. New York: McGraw-Hill, 1963 (pp. 814–815).

> Carl Rogers, essentially in the Rankian tradition, accepted the general principle that therapy could proceed—without an analysis of the past—through the client's ability to solve his problems as he saw more deeply into them as a result of the therapist's reflection of feelings.
> . . . It is apparent that such a view of therapy required an attitude and frame of mind or particular kind of personality on the part of the therapist more than some form of special training.

Transference. Rogerians and Freudians do not differ so much over the question of whether transference exists as they do over whether it is necessary to elicit an intense transference in order to successfully conduct psychotherapy. Rogers discusses this question at some length in *Client-centered therapy* (*op. cit*) in a section titled "Problem of transference" (pp. 198–218). He states that the occurrence of transference in client-centered therapy is both less intense and less problematic than in psychoanalysis. He believes that this difference results from the difference in impact of reflection and interpretation. The latter, in his view, is primarily responsible both for the creation and resolution of the psychoanalytic transference.

THE MOTIVES OF BEHAVIOR

It has been proposed that all Insight therapies presuppose that behavior is the consequence of some unseen motives, and

more important, that Insight therapies make the meanings of acts
virtually identical with their motives. That this is the case with existential analysts is illustrated in the quotation of Rollo May (p.
276). That it is no less true of classical psychoanalysis is suggested
in the work of Norman O. Brown,

> *Life against death.* New York: Random House, 1959.

Brown stipulates that the key concept in Freudian theory is that
of *repression*, and that the fundamental proposition of the entire
theory is that all events are *meaningful*.

Rogerian theory is less explicitly concerned with meaning
than with the concept of self, but the self-concept is itself significant only as a hypothetical construct for those psychological processes by which experience is interpreted and apparently separated
from its interpreter. This issue is discussed at length in an excellent
essay by C. Marshall Lowe,

> The self-concept: Fact or artifact. *Psychological Bulletin,*
> 1961, 58, 325–336.

> Is the self-concept a fact which, having an objective existence
> in nature, is observed and measured; or is it an epiphenomenon
> of deeper reality, invented by man that he might better study
> his behavior?
>
> The world has sought to be so sure of the self because
> there is so little else of which it can be certain. The self has
> become the anchor that man hopes will hold in the ebbtide of
> social change. But just as a fish could never know it was sur-
> rounded by water unless that water were to disappear, it is un-
> likely that Lecky (1945) would have known about self-con-
> sistency had he not lived in a culture which felt inconsistency.
> In Buberian terminology, the self is an It, which man invents
> because he cannot find a Thou.
>
> The position of this paper must be that the self is an
> artifact which is invented to explain experience. If the self-
> concept is a tool, it must be well designed and constructed. We
> will conclude therefore with that construct of the self which
> best serves the 1960's. Such a construction combines the self of
> ego-involvement with the self of feeling. It is a self which is ex-
> istential not to experience itself, but to mediate encounter be-

tween the organism and what is beyond. Such a self is what Pfuetze (1954) calls the "self-other dialogic theory of the self," being interpreted naturalistically through Mead and transcendentally through Buber. It is as an artifact that the self-concept finds meaning (p. 334).

The Definition of Insight. In this work, the term *Insight* has been used synonymously with consciousness, with the implication that consciousness could in turn be described verbally. There is some confusion in psychotherapeutic literature resulting from the fact that insight is sometimes restricted in meaning to an entirely intellectual process and at other times is used to incorporate quite different appearing behaviors, such as abreaction. A survey of the wide variety of usages will demonstrate, I believe, both that the way in which the term is used here is entirely legitimate, and that the basic psychotherapeutic objective of otherwise quite divergent psychotherapists is, as proposed here, the elicitation of insight.

A general description of the many uses of insight is given by Julian Rotter in

Social learning and clinical psychology. Englewood Cliffs, N.J.: Prentice-Hall, 1954.

. . . the term *insight* has taken on many meanings in the field of psychotherapy. It may refer to the understanding of one's own underlying or unconscious motivation. It may refer to the understanding of the relationship between past experience and present behavior. It is utilized sometimes as equivalent to any kind of learning that takes place in therapy. Sometimes it has the implication of sudden recognition; sometimes it does not. For some therapists it may be either verbal or nonverbal; for others it refers only to something that can be verbalized. Although almost all therapists stress the importance of insight, some may also state that it is not necessary that insight be verbalized or that the subject be aware of his insight. It is rather obvious that the term as used by some therapists has little in common at least from the measurement or referent point of view, with the way it is used by other therapists (p. 376).

Theodor Reik, a distinguished representative of the classical Freudian position, devotes a chapter to insight in

> *Listening with the third ear: The inner experience of a psychoanalyst.* New York: Grove, 1948.

Reik describes in considerable detail the personal experience of insight, emphasizing that this experience includes more than the simple verbal experience of a conscious cognition. The upshot of his description, however, is that insight nevertheless is defined by consciousness, even if not by simple cognition.

John Dollard and Neal E. Miller offer a perspective on psychoanalysis strikingly different from that of Reik in their

> *Personality and psychotherapy: An analysis in terms of learning, thinking, and culture.* New York: McGraw-Hill, 1950.

This work is an attempt to integrate Freudian theory of motivation and psychotherapy with the drive theory of Clark Hull. In effect, it is an elegant attempt to restate psychoanalysis in terms that would make it acceptable to scientific students of the learning process. The authors emphasize, nevertheless, that the development of insight, which they call "the labeling process," is the primary objective of psychotherapy. They even suggest that the use of emotional catharsis in classical psychoanalysis is important only insofar as this process itself leads to insight.

In his introduction to Alexander's essays (*The scope of psychoanalysis, op. cit.*), French points out that Alexander's view of psychoanalytic therapy demands a balance between the curative factors of "emotional abreaction" and "intellectual insight." Although he makes some academic distinction between these concepts, Alexander argues that every correct interpretation serves the purpose both of abreaction and insight, integrating them into a single act.

The meaning and significance of insight in the work of neo-Freudian revisionists do not differ particularly from the classical psychoanalytical position either. Frieda Fromm-Reichmann makes the following statements in

Psychoanalysis and psychotherapy. Chicago: Univer. of Chicago Press, 1950.

Interpretation means translating into the language of awareness, and thereby bringing into the open, what the patient communicates, without being conscious of its contents, its dynamics, its revealing connections with other experiences, or the various implications pertaining to its factual or emotional background (p. 94).

. . . Part of the previously hidden meaning of the patient's material reveals itself, and some of his dissociations resolve themselves by the mere process of relating the data to the doctor, that is, by bringing his hitherto private covert experiences into contact with outward reality.

No cure is accomplished, according to present classical and modified psychoanalytic knowledge, by any single, one-time understanding of any single symptom or any single previously dissociated experience. All emotional experiences which are made accessible to the patient's awareness and mature emotional judgment have to be recognized and accepted ("working through") repeatedly in various contexts. . . . Working through should be continued until the time is reached when the intellectual understanding of his problem, of its previously dissociated causes, and of its various interlocking mental and emotional ramifications is gradually transformed into real creative emotional insight (p. 95).

Erich Fromm also discusses insight in

Man for himself: An inquiry into the psychology of ethics. New York: Holt, 1947.

There is no situation which provides for a better opportunity to observe the strength and tenacity of the forces striving for health than that of psychoanalytic therapy. To be sure, the psychoanalyst is confronted with the strength of those forces which operate against a person's self-realization and happiness, but when he can understand the power of those conditions— particularly in childhood—which made for the crippling of productiveness he cannot fail to be impressed by the fact that most of his patients would long since have given up the fight were they not impelled by an impulse to achieve psychic health and happiness. This very impulse is the necessary condition for the cure of neurosis. While the process of psychoanalysis consists in gaining greater insight into the dissociated parts of a person's feelings and ideas, intellectual insight as such is not a sufficient condition for change. This kind of insight enables a person to recognize the blind alleys in which he is caught and to understand why his attempts to solve his problem were doomed to failure; but it only clears the way for those forces in him which strive for psychic health and happiness to operate and to become effective. Indeed, merely intellectual insight is not sufficient; the therapeutically effective insight is experiential insight in which knowledge of oneself has not only an intellectual but also an affective quality. Such experiential insight itself depends on the strength of man's inherent striving for health and happiness (pp. 223–224).

Measuring Unconscious Behavior. The references in the footnote on page 57 which describe relatively recent studies on the relationship between consciousness and behavior are from

Blum, G. S. *A model of the mind.* New York: Wiley, 1961.

Blum, G. S. Programming people to simulate machines. In S. S. Tomkins and S. Messick (Eds.), *Computer simulation of personality.* New York: Wiley, 1963.

Eriksen, C. W. Figments, fantasies, and follies: A search for the subconscious mind. In C. W. Eriksen (Ed.), *Behavior and awareness,* Durham, N.C.: Duke Univer. Press, 1962.

Razran, G. The observable unconscious and the inferable conscious in current Soviet psychophysiology: Interoceptive conditioning, semantic conditioning, and the orienting reflex. *Psychological Review,* 1961, 68, 81–147.

Critical reviews of *Model of the mind* may be found in

Kalish, H. I. The black box revisited. *Contemporary Psychology,* 1963, 8, 24–26,

London, P. *American Journal of Psychology*, 1963, 76, 526–528,

and of the entire field of current research on awareness in

London, P., and Rosenhan, D. Personality dynamics. In Paul Farnsworth (Ed.), *Annual review of psychology*, Vol. 15. Palo Alto, Calif.: Annual Reviews, 1964.

SCIENCE AND INSIGHT THERAPY

The upshot of the current research on awareness is that it is very doubtful whether any significant learning occurs without it. Of more immediate importance from a psychotherapeutic point of view, however, is the question of the pertinence of insight in the formulation and resolution of psychological problems. Here too the evidence is anything but encouraging. It is summarized, as is the status of "self" theory, by Ruth C. Wylie in

The self concept. Lincoln, Nebraska: Univer. Nebraska Press, 1961.

In short, there is no clear evidence that insight is significantly associated with adjustment or defensive behaviors.

It is clear that research on insight has not gotten us very far, due to methodological errors. What implications can now be drawn concerning the possibilities of ever doing fruitful research on the role of insight in behavior? Certainly many of the more gross sources of artifact can be avoided if a properly detailed and explicit analysis is made of the procedures used to define independent and dependent variables (p. 305).

However, as time has passed and a considerable body of research has accumulated, it seems that a crisis situation is at hand with regard to personality theories and research which emphasize the self. For one thing, the usefulness of these theories is called into question by the state of the empirical evidence, because the latter is partly a function of ambiguities in the theories.

If personality theories stressing self-referent constructs are going to be counted among scientifically useful theories, the time has come for them to move in the directions we have outlined above. If the theoretical difficulties cannot be overcome, both the theoretical and empirical efforts might just as well be abandoned, so far as their probable contribution to scientific psychology is concerned (p. 323).

Psychotherapy as Education. The notion that psychotherapy could function as an education in the subject of self whether or not it was successful in bringing relief from distress is neither new nor stated with tongue-in-cheek by most Insight therapists. Freud originated the position among psychoanalysts, though he did so as a pessimistic comment on the efficacy of the techniques he had invented. A modernized and optimized version of the same idea is presented by Karl Menninger:

> *Theory of psychoanalytic technique.* Menninger Clinic Monograph Series No. 12. New York: Basic, 1958 (preface).

> I once regarded it not only as a great educational experience but as also a therapeutic program par excellence. True, Freud warned us against the emphasis on the therapeutic effect. Now I know he was right; therapeutic effect it does have, but, in my opinion, were this its chief or only value, psychoanalysis would be doomed. Surely the continued development of our knowledge will help us to find quicker and less expensive ways of relieving symptoms and rerouting misdirected travellers. Psychoanalysis essays to change the structure of a patient's mind, to change his view of things, to change his motivations, to strengthen his sincerity; it strives, not just to diminish his sufferings, but to enable him to learn from them (xi).

MORALS AND INSIGHT THERAPY

Insight as an End unto Itself. Independent of its effect upon symptoms, the concept of insight as an end unto itself so attenuates the concrete therapeutic goals of Insight therapy that it forces this system out of a conventional scientific mold and into a moralistic one. However desirable or necessary the latter role might be, it has always seemed to me that the attenuation of their scientific claims would be a source of discomfort and despair to Insight therapists, considerably dampening the enthusiasm that conscientious and knowledgeable adherents of this system could manifest for it. This view receives some support in a recent essay by Allen Wheelis,

To be a god. *Commentary,* 1963, 36, 125–134 (August).

In the course of this passionate, rambling, and often quite beautiful discourse on psychoanalysis, determinism, and free will, Dr. Wheelis describes some analysts' views of analysis with great pathos. He speaks of the

> . . . psychoanalyst with the sad yellow face, shoulders stooped as if by an invisible weight . . . stretched on my couch (for I, too, am an analyst) . . . four times a week for—how many? —years; for a while analysis itself becoming for him the meaning of life, a kind of formal minuet in which the learning of new psychic steps replaced lost illusions; with insight to spare but no change, coming in time to feel betrayed, but still on the couch for years . . . years . . . saying, "I came to this hospital as a resident, and still remember how it was. And how I was. Patients would arrive sick and leave well. Something would happen—insight—that made a difference. So I thought. It's the same now; but I'm different, and they muddle along for a while with ups and downs, and then come back. And the second time is like the first—some new insights, some new "realizations," some new turning points—like the wind turns (p. 125).
>
> . . . I'm a clinician of despair, I know the little signs: the wordless shadow in the eye, the furtive pain around the mouth . . . It's there, and we know it at night when the wind blows. And it's there, too, after analysis; for when you have been completely analyzed—whatever that may mean—when, at the end of the last hour of your, perhaps, third analysis, you shake hands with your analyst and leave his office for the last time—at just that moment . . . you feel an ache of longing . . . for something . . . which has no name, lies beyond your grasp, and you know that analysis, however fine its net, could not capture this elusive anguish (p. 129).[1]

Self-consistency. Self-consistency has received more attention from Rogerian psychotherapists than from any others, and

[1] Reprinted by permission of the author and the American Jewish Committee.

researchers who adhere to this orientation have used increases in self-consistency as an operational criterion for improvement in psychotherapy. Such a hypothesis was first tested by Rosalind Dymond Cartwright, who reported her research in

> Effects of psychotherapy on self-consistency. *Journal of Consulting Psychology*, 1957, 4, 15–22.

Cartwright later extended and repeated her study, only to find that, while increases in self-consistency did characterize individuals who had apparently benefited from psychotherapy, the relationships were more subtle and equivocal than had originally been suspected. This is reported in

> The effects of psychotherapy on self-consistency: A replication and extension. *Journal of Consulting Psychology*, 1961, 25, 376–382.

> The general relationship of personal adjustment to discrepancies between the way people think they are and the way they would like to be is the subject of some controversy in the research literature. Current studies have been reviewed by London and Rosenhan in

> Personality dynamics. In *Annual review of psychology* (*op. cit.*).

Their upshot is that "large discrepancies between ratings of self and ideal self may be indicative of poor adjustment, but small discrepancies in these ratings are not conversely indicative of good adjustment."

THE PROBLEMS OF INSIGHT MORALITY

The implications of the morality of self knowledge are virtuous, of course, only in a society that is committed quite deeply to the positive valuation of individual autonomy. I have been particularly influenced to the view both that "psychological man" is the end product of Insight therapy and that this creature may be a kind of ideal type for democratic society by the work of Phillip Rieff, especially

Freud: The mind of the moralist. New York: Viking, 1959.

This position assumes that the moral canons of Insight therapy deliberately disdain to offer any positive prescription for the social order. This is not the unanimous view of students of this subject. Richard LaPiere, in

The Freudian ethic. New York: Duell, Sloan & Pearce, 1959,

views Insight morality as tantamount to a virtual conspiracy against the notion of social responsibility in general and the Protestant Ethic in particular.

Ernest Becker, on the other hand, in

The birth and death of meaning. New York: Free Press, 1962,

seems to regard the absence of a position vis-à-vis society as an error or oversight rather than an (unspoken) canon:

> Unless we use a theory that carries the implicit presuppositions of Natural Law, combined with our own definition of socially valued behavior, there is no point at which we can consider behavior abnormal. Psychoanalysis errs on both counts. And it is in this very double error that the picture is doubly obscured. Psychoanalysis, subscribing to the idea of an innate, biological developmental imperative, shuts its eyes at the same time to the inextricable immersion of the individual in a social context (p. 155).

In contrast to all of the foregoing, Herbert Marcuse proposes, in

Eros and civilization. Boston: Beacon, 1955,

that Freudian theory in particular, extended in the "antirepressive" direction supposedly implied within it, bears the seeds of a utopian social system.

Balakian. The quotation of Anna Balakian on p. 66 is from

"Asocial act of mercy," a review of *The executioner,* by Pierre Boulle. *Saturday Review,* Dec. 23, 1961, p. 24.

The asocial self. There is no overemphasizing that the doctrine of selfhood is not antisocial but asocial. Its consequences with respect to an individual's social values are not altogether predictable from this point alone. In his discussion of existential analysis, Franz Alexander (*The scope of psychoanalysis, op. cit.*) tells how this orientation distinguishes between the uniqueness of the individual and his social role without any mention of possible contradiction between them:

> . . . Primarily it is not a new contribution to the content of psychiatry or psychotherapy. It is a consistently formulated basic orientation. It is a vocal protest against the prevailing trend toward reducing the human individual to a cog in the social machinery. For such a society the uniqueness of the individual is useless; hence, it prefers to deal with him in his social role, and not as a distinct personality with the specific mission of realizing his unique potentialities. It emphasizes utility and adjustment—the polar opposite of creativity . . . adjustment means to accept and to conform with what is already there. . . . It is a desperate cry for preserving the most specifically human aspect of man, his self-awareness as a unique being different from all others (p. 554).

Abraham Maslow, on the other hand, argues very explicitly, in

Motivation and personality. New York: Harper, 1954,

that appropriate value systems are essentially self-oriented, and that a concern with morality is itself an epiphenomenon of implied neurotic nonacceptance or dissatisfaction with the self.

Snow. The quotation of C. P. Snow on page 67 is from

The two cultures and the scientific revolution. New York: Cambridge Univer. Press, 1959.

Rieff. The reference to Phillip Rieff on pages 67–68 concerns an unpublished paper entitled

A schema of therapeutic types.

Delivered orally at a symposium of the American Psychological Association in New York City in September 1961, the paper was prepared both for the symposium and as the first chapter in a forth-coming book.

The *misuse of self-knowledge* as an apology for impotence in fact may be dangerously characteristic of our times, and it is a possibility unwittingly reinforced by the very nature of Insight therapy. This tendency is observed by Alfred Kazin, commenting on modern novels in

> The alone generation. In *Contemporaries*. Boston: Little, Brown, 1962.

> . . . The age of "psychological man," of the herd of alones, has finally proved the truth of Tocqueville's observation that in modern times the average man is absorbed in a very puny object, himself, to the point of satiety. The whole interest of the reader seems to be summoned toward "understanding" and tolerance of the leading characters. We get an imaginative universe limited to the self and its detractors. The old-fashioned novel . . . showed a vulnerable hero . . . battling it out (a) for principles which he identified with himself and (b) against social enemies who were honestly opposed to the protagonists' demand of unlimited freedom. Now we get novels in which society is merely a backdrop to the aloneness of the hero.

Tolerance of social deviation, like sympathy to individual liberty, is more possible in a wealthy and well-developed society than in any other. This may be an important reason that Insight therapies have flourished in the United States in particular. David Potter considers the kind of liberality which would support such schemata to be indigenous in the American character. His theory is developed in

> *People of plenty: Economic abundance and the American character*. Chicago: Univer. Chicago Press, 1954. (Phoenix edition in paper.)

CHAPTER FIVE

REACTION AND ACTION

Action therapists generally seem to prefer the name *behavior therapists* to any other. This terminology is meant in part to convey the idea that they are concerned with observable behavior rather than with the "psyche," thus conferring some scientific stature on their trade. It also refers, however, to the Behavioristic school of psychology founded by John Watson, which has become the prototype of scientific psychology over the past generation. Hans Eysenck, one of the earliest and most eloquent expositors of Action therapy among current scholars, uses the term "behaviour therapy" in explicit opposition to the term "psychotherapy" in

Behaviour therapy and the neuroses. New York: Pergamon, 1960.

Still more recently, the term "behavior modification" has begun to gain some vogue among Actionists. The replacement of "therapy" with "modification" is meant to make unmistakably clear that the behaviors which are subject to these procedures are not illnesses, but miseducations; hence they are subject to modification or re-education but not to therapy or healing.

The erstwhile obscurity of Action therapies is ended with a vengeance by now, and the proliferation of relevant articles on the subject in the technical literature is such that it is already almost impossible for individual students to stay abreast of them. Professionalization of Actionists has not yet reached the guild stage, but is undoubtedly well on its way in that direction. Symptomatic of this development is the recent appearance (1963) of the first technical journal devoted entirely to this subject,

> *Behavior Research and Therapy: An International Multi-Disciplinary Journal.*

Published by Pergamon Press and with Hans Eysenck as its founding Editor-in-Chief, the journal's prepublication advertisements indicated that it would be devoted to things such as ". . . associations between specific behavior disorders and learning theory" and "empirical studies applying the principles of learning theory to clinical problems."

THE GENESIS OF ACTION THERAPY

The bases of Action therapy do not rest merely in theory of learning nor in the notion that neurosis is a learned disorder. These concepts are perfectly applicable to Insight therapy, and have indeed received elegant application to Insight in work like that of Dollard and Miller. It is the attempt to derive specific techniques of therapy from theory of learning that uniquely distinguishes the positions. Bandura takes this position in

> Psychotherapy as a learning process. *Psychological Bulletin,* 1961, 58, 143–159.

> If one seriously subscribes to the view that psychotherapy is a learning process, the methods of treatment should be derived

from our knowledge of learning and motivation. Such an orientation is likely to yield new techniques of treatment which, in many respects, may differ markedly from the procedures currently in use.

Pavlov, whose contributions to therapy would have been equally great even if he had not become interested in it late in life, actually suggested techniques on the basis of his studies of conditioning. For political as well as scientific reasons, his work became the basis of all Soviet psychotherapy. The scope of this work in the Soviet Union is suggested in a collection of papers translated and edited by Ralph B. Winn,

> *Psychotherapy in the Soviet Union.* New York: Philosophical Library, 1961.

Theoretical overdependency on interpretation and extrapolation of Pavlovian principles and technical overreliance on hypnosis and pep talks make the essays in this book seem hopelessly naive by comparison to the work of Action therapists in English-speaking countries. One cannot help but be favorably impressed, however, with the scope of conditions to which Soviet practitioners have applied their techniques, ranging from stuttering to dermatology.

The *psychotherapy of Andrew Salter* is described in his book,

> *Conditioned reflex therapy: The direct approach to the reconstruction of personality.* New York: Capricorn Books-Putnam, 1961 (original edition, 1949).

This work, which in important respects anticipates the therapy of Joseph Wolpe, is an attempt to make straightforward applications of Pavlovian principles of conditioning to the solution of psychological problems. Opening with an attack on psychoanalysis, Salter proceeds to describe conditioning and hypnosis. Like Soviet therapists, and unlike hypnosis researchers, he regards hypnosis as a form of conditioned behavior. Written in a semitechnical, semipopular tone, the work is in some sense a pioneering treatise on social learning theory, and also anticipates Eysenck's version of Pavlov's personality dimensions (CNS inhibition–excitation as the basis of extroversion–introversion). Like all Salter's writing, however, it is arrogant, oversimplified, and poorly organized.

Salter regards inhibition as the root of all personal problems, and sees the process of disinhibition through reconditioning as its solution:

> Unless the overwhelming proportion of humanity is freed from its shackles of inhibition, and made considerably more excitatory, the earth may be doomed to fear, hatred, hypocrisy, misery, war, and destruction. Only through excitation can we achieve mastery of ourselves. Only through excitation can we eliminate the fundamental unhappiness that haunts the entire earth (p. 46).

As is often the case with Action therapists, Salter has also been very concerned with what he considers the undeserved popularity of psychoanalysis. His second major work is a treatise entirely devoted to this subject:

> *The case against psychoanalysis* (rev. ed.). New York: Citadel, 1963 (original edition, 1952).

A very intemperate, vicious book in places, it also builds a rather good case, at least as far as classical psychoanalysis is concerned. On the positive side, he uses important materials, such as Knight's and Sears' respective studies of the results of analytic treatment and of research on analytic concepts (both now dated), also Landis' and Boring's essays on their personal analyses, later gathered into a single volume published by the American Psychological Association.

On the negative side, he not only writes with a pen dipped in gall, but occasionally distorts to the point of untruth (for example, on page 4 he says that analysts believe as a fundamental principle that "all boys want to have sexual intercourse with their mothers," and "murder their fathers") and makes some logical errors no less significant than those of which he accuses psychoanalysts (for example, on page 39: "Psychoanalytic therapy, of course, can only be as sound as the theories that underlie it").

THE ASSAULT ON INSIGHT

The humanistic orientation of Insight theories has been a significant subject of attack by Actionists. The possibility that scientific and humanistic concerns are mutually exclusive is a serious problem for psychologists, whose orientations in one or the other direction, as illustrated by Rogers and Skinner, have tended to be extreme. A brilliant attempt at reconciliation of these positions is represented in the work of Sigmund Koch,

> Psychological science versus the science-humanism antinomy: Intimations of a significant science of man. *American Psychologist*, 1961, 16, 629–639.

Koch points out that

> Ever since its stipulation into existence as an independent science, psychology has been far more concerned with being a science than with courageous and self-determining confrontation of its historically constituted subject matter.

Protesting the evident unconcern of scientific psychology with important human concerns, Koch develops the notion that psychology can contribute to the integration of science and humanities as a "third force."

It is probably true, in this connection, that the extreme scientific pose sometimes struck by Action therapists disposes them to overlook problems of significant human concern, especially when such problems are not neatly assailable by the application of principles of learning. But neither does appropriately humanistic concern justify the abandonment of scientific formulations, when these are possible, nor the anthropomorphization of the mechanics of behavior, however sentimentally satisfying that may be. In opposition to this kind of muddleheaded humanism, some Action therapists have deliberately formulated the processes of psychotherapy in terms of mechanical models. An excellent representation of this position is contained in a very well argued paper by Leonard Krasner,

The therapist as a social reinforcement machine. From *Research in psychotherapy*, Volume II, Proceedings of the 2nd Conference on Research in Psychotherapy, University of North Carolina, Chapel Hill, N.C., 1961.

A similar position is presented in a paper by Paul Bergman,

A general theory of psychotherapy. Paper presented at the annual meeting of the American Psychological Association, 1959.

Bergman's theory integrates some features of Rogers' and of psychoanalytic positions, interpreting both in terms of learning theory, which he feels is valuable largely because of its mechanical, non-human character.

Yet human thought has evolved by giving up anthropomorphic supports. . . . For a theory which does not give counter-conditioning comfort may give optimal manipulation of variables, and a machine model of man may show us the way to human uses for man and machines.

Bergman's position in this connection, like my own, leans heavily on views expressed by Norbert Wierner in

The human use of human beings: Cybernetics and society (ed. 2). Garden City, N.Y.: Doubleday Anchor Books, 1956.

The Economics of Insight Therapy is another significant source of attack, both in terms of relative improvement rates and actual costs to the persons treated. As the Joint Commission on Mental Illness and Health makes clear in its final report to the United States Congress,

Ewalt, J. (Ed.). *Action for mental health.* New York: Basic, 1961,

the insufficiency of our present national facilities for the treatment of even the most seriously mentally ill, let alone the multiple of that number who are troubled by relatively less serious impairments, requires the development of entirely new approaches to the problem of treatment, including the training of nonprofessional persons and those in other professions than the usual ones in therapeutic operations. But as is also made clear there, the problem is not merely the absence of personnel, but also the absence of effective treatment techniques. Among such techniques, psychotherapy has been almost completely dominated by Insight approaches. The effectiveness of these approaches has been equivocal, to say the least. A recent review of the literature is presented by Hans Eysenck in

> The effects of psychotherapy. In H. Eysenck (Ed.), *Handbook of abnormal psychology*. New York: Basic, 1961.

Eysenck calls attention particularly to the evidence which suggests that recovery rates in Insight therapy are no different from spontaneous remission rates among the same population.

The problem of base rate of recovery without treatment is a most critical one, and the failure to consider it in evaluations of therapy will necessarily mislead people into thinking that the techniques are more effective than they are. In effect, one must discount the effect of treatment for that proportion of patients who *might* have recovered as much and as quickly if simply left alone. Thus, if a study demonstrates that 70 percent of patients were favorably affected by treatment, and if it were demonstrated that 60 percent of troubled people from the same population will recover without any treatment, one must conclude that therapy is 10 percent effective rather than 70 percent. The theoretical upper limit on the effectiveness of a therapy is established by the base rate of spontaneous recovery. For that reason, it is quite impossible for any therapy to be 100 percent effective with respect to the general population to which it is applied. And assuming the adequacy of sampling procedures, it would be correct to say, were treatment effective in 60 percent of cases and spontaneous recovery to occur in 70 percent of a matched sample, that therapy was demonstrably harmful. Eysenck's article cites some work which points in this direction too.

A good discussion of this problem is given by Laurance F. Shaffer and E. J. Shoben, Jr. in a section on "Results of Psychotherapy" in

The Psychology of Adjustment (ed. 2). Boston: Houghton Mifflin, 1956.

Many studies have tabulated the percentage of clients who seemed to profit from psychotherapy, the improvement usually being judged by the therapists. In spite of their severe limitations, such data have at least a little value. Studies based on over 8,000 cases have shown with considerable uniformity that about two-thirds of the clients were judged to be cured, much improved, or improved; about one-third made little or no improvement. Two small samples have been evaluated under much better controlled conditions. One group was given analytically oriented psychotherapy based on the teachings of H. S. Sullivan, and was evaluated by other psychiatrists, not by the clients' own therapists. Of 25 clients, 17, or 68 per cent, were regarded as improved and the remaining 8 as unimproved. The conclusion seems well established that psychotherapy, as practiced by adherents of several different schools of theory, is evaluated as successful about two-thirds of the time. The most serious shortcoming of the evaluations is the lack of a comparison group of persons who need psychotherapy but do not receive it. Common observations show that at least some neurotic and maladjusted people overcome their problems without professional help. How many? It is almost impossible to tell. Some figures have been cited which might cause psychotherapy to be regarded very pessimistically. Of psychoneurotic patients admitted to mental hospitals in the United States, 66 per cent are discharged as recovered or improved within one year. An insurance company's study of 500 persons claiming disability for psychoneurosis, as diagnosed by general physicians, found that 72 per cent of them were back at work within two years. These two groups of persons were given some care and treatment, but few if any of them received formal psychotherapy. Critics have suggested that these figures cast doubt on the value of psychotherapy (pp. 545–546).

That therapy is often a luxury of the rich, whether or not its costs are justified by its effects, becomes obvious on consideration of the fact that, among private practitioners at least, a therapist is necessarily dependent upon a very few individuals for his entire livelihood. This notion is more fact than hypothesis, however, as indicated in the results of the official study conducted by the American Psychoanalytical Association among its members. By far the majority of individuals (60 percent) psychoanalyzed by this group had completed college educations and reported incomes very considerably in excess of $10,000 per annum (53 percent).

While private practitioners of psychotherapy do not make better livings than private practitioners of medicine, they make them from so many fewer people that they sometimes feel called upon to justify their high fees in more elegant-seeming terms than the mere claim that they are entitled to good livings. Even Freud was a little guilty of such rationalization, but the most grandiose instance of it I have seen is reported by Roland H. Berg (Medical Editor, *Look Magazine*), as told in

The Reporter (Notes), 1960, Feb. 4, 22, 6.

A Swedish psychoanalyst, Dr. Nils Haak, who has written extensively on the importance of high fees, says the belief that what is cheap is of little value is deeply rooted in the human mind. He argues that by demanding a high fee, the analyst appears to the patient as a forthright individual who dares to be honest about money. This makes the analyst a fine person for the patient to emulate. A high fee, Haak says, also prevents the patient from feeling infantile and becoming dependent upon his analyst. For the neurotic patient who likes to hurt himself, the making of large payments to the analyst, according to the Swedish doctor, is an excellent outlet for neurotic feelings. If the analyst were to allow the patient to pay only a small fee, it might give him a humiliating sense of gratitude that would interfere with his therapy. There is also the attitude of the analyst to consider, according to Dr. Haak. If he charges a low fee, the analyst may begin to doubt his own motives for doing so. He might wonder whether he is in love with his patient, and is trying to cover up by being kind. This sort of thing can seriously interfere with the analyst's ability to help.

POLICIES FOR ACTION

Learning theory has provided the basis for the development of Action therapy. Two works of classic proportions and remark-

able readability are particularly worthwhile for a general acquaintance with this field. Both are largely the work of Ernest R. Hilgard
of Stanford University, who is the most widely known general
expositor of the study of learning in modern psychology.

Hilgard, E. R. *Theories of learning* (ed. 2). New York:
Appleton, 1956.

Hilgard and Marquis' Conditioning and learning (ed. 2).
Revised by Gregory A. Kimble. New York: Appleton, 1961.

Talking in Action therapy is important for its "stimulus
value" but not for its "meaning." The distinction, at least in theory, sharply differentiates the two technical orientations, and it is
important to bear in mind that Action therapists are generally
unconcerned with cognition as a source of behavior control. The
meaning of meaning is, for them, either a moot point or a dubious
construct. Skinner even takes pains "to reject the traditional formulation of verbal behavior in terms of meaning" (p. 10) in

Verbal behavior. New York: Appleton, 1957.

The two major kinds of Action therapy, changing old behavior and shaping new behavior, are still further divisible, as illustrated in the particular schemata of Wolpe, Stampfl, and the
Skinnerians. They are not so different from each other, however,
but that focusing scholarly attention on one such scheme would
necessarily preclude an interest in or recognition of the others.
Indeed, E. R. Guthrie, who is probably the true sire of Action
therapy, seems to have described *all* the major systems more than
twenty-five years ago. He called them methods for "breaking undesirable habits," and expounded them in two books,

The psychology of learning. New York: Harper, 1935.

The psychology of human Conflict. New York: Harper,
1938.

Guthrie's methods include the following.

1. The Incompatible Response Method, which is Wolpe's
reciprocal inhibition, and was earlier described by Mary Cover
Jones as a treatment technique for eliminating children's fears,

and later by Mowrer and Mowrer as a treatment for enuresis (*American Journal of Orthopsychiatry*, 1938, 8, 436–459).

2. The Exhaustion Method, which is Stampfl's implosive therapy, and in which the response is repeatedly aroused till it is exhausted.

3. The Toleration Method, which is identical with Wolpe's systematic desensitization.

4. The Change of Environment method, which involves removal of stimulation, that is, the alteration of the conditions in which the undesirable response occurs. Conceptually, the notion seems to parallel operant treatment methods.

One wonders, under the circumstances, why Guthrie does not receive wider recognition from students of Action therapy for his pioneering contributions. The reason is not apparent, and he certainly deserves more attention. It is true that he inclined towards the use of horse breaking as illustrations of his methods, but such comparisons cause Actionists no distress. On the contrary, Skinnerians in particular, when talking about human conditioning, leap immediately to infrahuman species to illustrate their points. Greenspoon's article in Bachrach's compendium always uses rats as illustrations, and Isaacs, Thomas, and Goldiamond, in the tradition of Skinner, have a fondness for pigeons as examples. Personally, I prefer being compared to a horse, so perhaps the source of illustrations is not a factor.

DISCARDING BAD HABITS:

THE PSYCHOTHERAPY OF JOSEPH WOLPE

The main works of Joseph Wolpe that were used in preparation of the essay about him are:

Reciprocal inhibition as the main basis of psychotherapeutic effects. *A.M.A. Archives of Neurology & Psychiatry*, 1954, 72, 205–226.

The systematic desensitization treatment of neuroses. *Journal of Nervous & Mental Disease*, 1961, 132, 189–203.

Psychotherapy by reciprocal inhibition. Stanford, Calif.:
Stanford Univer. Press, 1958.

Isolation of a conditioning procedure as the crucial psychotherapeutic factor: A case study. *Journal of Nervous &
Mental Disease,* 1962, 134, 316–329.

The experimental foundations of some new psychotherapeutic methods. Chapter 16 in A. J. Bachrach (Ed.), *Experimental foundations of clinical psychology,* New York:
Basic, 1962.

Unless otherwise indicated, quotations are all taken from
his book.

Comparing Wolpe to Freud is not in any sense meant to
indicate that the psychotherapies are similar, but merely that some
critical features of the underlying theories are. The point might
be clarified by putting the sequence backwards, saying that
Freudian theory can be interpreted in a manner which would make
it structurally very similar to Wolpe's. Jules Masserman has, in
fact, done experimental work very much like Wolpe's experiments
on cats, developed similar methods of treatment (for cats only,
not people), and called it

*Behavior and neurosis: An experimental psychoanalytical
approach to psychobiologic principles.* Chicago: Univer.
Chicago Press, 1943.

Mowrer's attack on Wolpe as "thoroughly Freudian" was made in
his discussion of a paper which Wolpe presented at the meetings
of the American Psychological Association in New York in 1961.
The symposium in which they participated was titled: "Secular
Moralist or Behavior Technologist: The Psychotherapist's Dilemma." Wolpe's position was that psychotherapists are essentially
behavior technologists, but must occasionally be willing to assume
the responsibilities of arbiters of morality. He illustrated the point
by describing his successful treatment of a homosexual by attacking the man's religious beliefs.

The statistics of aftermath are far fewer in number than
the legends of symptom return. Since they are also far less dramatic, people often forget that they are far *more* important. Wolpe

has performed a particular service to the discipline by focusing attention on the evidence that has been collected. His article,

The prognosis in unpsychoanalyzed recovery from neurosis. *American Journal of Psychiatry*, 1961, 35–39,

is discussed in the context of his own and other Action therapy systems in his most recent review of the field:

The experimental foundations of some new psychotherapeutic methods. In A. J. Bachrach (Ed.), *Experimental foundations of clinical psychology*. New York: Basic, 1962.

Increasing numbers of clinical reports, meanwhile, testify impressively to the efficacy of behavioral methods of therapy. I have reported (Wolpe, 1958) that nearly 90 percent of 210 neurotic patients were either apparently cured or much improved after a mean of little over thirty sessions. Of forty-five patients followed up over two to seven years, only one relapsed. Eysenck (1960) has assembled more than thirty studies by many authors demonstrating successful elimination of neurotic habits by therapy based on principles of learning. Several further reports have recently appeared (Lazovik and Lang, 1960; Bond and Hutchinson, 1960; Freeman and Kendrick, 1960; Walton, 1961).

The allegation is frequently made that such methods of treating neuroses are only symptomatic and do not "get to the root." This allegation springs from an assumption of the correctness of the psychoanalytic account of the nature of neurosis. Leaving aside the fact that psychoanalytic theory contains logical inconsistencies (Wohlgemuth, 1923; Salter, 1952) and that much of the evidence by which it has been bolstered is inadmissible (Wolpe and Rachman, 1960) the practical implication of the question is whether recoveries obtained by conditioning methods endure and are free from repercussions to the patient. The answer, based on the evidence so far obtained, would seem to be in the affirmative. Psychoanalytic theory postulates that, in general, recoveries from neurosis without psychoanalysis are unreliable; but in a survey of follow-up studies of such cases (Wolpe, 1961a) only four relapses were found among 249 patients. This finding accords well with conditioning theory, which holds that the elimination of a neurotic habit is permanent unless there is reinstatement by specific new conditioning.

The statistics of outcome most recently obtained by the American Psychoanalytic Association may not have been officially suppressed, depending on how one chooses to define the term, but they certainly have not been published, in the usual meaning of that term. I tried to get a copy of the report for almost two years before succeeding, and the Association itself responded to my request merely by informing me that the person who had referred me to them was not a member. An undefensive member eventually did give me a copy of the summary issued to the membership under the chairmanship of Harry I. Weinstock:

> Summary and final report of the central factgathering committee of the American Psychoanalytic Association (mimeo). January 1958.

After all the trouble, and considering the dark hints of suppression (largely justified by the introduction to the report itself, which invites members to be circumspect about divulging its contents), the biggest mystery is why the report was not routinely published in a technical journal in the first place. Its authors protest that the study was poorly designed and executed, both of which claims are true, but it is no worse than most such studies, and in one respect a good deal better: it contains statistics of dropout rates. As for the content, the outcome is no less favorable to psychoanalysis than the pioneering report which Robert P. Knight freely published more than twenty years ago,

> Evaluation of the results of psychoanalytic therapy. American Journal of Psychiatry, 1941, 98, 434–446.

The upshot is that the chief psychoanalytic guild has acted somewhat scandalously, inviting appropriate contempt from the scientific community, for no good reason.

Wolpe's act of good faith in exposing his work is being increasingly rewarded by the favorable results that are reported by others using his methods. One typical such report is that of P. M. Bentler,

An infant's phobia treated with reciprocal inhibition therapy. *Journal of Child Psychology & Psychiatry*, 1962, 3, 185–189.

Some very well done research comparing Wolpe's to other methods is also appearing, such as A. R. Lazarus' well-designed comparsion of desensitization to interpretive therapy of phobias,

> Group therapy of phobic disorders by systematic desensitization. *Journal of Abnormal & Social Psychology*, 1961, 63, 504–510.

Lazarus' splendidly balanced discussion of his results states:

> It should be mentioned that the interpretive groups apparently enabled many of the patients to achieve a constructive modification of their self-evaluation, often clarified their evaluation of others, and enhanced their potentialities of interpersonal integration. These gains, however, appeared to have little bearing on their phobic symptoms, which usually persisted until desensitization procedures were administered.
>   . . . The treatment of phobias by interpretive methods, however, is well known to be difficult. Curran and Partridge (1955), for instance, state that "phobic symptoms are notoriously resistant to treatment, and their complete removal is rarely achieved." Similar views are expressed by Maslow and Mittelmann (1951), Henderson and Gillespie (1955), and Mayer-Gross, Slater, and Roth (1955). By contrast, phobias respond to desensitization exceedingly well (Eysenck, 1960: Lazarus and Rachman, 1957; Wolpe, 1958).
>   . . . The point may legitimately be raised as to whether desensitization achieves any result other than the elimination of the phobic symptom.
>   . . . The value of desensitization is limited to those conditions wherein appropriate hierarchies can be constructed and where specific rather than pervasive anxiety is present. In other words, it is only where reasonably well-defined stimulus configurations can be identified that desensitization techniques should be applied. For example, patients whose interpersonal relationships are clouded by specific fears of rejection, hyper-

sensitivity to criticism, clearcut areas of self-consciousness, or similar specific anxiety evoking stimuli often derive benefit from desensitization procedures. By contrast, desensitization cannot readily be applied in such cases as character neuroses, hysterical disorders, and chronic inadequacy. A further prerequisite for the effective application of desensitization is the ability to conjure up reasonably vivid visual images which elicit emotional reactions comparable to the feelings evoked in a real situation.

TEACHING FEARLESS BEHAVIOR: THE IMPLOSIVE THERAPY OF THOMAS G. STAMPFL

As indicated, none of Stampfl's work has been published. In addition to his two mimeographed papers,

Avoidance conditioning reconsidered: An extension of Mowrerian theory;

Implosive therapy: A learning theory derived psychodynamic therapeutic technique;

I have received written communications from time to time from Stampfl and from some of his students reporting recent developments with his techniques. One of his students, Robert Hogan, reports nearing completion of a formal research that evaluates the effects of implosive therapy in terms of changes in psychological test scores and hospital release rates. As of his communication (June 1963), the results appeared favorable. This study will presumably be published in due course.

The work of Mowrer on which Stampfl particularly relied for the development of his position is contained in the first of Mowrer's two recent major works on learning,

Learning theory and behavior. New York: Wiley, 1960;

Learning theory and the symbolic processes. New York: Wiley, 1960.

SHAPING NEW BEHAVIOR: THE OPERANT
TECHNIQUES OF B. F. SKINNER

Skinner has been a prolific writer and researcher for more than twenty-five years, and there are few areas of psychology that have not been affected by his penetrating analyses of behavior. In addition to the many honors bestowed on him and the wide recognition his work has gained, he has had the most unusual, if indirect, tribute, paid to him of the creation of a journal and society virtually completely devoted to "Skinnerian" research in every branch of psychology:

> *Journal for the Experimental Analysis of Behavior* (Ann Arbor, Michigan: Society for the Experimental Analysis of Behavior).

The works of Skinner used in preparation of this essay include

> *The behavior of organisms: An experimental analysis.* New York: Appleton, 1938;
>
> *Walden Two.* New York: Macmillan, 1948;
>
> *Science and human behavior.* New York: Macmillan, 1953;
>
> *Verbal behavior.* New York: Appleton, 1957;
>
> Behaviorism at fifty. *Science,* 1963, *140,* 951–958.

The basis of behavior shaping in practice is the principle of positive reinforcement, which is generally applied by what Skinnerians call the "method of successive approximation." As Isaacs, Thomas, and Goldiamond (1960) describe it in

> Application of operant conditioning to reinstate verbal behavior in psychotics. *Journal of Speech and Hearing Disorders,* 1960, *25,* 8–12,

> This method finds use where E desires to produce responses which are not present in the current repertoire of the organism

and which are considerably removed from those which are available. The E then attempts to "shape" the available behaviors into the desired form, capitalizing upon both the variability and regularity of successive behaviors. The shaping process involves the reinforcement of those parts of a selected response which are successively in the desired direction and the nonreinforcement of those which are not.

Total institutions offer maximum potential for operant psychotherapy. Erving Goffman develops the concept of total institutions in particular connection with mental hospitals in

Asylums. New York: Anchor Doubleday, 1961.

The work of Teodoro Ayllon and Jack Michael (p. 113) is reported in

The psychiatric nurse as a behavioral engineer. *Journal for the Experimental Analysis of Behavior*, 1959, 2, 323–334.

The use of chewing gum as a reinforcement for speech with psychotic patients is reported by W. Isaacs, J. Thomas, and I. Goldiamond, in

Application of operant conditioning to reinstate verbal behavior in psychotics (*op. cit.*).

The office practice of operant therapy probably has its greatest potential through the medium of counseling parents and teachers to assume appropriate roles as reinforcing agents—that is, therapists. The potential value of this notion is discussed at length by Albert Bandura in

Punishment revisited. *Journal of Consulting Psychology*, 1962, 26, 298–301.

Operant group psychotherapy (p. 114) might be a suitable title for the technique that Willard Mainord has developed for the hospital treatment of people with a considerable variety of problems. His methods are described in

A therapy for crazy—not sick—people (mimeo). Originally published as "A therapy in the *Research Bulletin* of the Mental Health Research Institute, Fort Steilacoom, Washington, 1962.

As implied by its title, Mainord's article, in addition to describing his procedures, attacks the conventional psychiatric notion that psychological disorder is disease. This gave rise to some hysteria among the state's psychiatric bureaucrats, who hastily ordered that Mainord's experimental treatment program be discontinued, issued a frantic bulletin to employees reassuring them that the mentally disturbed were indeed ill, and made some abortive and half-hearted efforts to suppress the article. Since it had been published in the official journal of the very bureau that sought to suppress it, some deserved embarrassment resulted to the bureau.

Skinner's disdain for theory and concern with rigorous analysis are nowhere more succinctly or clearly described than in The Behavior of Organisms (op. cit.) where he says of his system:

> It is positivistic. It confines itself to description rather than explanation. Its concepts are defined in terms of immediate observations and are not given local or physiological properties. A reflex is not an arc, a drive is not the state of a center . . . Terms of this sort are used merely to bring together groups of observations, . . . They are not hypotheses, in the sense of things to be proved or disproved, but convenient representations of things already known. As to hypotheses, the system does not require them—at least in the usual sense (p. 44).

This position is even more concretely demonstrated in his discussion of "The nature of drive," the near-sacred theoretical construct of Freud and Hull:

> The preceding formulation of drive may be summarized as follows. In measuring the strength of drive we are in reality only measuring strength of behavior. A complete account of the latter is to be obtained from an examination of the operations that are found to affect it. The "drive" is a hypothetical state interpolated between operation and behavior and is not actually required in a descriptive system (p. 368).

The social character of significant functions (p. 116) is as cherished an article of faith among Skinnerians, I believe, as is the method of "functional analysis" their sole permissible means of trying to understand anything. The social orientation, on the other hand, is more implied than advocated and is hardly visible through the antiseptic language of the seemingly technical discussion Skinnerians often have of the mechanics of social control. An interesting combination of sociality and functional analysis is contained in the distinguished discussion of childhood schizophrenia by C. B. Ferster,

> Positive reinforcement and behavioral deficits of autistic children. *Child Development*, 1961, 32, 437–456.

Ferster contends that the major difference between autistic and normal children lies

> . . . in the relative frequencies of the various kinds of performances. The major performance deficits of the autistic child are in the degree of social control: The kinds of performances which have their major effects through the mediation of other individuals (p. 439).

It is not particularly surprising that Skinnerians have been more concerned with the ethics of social control than have any other rigorously scientific psychologists. The reason for this is that one need not be very worried about the ethics of control unless he is pretty confident of having mastered the mechanics of it. Skinnerians show no lack of confidence in this connection. Boring describes this very well in

> When is human behavior predetermined? *Scientific Monthly*, April 1957, 189–196.

> Skinner claims to have better and surer methods for the design of behavior than have been available heretofore. You should see his pigeons, taught to earn their livings by the rewarding of their successes (not by punishment of their failures). So it is that he envisages a happy society, in which success and reward are the rule, and frustration has been reduced or eliminated by good social design. No one, of course, ever designs frustration into a machine so that it tries to make the same wheel go in opposite directions at the same moment.

SCIENCE AND ACTION THERAPY

That the efficacy of a system of therapeutics is no guarantee of the truth of its explanations is a stubborn principle which must be faced courageously before many tests of high quality can be designed. There is no reason, on the face of it, to think that Action therapists will have much more of this kind of courage than have most Insight therapists, especially when they have made profound personal and professional commitments to a particular body of principles and techniques. Carl Rogers is one of the few therapists who seems honestly willing to challenge the value of the system he himself created, and is the only therapist of my knowledge who is capable, in describing an extensive study of client-centered therapy of schizophrenics, of saying,

> For the first time in any of the research I've done on psychotherapy, we have rather clear evidence that we actually harm some people by psychotherapy (Colloquium delivered at Stanford University, January 30, 1963).

MORALS AND ACTION THERAPY

Cognitive dissonance is a term coined by Leon Festinger to describe the discomfort which is engendered by conflicting aspects of one's subjective experience. His major work on this subject,

A *theory of cognitive dissonance*. New York: Harper, 1957,

has been one of the most important stimuli to research and theory in social psychology and the study of personality ever since it appeared six years ago.

THE LIMITATIONS OF ACTION

The absence of circumscribed symptoms is a potential source of dismay to the Action therapist, if for no other reason, because it makes it very difficult for him to know where to sink in his therapeutic teeth. If he has many significant social concerns, the problem is especially great, for it is precisely those individuals whose deviance is from the norms of society rather than of personal comfort who constitute a major and chronic drain on the resources of the society and are least obviously amenable to the kinds of behavior modification methods that Actionists now have available. Not surprisingly, socially deviant conditions are less understood than any others, though they are more written about. Delinquency, crime, prostitution, alcoholism, and the like are generally as much beyond the *expertise* of the social scientist as of the clinical practitioner, and have been at least as resistant to intellectual penetration as to amelioration. Major studies of juvenile delinquency have been conducted for many years without many useful results; the same is true of alcoholism. Few similar studies have been conducted of sexual deviation, though an effective groundwork has been laid by the normative studies of Kinsey and others. The first major study of prostitution employing rigorous research procedures is currently in progress under the direction of James H. Bryan of the University of California at Los Angeles. No such studies have been conducted of criminal groups in vivo.

White's novel, referred to on page 123, is

White, T. H. *The once and future king*. New York: Putnam, 1958.

CONCLUSION

The *linear extension of conditioning and reinforcement* principles may not suffice to account for all those aspects of human behavior which are of relevance for psychotherapy, but Action therapists have all been rather consistent in discounting the relevance of other variables and principles than are involved in learning. Boring's discussion of the development of Lashley's thinking offers a historical context for the occurrence of this phenomenon in

Beach, F., *et al.* (Eds.) *The neuropsychology of Lashley: Selected papers of K. S. Lashley*. New York: McGraw-Hill, 1960.

Lashley was the pioneer neurophysiologist whose work, as Boring puts it, challenged

. . . nineteenth-century mechanism. Psychology had been caught in the toils of associationistic connectionism. The conception that learning occurs by the association of ideas . . . was paralleled by the neuron theory, which pictures the brain as a mass of neurons connected by synapses. This similarity of a synapse to an association proved irresistible, but Lashley's experiments denied such simple connectionism and brought him over toward the camp of the gestalt psychologists.

In 1929 Lashley delivered the Presidential Address of the American Psychological Association before the Ninth International Congress of Psychology at New Haven, Connecticut (13). It was called "Basic Neural Mechanisms in Behavior," and in it Lashley cited research and struck out against reflex theory. (Introduction, xiii)

Part of Lashley's speech will do for a critique of the simplistic connectionism which underlies Action therapy:

> The frantic search for sources of motivation and of emotion in visceral activity, though initiated by introspective analysis, has been supported by the faith that the nervous system is only a conductor having no sources of energy within itself. Our preoccupation with analysis of learning by trial and error, the denial of association by similarity, the belief that transfer of training can occur only through the training of common synapses— these are a result of the belief that learning is simply a linking together of elementary reflexes. The doctrine that the intelligent solution of problems results only through random activity and selection, and that intelligence itself is an algebraic sum of multitudinous capacities, is largely a deduction from the reflex theory. (p. 207)
>
> . . . The value of theories in science today depends chiefly upon their adequacy as a classification of unsolved problems, or rather as a grouping of phenomena which present similar problems. Behaviorism has offered one such classification, emphasizing the similarity of psychological and biological problems. Gestalt psychology has stressed a different aspect and reached a different grouping: purposive psychology still another. The facts of cerebral physiology are so varied, so diverse, as to suggest that for some of them each theory is true, for all of them every theory is false (p. 208).[2]

[2] Reprinted by permission of McGraw-Hill Book Company, Inc.

The practice of psychotherapy is so prolific in America, especially in urban and educated circles, that the public tends to be unaware of the extent to which it lacks scientific validation. This fact is a source of great concern within the profession, however. As Lowell Kelly puts it, in

Clinical psychology: The postwar decade. In *Current trends in psychological theory*. Pittsburgh: Univer. Pittsburgh Press, 1961 (pp. 31–49):

In a word, the *practice* of clinical psychology is of necessity still largely an art because the *science* of psychology has not yet provided the basic knowledge and techniques which permit clinical psychology (or psychiatry) to be practiced as an applied science.

THE LIMITS OF THE SYSTEMS

The fatal flaw of Insight therapy was the notion that consciousness somehow inevitably moved behavior. The discovery that this is not the case is difficult to come by, especially since virtually all practicing psychotherapists at this time have been schooled in the doctrine of the efficacy of insight. Nicholas Hobbs discusses this problem in his Presidential Address to the Division of Clinical Psychology of the American Psychological Association,

> Sources of gain in psychotherapy. *American Psychologist,* 1962, 17, 741–747.

> The promotion of insight is thus the tactic most heavily relied upon by most therapists who write about their work. Other strategies . . . are valued to the extent that they lay the groundwork for the achievement of insight . . . Furthermore, the achievement of insight by a client is a welcomed signal to the therapist that his efforts are paying off, and that his client, armed with new understanding, will gain a new measure of control over his life. All of this is a part of the folklore, both amateur and professional, of helping people by talking to them. But I have come seriously to doubt the presumed relationship between the achievement of insight and the achievement of more effective functioning.
>
> Once jarred from the point of usual perspective on this issue, I began to see a number of arguments for an alternate explanation, namely, that insight may have nothing to do with behavior change at all, or is, at best, an event that may or may not occur as a result of more fundamental personality reorganizations.

The flaw of the Action therapies, on the other hand, is that they have limited their attempts to understand behavior to the study of learning and have tried to extrapolate too neatly from the peckings of pigeons to the cognitions of men. They have been disinclined to examine the uses of consciousness in behavior, perhaps in reaction to the exaggerated valuations that Insight therapists have placed upon it. Ironically, biological scientists are often less reluctant to be involved in these problems than are psychologists. Neurophysiologists are particularly concerned, of course, with the sources of consciousness and one of them, Wilder Penfield, has recently turned up some exciting information about the recording of its contents. In the conclusion to a chapter on "The recording of consciousness and the function of the interpretive cortex," he writes in

Speech and brain mechanisms. Princeton, N.J.: Princeton Univer. Press, 1959.

Consciousness, "forever flowing" past us, makes no record of itself, and yet the recording of its counterpart within the brain is astonishingly complete . . . recorded in temporal succession between the experience which went before and that which follows.

The thread of time remains with us in the form of a succession of "abiding" facilitations. This thread travels through ganglion cells and synaptic junctions. It runs through the waking hours of each man, from childhood to the grave. On the thread of time are strung, like pearls in unending succession, the "meaningful" patterns that can still recall the vanished content of a former awareness.

No man can voluntarily reactivate the record. Perhaps, if he could, he might become hopelessly confused. Man's voluntary recollection must be achieved through other mechanisms. And yet the recorded patterns are useful to him, even after the passage of many years. They can still be appropriately selected by some scanning process and activated with amazing promptness for the purpose of comparative interpretation. It is, it seems to me, in this mechanism of recall and comparison and interpretation that the interpretive cortex of the temporal lobes plays its specialized role (pp. 54–55).

A COGNITIVE THEORY OF ACTION THERAPY

The essence of the position discussed in this section is that the connections between stimuli and responses are attenuated, altered, or even obviated by mediational processes, the most important of which in people may be thinking. Professor Albert Bandura pointed out to me that suppression may actually be a mediating response for extinction. Since response suppression is often a function of cognition in humans, this idea offers a clue for integrating thought processes into the stimulus–response theoretical scheme which guides Action therapies.

Existing positions do not incorporate it however. Stampfl never discusses the concept of mediation. Wolpe, on the other hand, may be dealing entirely with mediating responses; his antagonistic responses, in other words, may function primarily to suppress anxiety responses, but he never discusses extinction.

Jerome Bruner discusses the influence of cognition on behavior in

> On knowing: Essays for the left hand. Cambridge, Mass.:
> Belknap Press of Harvard Univer. Press, 1962.

> . . . this development has the effect of freeing learning from immediate stimulus control. When learning leads only to pellets of this or that in the short run rather than to mastery in the long run, the behavior can be readily "shaped" by extrinsic rewards. But when behavior becomes more extended and competence-oriented, it comes under the control of more complex cognitive structures and operates more from the inside out.

Bruner goes on to describe how Pavlov's early description of learning based it entirely on stimulus control by means of contiguity conditioning. Pavlov recognized, however, that this process would not account for higher order learning, so he postulated the existence of a "second-order signal system."

> It is interesting too that the final rejection of the universality of the doctrine of reinforcement in direct conditioning came from some of Pavlov's own students.
>
> A strange irony, then, that Russian psychology, which gave us the notion of the conditioned response and the assumption that higher order activities are built up out of colligations of such primitive units, has rejected this notion while much of American psychology of learning until quite recently has stayed within the early Pavlovian fold—as, for example, a 1959 article by Spence in the Harvard Educational Review, reiterating the

primacy of conditioning and the derivative nature of complex learning. It is even more noteworthy that Russian pedagogic theory has become deeply influenced by this new trend and is now placing much stress upon the importance of building up a more active symbolical approach to problem solving among children (pp. 90–92).

The Need for Meaningful Action

The context in which action becomes most meaningful is a social one. This has been recognized by many psychologists, but few have incorporated it into therapeutic systems. The best-known work on this subject at present is probably Erich Fromm's

The sane society. New York: Holt, 1955.

But this work, like Skinner's *Walden Two*, attacks the problem by reconstructing the entire social order rather than trying to find a way to help people achieve some decently balanced relationship with any existing one.

Alexander and French on the other hand, believe that the problem of relationship between individual and society is a function of the complexity of society rather than its inequities:

> Contemporary man now faces the problem of living together harmoniously in a highly differentiated civilization. The majority of mental disturbances are failures of adjustment by the individual to social living—an adjustment which is becoming more and more difficult in this era of transition wherein social values and standards are so rapidly changing.

Psycho-analytic therapy. New York: Ronald, 1946.

Some empirical evidence in support of the foregoing is contained in the research of Edward Zigler and Leslie Phillips on the relationship of social competence to psychiatric disorder. Their general hypothesis is that social competence, defined by variables such as age, intelligence, education, occupation, employment history, and marital status (together approximating "personal and social maturity"), predicts the incidence, form, and prognosis of mental disorders. With some reservation, the data bear this out, as reported in

Social competence and outcome in psychiatric disorder. *Journal of Abnormal & Social Psychology*, 1961, 63, 264–271.

Social competence and the process-reactive distinction in psychopathology. *Journal of Abnormal & Social Psychology*, 1962, 65, 215–222.

Rotter (1963) points out, in

Analysis of trends in clinical psychology. In S. Koch (Ed.), *Psychology: A study of a science.* Vol. 5. New York: McGraw-Hill, 1963.

that, among psychological theorists who devoted primary attention to the original development of learned behavior in a social context, Mowrer, Dollard, and Miller all served pioneering functions. So did Rotter himself, but as he says,

> . . . Rotter described a social-learning theory and its implications for psychotherapy, but formulated no extensive descriptions of specific psychotherapeutic techniques.

Social learning theory, as it is now formally known, is receiving increased attention from personality and developmental psychologists. It is discussed at some length in

London, P., and Rosenhan, D. Personality dynamics. In Paul Farnsworth (Ed.) *Annual review of psychology*, Vol. 15. Palo Alto, Calif.: Annual Reviews, 1964,

and a very important work discussing the development of socialization and offering considerable experimental evidence in favor of its position has recently been written by Albert Bandura and Richard Walters:

Social learning and personality development. New York: Holt, 1963.

The major work of George Kelly (p. 134), which is regrettably not discussed, is

The psychology of personal constructs. Volume I: *A theory of personality.* Volume II. *Clinical diagnosis and psychotherapy.* New York: Norton, 1955.

THE PRICE OF PERSONAL INTEGRITY:
AN INTERPRETATION OF O. H. MOWRER

As in the case of Skinner, Mowrer has been a prolific theoretician and empirical scientist whose work has significantly and influentially affected much of psychology for almost a generation. His specific writings which were used in preparation of this essay are:

Learning theory and personality dynamics. New York: Ronald, 1950.

The crisis in psychiatry and religion. Princeton, N.J.: Van Nostrand, 1961.

The new group therapy. (In preparation.)

Morality and mental health. (In preparation.)

Payment or repayment? The problem of private practice. *American Psychologist,* 1963, 18, 577–580.

The Guilt Theory of Neurosis

"Significant others" is a term which Mowrer borrows from George Herbert Mead, along with the general position which Mead developed that the self is a product of and representation of social processes. As Mead writes in

Language and the development of the self. In C. W. Morris (Ed.), *Mind, self, and society.* Chicago: Univ. Chicago Press, 1934.

I have . . . emphasized what I have called the structures upon which the self is constructed, the framework of the self, as it were. Of course, we are not only what is common to all; each one of the selves is different from everyone else; but there has to be such a common structure as I have sketched in order that we may be members of a community at all. We cannot be ourselves unless we are also members in whom there is a community of attitudes which control the attitudes of all. We cannot have rights unless we have common attitudes. That which we have acquired as self-conscious persons makes us such members of society and gives us selves.

Mowrer's position is sometimes mistakenly understood as a defense of the social status quo. This is not the case, any more than it is the case with G. H. Mead, whose position, substantially the sire of Mowrer's own, incorporates a quite explicit statement of the relationship between individual and society, in

> The self, the generalized other, and the individual. In *Mind, self, and society* (*op. cit.*)

> The fact that all selves are constituted by or in terms of the social process, and are individual reflections of it—or rather of this organized behavior pattern which it exhibits, and which they prehend in their respective structures—is not in the least incompatible with, or destructive of, the fact that every individual self has its own peculiar individuality, its own unique pattern; because each individual self within that process, while it reflects in its organized structure the behavior pattern of that process as a whole, does so from its own particular and unique standpoint within that process . . . In other words, the organized structure of every individual self . . . reflects, and is constituted by, the organized relational pattern of that process as a whole; but each . . . reflects this relational pattern from its own unique standpoint; so that the common social origin . . . does not preclude wide individual difference and variations among them, or contradict the peculiar and more or less distinctive individuality which each of them in fact possesses."

Psychopaths and some other disordered groups are, by definition, outside the scope of Mowrer's theory because they have not been sufficiently well socialized for the experience of guilt to exercise a determining influence over their behavior. Hervey Cleckley describes adult psychopaths very tellingly in

> The mask of sanity: An attempt to clarify some issues about the so-called psychopathic personality. St. Louis, Mo.: Mosby, 1955.

The study of severe personality disturbances originating in infancy has been pioneered by Margaret Ribble and Rene A. Spitz. Some of Ribble's work on this subject is reported in

> Disorganizing factors of infant personality. American Journal of Psychiatry, 1941, 98, 459;
>
> Infantile experience in relation to personality development. In J. McV. Hunt (Ed.), Personality and the behavior disorders, Vol. II. New York: Ronald, 1944.

Spitz' work in this area includes

> Hospitalism: An inquiry into the genesis of psychiatric conditions in early childhood. In Psychoanalytic study of the child. Vol. I. New York: International Universities, 1945;
>
> Anaclitic depression. In Psychoanalytic study of the child. Vol. II. New York: International Universities, 1946.

The dubious significance of repression is suggested by some of the research cited earlier on the general subject of awareness. More specifically relevant work in this area is that of

> Zeller, A. F. An experimental analogue of repression: I. Historical summary. Psychological Bulletin, 1950, 47 (93 references). II. The effect of individual failure and success on memory measured by relearning. Journal of Experimental Psychology, 1950b, 40.
>
> Eriksen, C. W., and Kuethe, J. L. Avoidance conditioning of verbal behavior without awareness: A paradigm of repression. Journal of Abnormal & Social Psychology, 1956, 53.

In all these and others, it is clear enough that experiments can be designed to meet the requirements for the Freudian analogue of repression; there plainly is such a phenomenon. But none of the studies cited give any particular evidence of its centrality in personality or in pathology. The same conclusion seems warranted in Ruth C. Wylie's more recent review:

> *The self concept.* Lincoln, Neb.: Univer. Nebraska Press, 1961.

> Even if these proposed studies warrant the conclusion that S's behavior is a function of "insight," they still would not warrant the dynamic interpretation which investigators interested in insight studies wish to assign. That is, further converging operations would be necessary before one could say that the predictive descrepancy between S's self-report and the objective index involves repression or active avoidance of perception on S's part (p. 306).

The Insight–Action dichotomy was only implicit in Mowrer's earlier writings on guilt and neurosis, but it has become more explicit in his most recent publications, evidently justifying the interpretation of his work which is presented here:

> We psychologists and psychiatrists have been putting great emphasis upon the patient's emotions, his *feelings,* rather than his actions. . . . so it is not surprising that we are often not very helpful to him. Now we are coming to see that the way to *feel better* is to *be better,* in the ethical and interpersonal sense of the term. Thus, *behavior therapy* is the method of choice. But this is very different from the "behavioristic," or "conditioning," approach of Wolpe and others, who assume that all that is wrong with neurotics is that they have some unrealistic fears which need to be extinguished, or counter-conditioned. . . . the neurotic's fears ("anxieties," "feelings,") are eminently realistic and justified, i.e. his "insecurity" stems from *real guilt,* which can be satisfactorily resolved only by radical openness and restitution. Anything less than this will be only temporarily effective, if not, in the long run, positively harmful.

> Payment or repayment? The problem of private practice. *American Psychologist, op. cit.*

Professional people nowadays are very reluctant to see themselves as having significant kinship with the guilds of the past because they are more sensitive to the implications of blatant self-interest of which their hardier and more brutal forebears were so proud. Both the guild structure and its implications are pretty obvious nevertheless. Edward T. Chase discusses the guild phenomenon in American medicine in

> The politics of medicine. From *The crisis in American medicine*, originally a special supplement to *Harper's Magazine*, October 1960, *221*, 125–131.

> *The Mighty Guilds* . . . Hippocrates devised his oath to regulate the admission of new physicians into guilds, which the ruling families tightly controlled. These guilds of antiquity

looked after the professional and economic interests of medicine. This remains the prime purpose of their successors, the medical societies. One of their chief concerns, as with business trade associations, is to help the membership make money, substantial money.

The modern guilds are run by the top practitioners—in income and prestige—in each community. Like their Greek forebears they have seen to it that there are not too many doctors and that those who are admitted to the fraternity abide by the rules. In theory, this is not a sinister function—it is fitting and necessary that those of highest competence set and maintain professional standards. But in practice the system controls a good deal more than medical excellence (pp. 126–127).

Chase also indicates that an even more extensive analysis is provided by E. G. Jaco in

Patients, physicians, and illness. New York: Free Press, 1958.

PSYCHOTHERAPY AS A SERVICE GUILD

The psychotherapy guilds have been split among several professions, but this has had little effect on their guild character, and has been reflected chiefly in internecine warfare over control of a largely economic pie. A very considerable number of articles and essays have been written on this subject. The most cogent one that I have seen by a psychiatrist is by Thomas S. Szasz,

Psychiatry, psychotherapy, and psychology. A.M.A. Archives of General Psychiatry, 1959, 1, 455–463.

Szasz dissents from the common psychiatric position, which simply wishes to restrict control of psychotherapeutic practice entirely to physicians:

Let us . . . regard the official psychiatric position as a law enacting prohibition—in this instance, prohibiting psychologists (and others) from the nonmedical use of psychotherapy (i.e. from using psychotherapy independently of physicians).

If we regard this as a majority opinion, enacting a social law
. . . it will be useful to consider contrary opinions. Such opinions—at least from psychiatrists—have been curiously lacking.

I do not wish to dignify an inevitably somewhat sordid conflict with an excess of discussion of it, so will merely cite a few
more articles by both psychiatrists and psychologists of good will
and intelligence. The following are all easily available through the
American Psychologist, where they originally appeared, or through
Braun's anthology:

> *Clinical psychology in transition*. Cleveland: Howard Allen,
> 1961:
> Ausubel, D. P. Relationships between psychology and psy-
> chiatry: The hidden issues. *American Psychologist*, 1956,
> 11, 99–104;
>
> Kelly, G. A. Issues: Hidden or mislaid. *American Psychol-
> ogist*, 1956, 11, 112–113;
>
> Handler, J. S., and Kelly, G. Joint reports on relations be-
> tween psychology and psychiatry. *American Psychologist*,
> 1960, 15, 198–200.

The *disease model of disorder* has inevitably served to sustain the medical claim to jurisdiction over it, but there is no concept within psychiatry that is currently so subject to concentrated,
acerb, and accurate attack. The most articulate spokesman of this
attack is undoubtedly Thomas Szasz, himself a psychiatrist, whose
original article in the *American Psychologist* was shortly expanded
to a full-length work,

> *The myth of mental illness: Foundations of a theory of
> personal conduct*. New York: Hoeber, 1961.

It is customary to define psychiatry as a medical specialty concerned with the study, diagnosis, and treatment of mental illnesses. This is a worthless and misleading definition. Mental
illness is a myth.

Although powerful institutional pressures lend massive
weight to the tradition of keeping psychiatric problems within

the conceptual fold of medicine, the scientific challenge seems clear. The task is to redefine the problem of mental illness so that it may be encompassed under the general category of the science of man.

. . . the omission from psychiatric theories of moral issues and normative standards, as explicitly stated goals and rules of conduct, has divorced psychiatry from precisely that reality which it has tried to describe and explain. I have endeavored to correct this defect by means of a game theory of human living, which enables us to combine ethical, political, religious, and social considerations with the more traditional concerns of medicine and psychiatry.

Another approach to the scientific understanding of the development of disorder is implicit in the social learning theory point of view, as characterized by Bandura and Walters:

Social learning and personality development. New York: Holt, 1963.

It is similarly attacked by Edward Sulzer in

Research frontier: Reinforcement and the therapeutic contract. *Journal of Counseling Psychology*, 1962, 9, 271–276.

and it has already even been attacked in undergraduate textbooks, as in Jesse Gordon's

Personality and behavior. New York: Macmillan, 1963.

The day is apparently nearing when it will be as necessary for a psychology book to reserve a paragraph for specifying that mental illness is not disease as it once was for a psychoanalytic essay to open with an obeisance to Freud. Meanwhile, an occasional good word is still said for the disease model with the reservation that "disease" is not limited to the notion of invasion of foreign agents. So Alexander Leighton, in

My name is legion: Foundations for a theory of man in relation to culture. New York: Basic, 1959,

presents a sociocultural approach to disorder which nevertheless speaks of the disease characteristics of it. His comparison of psychiatric disorder is more with something like hyperthyroidism than like tuberculosis, however:

> . . . it is an illness in that it comprises malfunction, unpleasant affect, and is beyond the reach of voluntary control, and also . . . "the cause" must be sought in multiple factors which may be conceived as predisposing and precipitating, and which stretch over the whole life-arc, including anticipations of the future (p. 44).

The issue, of course, is one of fact rather than terminology. The term *disease* probably does tend to be misleading, but as long as it is not used to reinforce demonological explanations of disorder or to sustain the hopeless quest for physiological "magic bullets" in situations which require educational ones, perhaps its use may still be countenanced.

THE MANIPULATION OF BEHAVIOR

A *comprehensive psychotherapy* must function, among other things, to tell people some purposes that lend meaning to their lives and some means for pursuing those purposes. The idea that such telling is literally possible is explored by Ernest Becker, in

Birth and death of meaning. New York: Free Press, 1962.

By "choices" I mean, obviously, other verbal formulas. The therapist educates the patient to new performance vocabularies to replace the constrictive old vocabularies, learned in childhood—but which no longer fit complex, contemporary situations to which the patient strives to adapt. The patient must come to dissociate his feeling of self-value from the old vocabularies learned from the parents. When he learns new words with which to dress his action, he acquires new motives for that action. For a symbolic animal motives are words. Words facilitate action; words dress action in meaning; words convey an image of the self. The individual discovers himself in words. Our whole discussion in this chapter is based on the idea of the primary derivation of meaning from words alone (Note 6, p. 186).

THE SECULAR PRIESTHOOD

Irresponsibility from unconsciousness was a conclusion that seemed entirely justified by the assumption of the compelling power of Unconsciousness, while the equally compelling subjective experience of freedom came to be regarded as epiphenomenal. Allan Wheelis comments tellingly on this, in

To be a god. *Commentary*, 1963, 36, 125–134.

No one could have been more explicit or passionate than Freud in insisting that every wisp and shred of psychic occurrence is rigidly determined . . . Yet it was Freud who found it necessary to say that the object of analysis is "to give the patient's ego *freedom* [his italics] to choose one way or the other." We, as psychoanalysts, expose to a patient why he *has* to be the way he is, then expect him to use this insight to become different from the way we have proved to him that he can't help being.

NEW THEORIES OF HUMAN NATURE

The references to Gardner Murphy's work (p. 168) are to

Human potentialities. New York: Basic, 1958.

The major work of Daniel Berlyne (p. 168), which describes his research on the "curiosity drive," is

Conflict, arousal, and curiosity. New York: McGraw-Hill, 1960.

Computer simulations of personality (p. 169) are most recently described in a work edited by Sylvan Tomkins and Samuel Messick,

Computer simulation of personality: Frontier of psychological theory. New York: Wiley, 1963.

The issue of freedom of will is not only a matter of therapeutics, but ultimately one of scientific theory that must have some kind of satisfactory interpretation of human experience in connection with it before any really adequate understanding of human nature will be possible. Sir Charles Sherrington approached this problem in the Gifford Lectures, Edinburgh, 1937–1938, later published as

Man on his nature. Baltimore, Md.: Penguin, 1940.

". . . Will cannot be called a 'free cause,' but only a 'necessary cause.' The will is nothing else than a manner of thinking just as is the understanding. Men think themselves free, because they are conscious of their volitions and of their desires and are oblivious to the causes which dispose them to desire and to will." (From Spinoza's *Ethics*, ii, prop. 49)

Perhaps to this a comment, wholly without cynicism, might be that, from the human standpoint, the important thing is less that man's will should be free than that man should think that it is free. That can indeed serve to activate and sustain his zest-for-life. This last, if he have it not, he is a biological failure and will die out."

Edwin G. Boring deals with the same issue, but instead of proposing an explanation, as does Sherrington, he warns of the necessity for avoiding the confusion of dimensions of discourse with each other:

When is human behavior predetermined? *Scientific Monthly*, April 1957, 189–196.

It is in this way that the determinist gets trapped in the egocentric predicament. He has to be outside the system in order to recommend it. He would be more convincing if he would take up his stand firmly on the outside—the man from Mars viewing human society—and describe what is going on, that and nothing more, just as a human being may describe the behavior of ants, without praise or blame for their conduct, or suggestions for improving their social structure, or even the admonition that ants could be happier if they were controlled by positive reinforcement and not by aversive stimulation.

Perhaps I have already made my point. It is that fact and value, as surely everyone knows, belong in different worlds, each with its own language, and that the wise man must keep both in his repertoire if he is to get along in the culture in which he lives. To me this view means that the wise man is something more than the scientist, who does indeed need, as scientist, to stick to determinism and thus to description. I am saying that science must be something less than the one way to truth . . . Today we hear less about theories and more about models. What is the difference? The theory claims to be true, even though we all know that assurance about the validity of these claims varies greatly from theory to theory and from time to time for the same theory. The theory is an *as*, whereas the model is an *as-if*. The theory is indicative; the model, subjunctive. The model is a pattern to be abandoned easily at the demand of progress (p. 191).

INDEX OF NAMES